Your sister and I
are very close. You are
her number one brother.
I am looking forward to meeting
you in August.

K

Across The Creek

By

Kaaren Terry

authorHOUSE™
1663 Liberty Drive, Suite 200
Bloomington, Indiana 47403
(800) 839-8640
www.AuthorHouse.com

This book is a work of fiction. Places, events, and situations in this story are purely fictional and any resemblance to actual persons, living or dead, is coincidental.

First published by AuthorHouse 02/21/05

ISBN: 1-4184-6129-6 (e)
ISBN: 1-4184-4513-4 (sc)
ISBN: 1-4184-4514-2 (dj)

Library of Congress Control Number: 2003097704

Printed in the United States of America
Bloomington, Indiana

This book is printed on acid-free paper.

Teresa Kane, 1890-1983

To Nana, my paternal grandmother, who was a great storyteller and family historian.

She always accepted me for who I was and encouraged me to believe in endless opportunities. I still hear her voice in my heart.

Chapter One
The Invisible Tourist

This was his first day in San Diego. He had come here to work, to advance his career. Why not choose the city of perpetual sunshine, America's Finest, to make a killing. What a place to make a killing!

He was walking along the Embarcadero where the sidewalk was wide and crowded with the people out enjoying the sunshine on Easter Break. He pretended to be watching the sailboats in the harbor when he hit his first patsy. He had picked the man's pocket as he casually walked, never looking around or changing his gait. Within twenty paces, he had memorized the man's address from the driver's license. The wallet slid to the ground after hands covered with thin transparent gloves had removed the cash. If he was feeling particularly ambitious, fifteen marks could have their wallets removed and each address memorized in an afternoon. Of course, only the addresses of the locals were worth remembering. The cash was worth the risk from the tourists.

When he had a pocket full of cash and a head full of addresses he would sit in a public place, and study the local map. A local map was the first purchase he would make in each city he would visit. He loved the way the *San Diego County Thomas Brothers Map* took the city and divided it onto pages with columns and rows. He would locate each residence from the recently memorized driver's license in the index and find its location as he flipped through the pages. With help from the big foldout map in the back of the book, he would plan an efficient tour of his victims' addresses. First, he would cruise by and check out the potential for rewards versus risks, and then if he liked the looks of the place he would later return and stake out the residents for their schedules and habits. Once he learned when the house was empty, he found even the most sophisticated of alarms and locks child's play. He avoided the homes where there was a dog. He affectionately thought of himself as a cat burglar, and any cat knew that messing with a strange dog was just plain stupid! He knew he wasn't stupid; he was brilliant, even bordering on genius! He had only to remind himself that by being smarter than his vics would he prosper.

He thought himself clever to call his victims that, unaware that the police used the term too. He was often unaware that others had the same idea or used the same word that he privately claimed as his own. Being clueless was an occupational hazard for a man who worked solo. However, being clueless made less conflict and gave him greater confidence. He was a loner and had great conversations with himself. When he became nervous he spoke loudly to himself, repeating a simple sentence in his head until it became a mantra, and relaxing him and keeping him directed during a burglary. The key to success was staying in control!

He did his work from his van or on foot. He loved his van and it gave him the ability to stake out a place, hide the stash, and lay low when necessary. He silently referred to his van as his office. He had stolen it in Houston about a year ago. He changed the plates as often as his briefs; and since he thought of himself as fastidiously clean, he was always on the lookout for a new license plate. He would take a plate from a car in a public place and always replace it with another plate, often from another state. He had great fun visualizing the police trying to play musical license plates.

It was a plain white van, no identifying marks and the only windows were in the back doors. He had placed film over the glass that made it possible to see out but no one could look in. There were curtains he could pull over the back windows when he needed to use the light inside. He had many disguises for the van. In Salt Lake City he had bought large sheets of thin magnets and had covered them in several colors of bright vinyl and cut out shapes that fit together. It looked like a custom paint job and some of the graphics had lettering for businesses with an eight-hundred-phone number. He could change the graphics almost instantly, different job, different van. He knew this clever ruse must be working because he had remained free from the police, able to live and work invisibly unhassled.

As he was on his tour of San Diego, he'd quickly put together the neighborhoods where he would begin his work. The neighborhoods he liked had big houses, lots of trees, and big yards. He had only been on tour less than an hour when he saw a family leaving their house all dressed up and climbing into their car. He waited for them to back out of the driveway before he quickly made the decision that this would be the first house to hit in San Diego. He hadn't picked this man's pocket, but an empty house was just too easy, and it met all his criteria. He drove up a block, turned right, and parked his van in a Jack in the Box parking lot. He went in, bought a drink, and casually walked back to the van.

Once inside, he slid into the back and changed into a light blue jogging outfit, the expensive kind. He knew that in this disguise he would fit into the neighborhood. Just another health-hungry Californian out for his heart exercises, he said smugly to himself.

He got out of the van and jogged toward the vacant house. At the front yard, he slid between the hedge and the driveway, and made his way to the back. The hedge gave him total cover from the neighbors and the street. When he reached the back gate, he pulled a small nickel-plated whistle from the zippered chest pocket and blew a silent sound that only dogs could hear. He could hear dogs on the next street go crazy but none in this backyard. He slipped inside the enclosed yard. He surveyed it and gave himself a silent whistle. Wow, he thought, this place is beautiful; I think I am going to love San Diego! As he tried the back door, he found it unlocked. He was in and out of the house in less than five minutes. He always prided himself with his calm intelligence and ability to size up a floor plan to determine where the valuables were most likely stashed. He only took what was small and expensive. Small enough to put into the pockets of his jogging suit and not have anything bulge. Small enough that the owners might take weeks to notice they had been robbed.

He was back in the van in another five minutes. Only twenty minutes had elapsed since the family had climbed into their car. He sat in the driver's seat and slowly sipped the Coke.

He wondered if he should get back on tour again. After all, the evening was still young. He could hit three to four places in an evening if he felt motivated, maybe the term should be excited. Sometimes he would stake out a place for weeks, and then decide to strike or not. Often after watching a place, the excitement wore off and he would just move on to another location or another city.

He would give the people in the house he was watching personalities, professions, and possessions. Often he would know the name of the family from the drivers' license that he had previously lifted. Part of the thrill when he broke in was to compare his *fantasy family* with what he found once he was inside. He liked to think of the house as a present, all wrapped up, and only he could guess what was inside. He liked the suspense, and the anticipation would keep him stimulated until he entered the house. He hated the feeling that swallowed him when he discovered the fantasy was better than what he found, and often he would be depressed for days with his disappointment.

He was pleased with his winnings from his first burglary in San Diego. He didn't take all the cash this time. He thought he would leave some. He liked to believe it always made his vics a little crazy. He could imagine them wondering what happened to the money. Did they drop some, where did they spend it, did someone take it, could it be the kids?

He got some prized jewelry this time, really unique. He recognized good artisanship and beautiful design. Of course he would later disassemble it. He had a small workshop in his van and he would separate the stones from the gold, and melt down the gold to be unrecognizable. He smiled to himself as he carefully hid his bootie in a secret compartment in the wall of the van.

He would send the stones and the gold to an exquisite jewelry artist he had been doing business with for the last fifteen years. What a lucky find this woman had been, and not bad in bed either. However, he was doing less and less business with Suzanne lately. She wanted more from him than the huge percentage she already took. Lately she had started hounding him about her biological clock. She was becoming a fucking time bomb to him!

He remembered the first summer he had met her. He had seen her at a jewelry show. He went there to size up the place and became totally absorbed in the beauty of the craft. He found some pieces that kept him transfixed. He stopped to talk, and met the young woman who had designed and crafted the exquisite pieces. She was barely twenty and in the fall, she would be a senior at the University. She hoped she could pick up a position to teach art in a year or two. He could spot talent, and he also spotted the long slender body and the intelligent eyes. He could sense her free spirit.

Suzanne was sexy and funny, and slowly he fell for her. They traveled that summer, made passionate love, ate in the best restaurants, and planned for their future together. They traveled in his old VW van, the kind that was a camper. He would leave her while he went out to pick up food. The money just kept rolling in and she began to figure out where it was coming from. She never judged him, and soon she began planning with him. She was the first person he had ever connected with.

Reluctantly, at first, he told her of his rotten childhood, the abuse he had taken from his mother and her johns. He told her that one of them had taught him his trade at eight. The boyfriend had convinced his mother to let the kid become his accomplice: learn the craft because no one would suspect a raggedy looking kid. If the boyfriend got busted, he would be breaking parole and do some serious time. His mother was a sucker for a loser. She would shack up with any man who would give her a minimum of attention and a few bucks to keep her from doing tricks on the street.

He and Suzanne had devised a plan that summer. She would finish at the University and begin to teach. It would give her both the time to hone her skills as a jewelry artist, and the perfect cover of respectability. He would travel and do the thefts while Suzanne would use the stones and the melted gold to re-create a new work of art. He would supply her with her raw materials, and she would sell her jewelry at shows. The money would go into separate accounts where they would buy property under dummy corporations. He convinced her that if one of them were ever caught, the other partner would still have half of the assets and be set for life. They were going to become wealthy in just ten years. They could then retire together and appear to the world that they were respectable. Suzanne bought the plan.

By the end of summer, he felt that he and Suzanne were a passing thing. He discovered that he liked being alone, and she was crowding him, pushing him into domesticity. He was trying to flee, but he was so enamored with their plan for riches that he knew she would have to remain in his life. He didn't mind sharing the profits with her, but sharing himself was something he was not about to let happen!

As business partners they had endured and prospered. They were definitely wealthy. Suzanne believed he could step into respectability with her. She was making louder and louder noises about how much she loved him, was tired of teaching, and wanted his baby. She didn't get it, get that it was the love of the game, not the money that kept him going. He was tired of making excuses to her. She kept whining about how they had planned to do this for ten years, and fifteen years had already passed. She was running out of time! He needed her all right, but not like she wanted. He kept sending her his hot property, minus the cash, but the shipments were fewer and the cities were further and further away from her. Now he was hardly lifting any jewelry, mostly cash.

In his booty he saw two Padre baseball tickets to the Opening Game. He began to plan tomorrow afternoon and all the fans that would be there. San Diego just gets better and better, he thought to himself.

He opened the accordion doors, climbed into the driver 's seat, and headed out of the parking lot. Dinner and a nice motel with a hot shower will put the perfect end to a perfect day, he thought. He spotted a Denny's and pulled in. As he was opening the restaurant door, a young couple with two small children left. He held the door open for them, and they never knew he now had the woman's wallet and address. He walked towards the restroom, and in the hall he dropped the wallet, minus the cash, on the floor. He walked to a booth, slid in, and pointed to the picture of the food he wanted to the waitress. When his steak and eggs arrived, he ate quickly, left a good tip, and paid for his dinner at the counter. He smiled to himself about the vic in the big house who had just bought him dinner.

He sat propped up against the pillows on the bed in the motel. He had bought a six-pack of Coors and a bag of Fritos at a 7-11 next door to the Denny's. As he drank his beer and munched on the chips, he surveyed the layout of San Diego with his new *Thomas Brothers Map.* He had on the 11:00 news, and they were hyping the Opening Day of baseball season tomorrow. It was a sell out and they expected sixty-five thousand fans. The weekend anchor was advising everyone going to the game to take the trolley and avoid the traffic. "Great idea," he said to the TV, "and thanks John Harvard and Channel 8."

He began to plan tomorrow. The game started at 3:00 p.m., and he needed time to ride the trolley and get to the stadium. He figured he would do his best work after 2:00 p.m. when everyone was rushing to their seats. He took the last swig from his beer, set it onto the nightstand, and smashed the empty Frito bag between both hands. He heard the small pieces of chips crunch before he slam-dunked the bag into the wastebasket across the room. "Purrrfeect!" He yelled at John Harvard and the news team. He punched the remote, and the TV went black. He slid down from the headboard, pulled the bedspread under his chin, and fell asleep with visions of addresses and cash floating through his head.

He walked the perimeter of the stadium until he saw the ticket windows. People were waiting in long lines to pick up their tickets from will-call. He waited while a couple walked towards him and he exchanged their tickets for his. He did the ticket exchange several more times and smiled knowing all the confusion the swapped tickets would cause.

Once inside the stadium, he found the Padre Store and bought himself a team shirt. He paid for it with some of last night's take. He smiled when he thought they were bigger thieves: selling shit at these jacked up prices. He acted excited and said thank-you to the clerk. Once outside of the store he pulled off the tags and put it on over his other shirt. From his back pocket, he pulled out the hat he was given at the gate as he entered the stadium and placed the bill low over his eyes. Now, I look just like all the other fans at the game today, he said to himself with a grin.

There was a big diagram of the stadium mounted on a pillar. The *Seat Locator* was color-coded and showed the sections, levels, and ramps. He had memorized the numbers on his ticket and quickly found his seat on the diagram. He walked quickly to the left and headed for the plaza level. Now he was ready to begin his day of work.

On the plaza level, he strolled along with his ticket in one hand, pretending to look for the section. Actually, he was taking a wallet out of the pocket of a man waiting in line to buy beer. At the opening to the section, he stopped and appeared to be searching for his seat. A young family walked past loaded with food and drinks. They were preoccupied with trying to herd the children towards the seats with the fear that the kids might spill their four-dollar cokes. He took a wallet from the mother who had it stashed in a backpack that she slung over her shoulder. He stepped back from the section entrance and dropped the mother's wallet near the entrance to the women's restroom. He continued to the next level by way of a huge circular ramp where he followed a man balancing a tray with four beers. He took the man's wallet and dropped it a few feet up the ramp in the crushing crowds. Everyone was rushing to their seats, in fear of missing the opening ceremonies. From each wallet, he took the cash. With the cover of the crowds, he believed it was too, too easy. This was better than the waterfront where he often found only travelers' checks.

Soon he had worked his way to the top; the sign said *View Level.* As he tried to appear as if he was looking for his seat, the most horrific noise came from overhead. It was four fighter jets flying in formation. After the jets were out of view, everyone around him screamed and raised their arms while they jumped and shouted. The noise of everyone was as deafening as the jets. They too had become easy prey. He found an empty seat, sat there until the inning was almost over and then joined the crowds in the aisle again.

By the end of the fifth inning, he was tired from all the walking and the concentration he needed to do an undetected lift. He bought a beer and worked his way to the closest seat that was empty by the field. He couldn't believe his luck when he found an empty seat in the second row, near third base. He nodded to the man sitting next to him and when the man didn't question his seat choice, he leaned back and began to sip his beer. He was enjoying the game and watching the people in his immediate area. It soon became apparent to him that everyone knew each other; they visited, teased and brought each other food when someone returned from a bathroom run.

The man sitting in front of him was telling the person in the seat next to him about his place in the mountains, some place called Julian. Julian? That name really sounded familiar. Then it clicked. His grandmother would tell him about her life in Julian when she was a young girl, just here in the United States. He was curious and started to ask the man in the front row questions until he noticed this man's wife watching him. As the woman observed him, he sat back in his seat and appeared to watch the game again. He watched her from the corner of his eye and hoped she would ignore him. She made him nervous, and if she didn't turn around, he would have to move on. He didn't like to be noticed. He lived his whole life trying to be invisible. He placed his hat back onto his head and pulled the bill low, shading his eyes.

He wanted to find out more about Julian, and definitely more about the ring the woman was wearing. She had her arm across the back of the seat, and he could see a gold ring with a huge diamond. He wondered how tight it fit. Then he wondered if she always wore it. Oh well, he said to himself, go slow and don't get too greedy. It had been a profitable day and he had many new addresses memorized.

Everyone stood for the seventh inning stretch and he decided that he wanted to visit their place in Julian. He would set the ball in motion to pick up a stone for Suzanne along with a little family history. He tapped the shoulder of the man in front, extended his hand, and gave his name as Mike Jenkins.

Chapter Two
Opening Day

Cathy stepped outside her door and sucked in a deep breath of pure mountain air. She looked up through the trees and saw nothing but the bluest sky. It was spring, and Cathy could feel it in every cell of her body. This was the fourth spring since she had moved to the mountains, the fourth rebirth of new life she was fortunate enough to witness.

She was from San Diego where nature lies and shows no seasons. It was the city of perpetual spring, continual sunshine, evergreen trees, and blooming flowers. The city of imported water bought and pumped from far away, delivered to sustain almost three million people and make the flowers bloom and the landscapes flourish.

She knew spring, even as a child she knew. Was it some biological clock, or was it like the pull of the tide? Either way, the pull was strong today. She could feel it internally, and just the filling of her lungs with air made her feel like her troubles, bills, and the dirty dishes she had just left in the sink, would slide off her back and be gone forever.

Humph, she thought as the vision of the mess she left stacked in the sink jerked her back to reality. Was that reality, or the door that just hit her? Tim threw the door wide to make room for him and the backpack he was carrying, and it caught Cathy on the elbow. She jerked aside as he plowed on through, totally oblivious of how she was rubbing her elbow.

"Are you finally ready to go? You know how jammed the parking lot gets, I want to get there early." he said impatiently.

Cathy fought the urge to point out the fact that he had just about knocked her off the porch when he hit her with the door, let alone how many hours it was until the game started. She had learned that facts didn't fly, but words usually would when she would point out the obvious to him. She was sucking in a small bit of that pure air when she noticed the smile on Tim's face. His expression showed total bliss. A kind of happiness radiated from his eyes like a little boy on Christmas morning when he caught a glimpse of his first bicycle. Why not, Cathy thought, it was Opening Day of the baseball season, and they were on their way to the game.

They climbed into the truck and Cathy settled into the trip that would take over an hour. A lot more than an hour, she thought, with the pre-game traffic. She leaned back, pushed her bag aside with her foot and stretched out. Sometimes she knitted on the ride, sometimes she read. Today she just wanted to experience spring and observe the changes in the scenery as she rode. It was more than just observing the rebirth of the forest, because she could feel it inside herself too. It was this sort of anxious feeling gnawing in the pit of her stomach like something was about to happen. She hoped it wasn't another damn premonition, and she knew better than to believe that the numbers for Saturday night's lottery were going to be revealed to her. Damn, she could sure use that money! She had worked hard to get her life with Tim and their mountain retreat just like they had dreamed. Don't mess with me, she shouted in her mind. I am happy with the way things are.

Cathy had many conversations with herself, God, and other people in her mind, some were friends and some were fictitious faces. Since she was known to many to say too much, these internal conversations often made her life a little smoother. It had become sort of a safety zone for her. Talk it out in your mind before you open mouth and insert foot! She had learned early in life that people were not very interested in her observations, and their lack of interest increased in inverse proportion to the correctness of her perceptions. Therefore, over the years she had tried to become more of an observer of people and their behavior. It generally served her well, especially when she could keep her comments to herself.

She had learned to remove herself from the scene and watch the participants and their reactions to each other. She learned that it was not necessarily the words but the expressions and the body language that said more. She thought of this technique as mentally filming the experience and saving her memories as little videos in her mind and storing them in her subconscious.

"Ok God," she whispered, "have you got something you are trying to tell me or have I just caught a bad case of spring fever?"

Tim looked over at her to see if she had spoken as he rounded a bend on the road and Cathy's elbow hit against the door. The soreness from the door hitting her at home felt like her funny bone was screaming. Funny bone, humph, not funny at all! She looked over at Tim, sucked in a quick breath as she tried to choose her words and noticed how intent he had become with his driving. She filled her lungs to calm her elbow as she began to rub the soreness and then thought how cute he looked in his Padre Baseball shirt and hat. She loved him dearly, but he could definitely rile her. Today, Cathy decided, nothing was going to rile her!

He was driving faster than she liked, but she knew that he was on a mission to beat the other sixty-four thousand nine hundred ninety-eight spectators to the parking lot at the stadium. They were already planning to arrive at least two hours before the game. Tim had this obsession about finding a parking place. He actually had many obsessions about his love of baseball. The new season was just beginning, and his little rituals were spilling out of only God knows where, and he was clueless that he was gearing up.

She smiled to herself, leaned her head against the door of the truck and watched Tim as the ride progressed. She decided that this was becoming a re-run of last season and every season since they had met.

"What's so funny?" Tim asked after he caught her grin from the corner of his eye.

"Oh nothing," she fibbed, "I was just thinking about the crowds at the opening game. I was wondering if they would return to singing *Take Me Out To the Ballgame* during the seventh inning stretch. I loved it when they sang *America the Beautiful* after 9-11, but I feel so good I don't know if I want to sing it today. You know how it always makes me start to cry." Tim just sort of shrugged and continued driving. Tim always played tough, but Cathy knew his voice would crack if he answered her.

Arriving at the parking lot two hours before the game meant there were plenty of spaces left. Cathy fought the urge to point out all the empty handicapped parking spaces as she scanned the exterior of the stadium, silently counting all the painted blue lines. Tim had bad knees and a long walk set him back with his feet up in his recliner for days after a walk on hard pavement. She knew he suffered with pain but she was always amazed at how he was able to climb down three flights of stairs to reach his field level seat.

Cathy wasn't a big baseball fan, but enjoyed sharing the game, the crowds, and the experience with Tim. She didn't concern herself with the statistics, player trades, and team standings because Tim was her baseball-database and if she wanted any information, she could just ask. Please, no tied games with extra innings! The extra innings in those skimpy plastic seats made her butt hurt! She tried hard to understand the drama and emotion a true fan felt when a play changed the course of the game or to understand the heartbreak over a lost game. It was just a game to her, more of a social occasion. She worried about getting bored with her favorite player gone, now retired. Tony Gwynn had made the game fun for her. Tony was more to Cathy than a great athlete, she liked the way he lived his life. He could have made more money by leaving San Diego and playing for another team, but San Diego was where he played college ball, raised his family, and made his home, so he stayed. There had never been any big scandal about Tony, and she liked that. That was becoming rare these days with celebrity athletes. Cathy didn't follow such scandals but knew Tim would have told her all the gory details if there had been a scandal about Tony. After all, he was Tim's very favorite player! Tim had followed his career and bragged to anyone who would listen how he had seen Tony's first pro game, been there for each of his milestones and went daily to a game trying to catch sight of the 3,000th hit. Tim always finished the story of his baseball affair with Tony by pointing out how sad he was to watch his last pro game. She smiled when she thought of all the Tony Gwynn memorabilia that decorated the wall in the family room.

Cathy admitted that she probably would never *get it*, but decided that today was going to be a day to observe people and enjoy the ceremonies. What better place than the stadium with sixty-five thousand baseball fans on Opening Day! Cathy opened the door to the truck and took in a deep breath to psych herself up for the crowd. She was back in the spirit of the day and looking forward to seeing everyone.

She hoped that Tim would be mellow with the wait and decided she would set the mood by playing a game that always made him laugh. She would gently elbow him and point out some strange looking couple. She would then give him a rundown on their lives. When Tim asked her questions, the fantasy statistics got more bizarre and their fictitious life more humorous. Sometimes this game would last only a few minutes, or they could play it in small vignettes over several days with Tim adding his own absurd incidents to the fantasy couple's life.

Cathy started her routine and Tim immediately jumped aboard. As they waited for their friends to arrive, they began watching the crowd and adding more couples' lives to their game. Opening Day was a great place to do this. Every baseball fan had dug out his baseball outfit from years past and dressed up as if it were baseball Halloween. Young and old, rich and poor, they were all there today. They were all Padre Fans.

On Opening Day, the seats were as prized as hens' teeth; so four of their seats were together in their usual place by third base and four of the seats were in the view level, commonly referred to as the nosebleed section. Tim had given explicit instructions to their friends on where and what time they would meet. Tim orchestrated this seat exchange, but historically Cathy knew that someone was always late, didn't get the instructions correct, and really came today for the fun and not the religion of baseball.

As they waited for their friends, Cathy felt the sun start to burn her nose and remembered last year and how she suffered the next day from sunburn. Then she thought of all the wrinkles that sun damage made. She was telling herself to quit obsessing when she spotted her daughter, son-in law, ex-husband, and a friend from work. Cathy stretched up on her toes and waved to them. Well, this is my part of the group she thought. The others belonged to Tim. It was a little while more when Tim's friend and one of his friend's showed up. They all shared the introductions, and Tim began the drill on the seat exchange.

Cathy wasn't listening to the details but was trying to catch up on a visit with Carmen. They worked together and didn't get much time to visit because they were seldom in the office at the same time. The two women worked for the same Real Estate firm and had hit it off the first time they worked on a sale together, becoming fast friends. Cathy loved the way Carmen could handle a problem with a buyer and smooth over all the rough questions at document signing. She had a keen sense of how people ticked and glided the buyers through a transaction with her great sense of humor. Her clients loved her.

Tim cleared his throat as a reminder that their side conversation was holding up the seat exchange. The two women rolled their eyes as if they could speak some secret language and felt like their 3rd grade teacher had busted them.

The first group descended the stairs to the field and the remainder of the group walked to the escalators to climb to the highest level. Cathy went with the cheap seats this shift. She actually liked the fun of sitting in the View Level because the perspective was so different from their front row seats. From the top of the stadium, it looked like ants were playing the game on the field.

They found their seats, settled in, and looked for a vendor wearing a day-glow orange hat. When the young man had climbed the stairs to their seats, the ritual began. They held up their fingers to show him how many they wanted, and as he passed them their popcorn, they passed their money to the aisle. Cathy put her hand in the bag, sat back, and watched the ants warming up on the field, the crowds searching for their seats, and the vendors in their bright hats running up and down the stairs in pursuit of the sale. She also felt the sun cooking her neck. She felt like she was in a time warp, and yet everything was clean and crisp, the seats repaired, the stairs freshly painted.

Out marched at least a hundred sailors in uniform. They unfurled a giant flag that completely covered the outfield as the crowd stood and held their free Opening Day hats to their hearts and sang the *Star Spangled Banner*. Four fighter jets flying with their wings almost touching, barely clearing the lights on the rim of the stadium followed the National Anthem. Since San Diego is a military town, every fan shared this display of patriotism, especially with 9-11 still too fresh. The crowd went wild! The boy on the field yelled, "PLAY BALL!," and the game began.

When it was time to change seats, Cathy felt like it was old home week. All the people who had season tickets around them were there. Obviously, Tim had been talking because they got up to give her a big hug and congratulate her on their recent marriage. "That's right," she replied, "last season we weren't married yet." It felt good to see the old seasoned fans who had become friends.

Between innings and plays, the teasing began, just like the previous years since she had been with Tim. They wanted to see her socks. Cathy brought up her feet and stuck them up on the rail to show off the hand knit socks she was wearing. A round of applause went up for her socks.

"Show me your weapons," Joe chided her.

"Hey," she said to Joe, and all the teasers, "I was afraid to sneak my knitting needles past security," she mocked, "This is Opening Day, and the first game of the season is a day too sacred to knit!" A round of applause went up for her Padre loyalty.

Cathy often brought her sock knitting to the games and knitted while she visited and watched the games. Once she overheard someone a few rows back saying, "If that lady in the front row wants to knit, I sure would love to change seats with her."

After a couple of innings, Tim came back to his seat next to Cathy. Joe, who had seats behind Cathy, started asking what they had done on their property in the mountains since the end of last year's baseball season. Whack, sounded the bat, and the ball sailed over the wall and the crowd stood up and screamed. It was a while before Tim answered Joe's question.

Cathy always liked watching Joe and Tim talk. It had a rhythm and some rules they honored. She didn't know how they each knew the rules or who had made them, but they were honored religiously. Talking about baseball could go on during plays. It was sort of an information exchange, a honing of the knowledge about the game, learning the latest statistics. Talking about one's job, interests, or life, was only allowed during warm-ups, time outs, and between innings. A question could be asked and not immediately answered. Somehow, it worked, and Cathy enjoyed these conversations better than watching the professionals on the field.

Since both of the men were such baseball addicts, it wasn't long before others, sitting within earshot, wanted in on all this knowledge and started asking questions. The rules never mentioned; the plays and the innings set the timing. Cathy wondered if it was a guy thing. It was amazing to watch how quickly the eavesdroppers caught on to the rules. When men could catch on to these rules so quickly why couldn't they find the box of cold cereal in front of their eyes on the counter? Such paradoxes had infuriated Cathy in her youth. Now she accepted the differences between the sexes and generally chuckled. It was between innings when Tim got to Joe's question.

"Well, we have been trying to recover from the cost of the wedding. I bought a new truck, helping the economy after 9-11 and all. Cathy's mom needs a lot of help, we got a new hot water heater, and you know all the crap of life." Tim began speaking again by telling Joe of his plans to have a waterfall and pond built in the creek for a wedding gift to Cathy.

"She wants a place for the grandkids to come and get their butts wet in the summer. First I have to put in a water tank so I'll have the extra water to re-circulate." Tim continued telling Joe of his plans.

"We found out that about a hundred years ago there was a lumber mill on our property. They milled for timber and firewood for the gold mines. There were about 40 or 400 Russian immigrants working the mill, depending on what book you quote as a resource. I'll go with the 40 lumbermen, because Julian was not much more than a little Wild West mining camp. Four hundred men would have made lumber the primary industry. We always wondered why such an isolated place would have stonewalls lining the creek and a stone dam. We didn't have a clue when we bought the place."

As Cathy watched the men visit, she noticed Joe lose interest in Tim's dissertation on his love of their home. He had only asked a simple friendly question. It had become TMI, Too Much Information. A man sitting next to Joe leaned closer to hear Tim's report. He started asking Tim questions about the mill, where they lived, and was it far from the stadium. Tim loved to talk and threw the answers over his shoulder as he kept his eyes on the new batter. He didn't look back to watch the man as he became more persistent with his questions. Tim just continued telling the stranger about their hide-a-way and his plans for it. Cathy was watching the man from the corner of her eye. She noted he was breaking the rules and his timing was wrong. These were not baseball questions, but personal ones. He was a little too personal with his questions and she wished she had a way to stop Tim from telling all the family secrets.

Joe had two season tickets and this man was sitting in one of his seats. Earlier, Joe's friend Margaret was using one of the seats, so Cathy shot a question to Joe and asked where Margaret had gone.

"She got a call from her son. His car broke down. She left all pissed because she really hated to miss the first game of the season. I hate those damn cell phones!" Joe impatiently shot Cathy his answer. Now she was breaking the rules!

Usually about the fifth inning, security stopped checking tickets and the ambitious fans slowly descended towards the field. The higher the inning, the more deserted the nosebleed section became. Joe had every right to run this guy out of his seat, but Cathy knew that Joe loved to share his baseball knowledge with a true fan. If the guy was respectful, he could stay.

Cathy continued observing the stranger in Joe's seat and noted he was good looking, probably in his early 40s. He appeared to be fit and tan. His hair was just beginning to thin, and he wore it short. It was a honey-color of blonde, maybe more sun-bleached than light-colored. She wondered if he bleached it, so many men were doing that these days. He was wearing Levis and a Padre shirt; the shirt looked brand new. It was not the kind that was a give-a-way on Saturday night, but an expensive one from the team store. He must truly be a Tony Gwynn fan to spend so much on that shirt! He caught Cathy watching him, gave her a big smile, and quickly looked away as he nervously placed his freebie hat on his head pulling the bill low, covering his eyes. There seemed something artificial about his grin and Cathy couldn't quite put her finger on why he bothered her. Was he shy or embarrassed that she caught him watching her?

Carmen and Cathy visited and swapped stories about work since they were sitting next to each other again. Carmen was such a fun person, and she had this not-so-secret desire to be an entertainer. She had a boatload of voices and accents, and hardly ever carried on a conversation without lapsing into some character. Half the fun for Cathy was trying to catch the plot or the impersonation. Cathy whispered to Carmen about the new man that was pumping Tim for information. That was all the permission Carmen needed to spin off into a routine. She went into a Russian accent and acted the part of this man's old grandmother. Cathy was laughing so hard that she was afraid he would catch on that he was the center of this outburst. She was poking Carmen in the arm to stop because she couldn't handle laughing any more. Her face hurt. It wasn't what Carmen said that was so funny; it was how she said it. She scrunched her features to look like an old woman, made her voice sound thin and crack, her bright red hair defying the illusion of her comedic role.

Then Cathy caught the stranger staring at the large diamond in her ring. His scrutiny of the stone made her so self-conscious she pulled her arm off the back of the seat and put it into her lap. Carmen stopped her routine immediately when she saw how Cathy's mood had changed. Cathy turned her hand over to show Carmen the ring and rolled her eyes in the stranger's direction. Carmen rolled her eyes in return and shrugged her shoulders. Since the mood was gone, Carmen went back to watching the baseball game. Timing, timing, she said to herself, it is all in the timing. Carmen never thought it was anything more than perfecting her routine.

In a couple of innings, the game would be over. Cathy was having a wonderful time, but she noted the anxious feeling was growing within, beginning to cloud her day. She tried to shake off the feeling as she kept observing the stranger in Joe's seat. She could feel him watching her. He wasn't flirting with her, but more like sizing her up as friend or foe. Damn, she thought, a good-looking man flirting with me at my age, on a spring day, would not be too bad. But not from this guy! He was starting to give her the willies. She couldn't put her finger on it, but he made her feel like he could be trouble and that he had some motive to his friendliness. Why had he been so interested in asking Tim questions about their place? Cathy kept her hand with the ring in her lap.

The music geared up and everyone stood for the seventh inning stretch. The man tapped Tim on the shoulder and extended his hand. Tim turned toward the tap and as he recognized the gesture, he extended his hand. "Hi," he said, "My name is Mike Jenkins and I would sure love to see that place of yours."

The organ volume cranked up and *God Bless America* began to play. Cathy and Tim leaned together with their heads touching and began to sing, their bodies swaying with the row of fans in time with the music. While they sang they looked into each other's eyes, enjoying this ritual together, another year of opening games shared together. Neither cared that *Take Me Out To The Ballgame* wasn't to be sung this Opening Day. When the game ended, the Padres had won! Tim gave Mike directions to their place and the rush was on to leave the stadium with Tim trying to outsmart the fans and beat the traffic.

Chapter Three
A Day in Julian

When he paid for his breakfast the next morning, Mike remarked to the cashier about hearing that San Diego always had sunshine. "What's with the wet mist?"

"June Gloom, the city is just having it in April." She answered in her most polite voice, the one she used as a disgruntled employee of a fast food restaurant. He recognized the tone immediately. He just smiled at her and agreed she was probably correct. He did not intend to engage in a conversation with some cashier. He was only trying to be casual and friendly. His experiences had taught him that by being pleasant and giving no information, he became nearly invisible.

With the weather so gray and the boardwalk along the harbor almost empty, he decided to take a drive to the mountains and see what that little town called Julian was like. He had heard so many stories about Julian from his Grandmother when he was a child. She had held him on her lap and told him of her life as a young immigrant in a new country. He could still hear her voice in his head and feel her warmth as she held him. Remembering the only time he felt loved and safe. He knew she had had such a hard life in California, and yet she spun a warm glow around the tales she told while protecting him from his mother and her boyfriends.

In preparation for his drive east, he sat on the bed in the motel. The *Thomas Brothers* was open to the large foldout map in the back. As he chose his route, he ran his fingers along the lines on the map. He did this several times and then he did it several more times with his eyes closed. Once he had the shape of the lines imprinted in his memory, he folded up the map and closed the book. He knew he would drive there with no need for the map or directions from the locals. He prided himself on his memory and his independence.

As he drove east, the weather became bright and cloudless. The day grew exceptionally warm for early spring, and he turned on the air conditioner in the van. This was the first time he had driven east on Highway 8 and he was enjoying the un-crowded freeway on a Saturday morning.

Within a half an hour, he was past Lemon Grove, past La Mesa, past El Cajon, past Lakeside and almost to Alpine. He remembered the names of these cities from memorizing the map, and they seemed more like suburbs to him than separate cities. He was now nearing the mountains as he sped uphill on the freeway.

He began to remember the story his grandmother had told him about her father. He was a poor Russian immigrant who had come to Julian by way of Mexico. He had joined a religious sect known as the Molokans in the old country. The sect denied the Orthodox faith, and the young men refused conscription. To escape prosecution, they decided to immigrate to Los Angeles. They loved the name of the city and prayed that a city named for the angels would protect them and give them the freedom they were searching for in a new land. However, they were soon unhappy in Los Angeles and relocated to Mexico, where they purchased from the President, a large amount of land in Baja California. They wanted to farm. Their life in Mexico was soon in turmoil with the continuing Revolution. It became evident the government would not help the congregation establish their rights, and the locals did not accept their purchase of land from the President. They feared squatters were going to take back their land! He remembered his Grandmother telling him, "It is all the same, another country, another government to fear!"

The men in the group left Mexico in search of work and reentered the United States, where they ended up in the small mining town of Julian. They lived together and operated as a cooperative work party. His Great-Grandfather had to contribute to the sect in Mexico while also trying to save money to bring his family from Russia. There were few jobs with the gold mines petering out, and most of the residents who had stayed were planting orchards or becoming merchants. Life was difficult in Julian in the early 1900s and he was pleased he had found work in the lumber mill.

He loved best the story his Grandmother told him of a love of all loves, that of his Great-Grandfather and his Great-Grandmother. As was the custom, they had married when they were in their late teens. Before his Great-Grandfather left for the new country, searching for a better life, his beloved wife was pregnant again. They were still mourning the three children they had buried the year before, all dead of scarlet fever. Only the eldest daughter survived, his precious Marina, she was fourteen. He had left his wife and daughter with her family in the little village where they had been born, where the family had lived for generations. He kissed them good-by and promised to send for them, and promised they would become rich in the great new land named America.

There had been only one letter, and written in it was the promise he would send the money for their passage soon. He was doing well with his trusted position at the mill. He was in charge of all the shipping. In the letter it sounded like he was a partner with another man, and they had devised a way to make money from both the owner of the mill and the buyer at the other destination. He apologized to his beloved wife for his larceny, explaining that life was difficult in a new land with a strange new language, new customs, and people of many different beliefs. He must do what he could to raise the money quickly to bring them here. He loved her and his children so deeply and cried everyday they were apart. He wrote of keeping his gold coins buried in a can in a secret place, very near the mill. He would use this gold to bring his beloved family to a new life in America.

This family was simple, rural people and their education had been poor, so many of the details written in the letter were unclear due to poor grammar or misspelled words. When he was a small child, his Grandmother had unfolded that very letter several times, showing it to him, reading what she could. She had told these stories to him in her native tongue, never having learned English well. It made her life more difficult in California. Therefore, she clung to her native tongue, her memories, and tried to give what she could to her only grandchild. He was too young to understand the heartbreak and loss his Grandmother had felt when she carried the letter halfway around the world in search of her father.

By now, he was driving on a two-lane highway where the oaks were old and huge, the pines at least fifty-feet tall, and the grass the prettiest shade of green. He passed campgrounds, a lake, and by reading the road signs, knew he would soon be in Julian. He was amazed at the vast expanses of raw land and forest. He found this new environment very relaxing, his hyper-personality slowing. He was glad he had taken the morning off from work to take this trip.

He pulled over at a sign that said Inspiration Point. A circular road hung to the side of the mountain, offering a spectacular view to the East before it returned to the road he had just left. He stopped the van, got out to stretch his legs, and noted that he was not looking at the forest from here, but the desert. The colors were so different from the greens through which he had been driving. The desert was cream, lavender, mauve, and shades of silver gray. He had driven through deserts before, but these colors were so different from the reds of Arizona and the oranges of Utah.

He found himself alone and decided to walk into the chaparral and take a leak. While he was there, an animal ran out in front of him. It startled him, and upon inspection he noted it was not a wild animal at all, but a common alley cat. The cat would watch him and then dart into a drainage pipe under the road when he would move. He spoke to it and it stuck its head out of the pipe when it heard his voice. It carefully moved closer, but stayed out of reach. The cat paced back and forth in front of him and acted as if it were waiting for something.

"Ah," he said, "A little beggar out in the wild. I bet you are hungry. What a little con you have going my man." He returned to the van and opened a bag with his lunch. He walked halfway to where he had last seen the cat and called to him. He then threw down pieces of the sandwich. The cat approached carefully, watching both the donor and the food. It would grab a piece and retreat to eat it, keeping the man in view. Piece by piece the cat continued this ritual, growing more contented with each trip, but never trusting the benefactor. He took his time tearing up the sandwich and throwing down the pieces, watching the cat eat. This exchange with the cat relaxed him and he believed the cat liked the sound of his voice.

"I will tell you things about myself I have never told anyone, not even Suzanne when I was passionately in love with her." He crouched down to be closer to eye level with the cat in a gesture of friendliness.

"My mother was a prostitute and supported me and my grandmother. Many men would come into our apartment, and when I was about eight years old, I knew what kind of a man had come home that evening. I got so I knew what kind of a man they were before they had gone into my mother's bedroom. Alcohol was a big part of the life in our house," he told the cat. "Some men would fall asleep before sex and some after. Some got real mean. The violent ones usually came back more than once. My mother would pretend to send them away until the man promised more money. She always let them stay again, and they always became violent again."

He looked from the right to the left to see if he and the cat were still alone before he began speaking again. The cat seemed to look each way after the man, as if he was afraid he might have let his guard down listening to the man's voice while he ate. Had the man caught sight of a predator before he had? The man continued with his story.

"One night my mother had come home drunk with an old boyfriend. Once inside the bedroom the man began to beat my mother. I could hear this through the wall, it was so thin, and I started to cry. My Grandmother held me very tight and started to hum my favorite Russian lullaby in my ear. When I stopped crying, she brought out an old worn and tattered letter from her pocket and began to read it to me again."

"Then," he said to the cat, "the man began yelling about what kind of a sick whore my mother was, to have other people in the apartment when he had paid her for her time. He knew we lived with her because he had seen us there on previous nights. The man bashed into our bedroom and started yelling at my Grandmother. She tried to act old and deaf, trying to be no threat to this violent man. He grabbed the letter from her hands and tried to light it with his cigarette. He threw the letter into an ashtray and lit it with a match. My Grandmother jumped up," he continued telling the cat, "and I ended up on the floor, falling from her lap. She reached for the letter and the man yelled and hit her with his arm. He just raised his arm, swung, and smack! She fell unconscious onto the table, the letter now in flames. I can still see the flames almost touching her hair. The man yelled some more, calling us all horrible names, and snatched the money from my Mother's hand while she was watching at the bedroom door. He left yelling and hitting the walls all the way down the stairs. There was so much noise and banging! I held my hands over my ears. My Mother began to yell and she grabbed my Grandmother's arm and told her to get up, calling her an old whore. When my Mother let go, my Grandmother just slid to the floor. She was dead. Then, my Mother came, slapped me hard across the face, called me a sniveling baby, and told me it was my fault that the man had grabbed back the money!"

He tried to shake the memory of the day his Grandmother had died. It was like an old horror movie that just kept replaying itself in his head. It was definitely the day that had changed his life forever. He shook his head again because didn't want the memory to cloud what may lie ahead today, what he might find out about Julian and his Great-Grandfather. He began to tell the cat funny stories, like the time he fell off a wall when he was trying to climb into a window.

After the cat had eaten the remains of the sandwich and two cookies, he sat back on his haunches and began to wash his face with his paws. The cat looked bored and Mike knew the cat would soon leave him and melt back into the drainpipe. He knew the cat was so much like himself, both of them living off strangers, and never trusting anyone. They both only invested enough time in being social so they could get what they wanted and then vanish without a trace. He wondered if the cat had never known humans, and if that was why it didn't trust them. Or, was the cat truly like himself, had lived with people and learned they could not be trusted?

"You can go my friend, I know you are ready, you're secret for survival is safe with me. We are both alike."

He turned back to the van and once inside he rolled down the windows and turned off the air conditioner. The time he spent feeding the cat had been truly enjoyable and yet it saddened him. He had never stayed long enough in one place to own a scruffy cat. He longed to stroke the cat and feel the softness of its fur. He knew the cat would never allow such a breech of security, but the urge to pet it was strong.

Soon a sweet perfume drifted through the windows of his van. He looked for the source of the fragrance and saw apple orchards in bloom on both sides of the highway. He realized he had been so preoccupied with being aware of the people around him when he was picking pockets that he literally had not taken the time to smell the flowers. He liked how he was beginning to relax and decided he had definitely earned the right to cut back, to work less.

He took a mental accounting of his assets and wondered how much money a man really needs in a lifetime. Suzanne had been continually haranguing him on this same topic for the last couple of years. Today he could agree with her: he would cut back and relax. No way was he going to agree with her about the part of them finally getting together and having a family. They were finished, done, over, even if she refused to *get it.*

He remembered today's date and made a mental note about calling Suzanne on Monday, the 15th. He called her on the 15th of every month, unless it fell on a weekend and then he called her on the following Monday. He didn't want to cloud this beautiful day with thinking about the shit, and guilt, Suzanne would throw on him when he called. He drove the thought of her from his mind while slowing for the traffic jam as he arrived in Julian.

"Jesus Christ, where did all these people come from?" He complained to the faceless drivers in their cars. People were four deep on the sidewalks and spilling out into the street between the cars that were wedged together along the curb. It appeared the three-block town had mostly gift shops and restaurants. "My God," he groaned, "this place is nothing more than an East County Seaport Village, a tourist trap!"

People were waiting in line to enter the restaurants and pie shops. The smell of the orchard blossoms had given way to the fragrance of apple pies baking. He stopped to let a car out of a parking space and then stole it before the car behind him could. “Screw you,” he said to the car behind that honked its horn. He raised his hand, giving that infamous gesture.

Chapter Four
Candy Apples

The grandkids were spending the weekend with their Grandma and Papa Tim while Mom was walking on a three-day fundraiser for breast cancer. Dad was staying home playing catch-up on long over due projects. This was the first time Elaine had let go of the baby for an overnighter, and to think she was almost two. Elaine admitted to her mother the baby was ready to spend the night away, but she wasn't sure if she was ready to let her.

Cathy had promised the kids a candy apple from the Cider Mill when they were in town to pick up the mail. She rationalized that a candy-covered apple was somehow easier than ice cream dripping down the kids' arms. Cathy tried to make her visits with the grandkids as easy on her as possible. She believed that ice cream pooling on the leather upholstery in her car was not what she considered easy; apple cores with sticky hands were easy.

As they were walking towards Jack's Market, she heard her name. She instinctively looked in the direction of the sound, and saw a face with a big wide grin plastered across it. Shit, she said to herself, it's that man from the baseball game. What were the odds of running into him here?

"Your name's Cathy, isn't it?" He said with a warmth that gave her a chill.

"It's Mike, isn't it?" She mimicked with the same phony tone to her voice. He nodded his head, not acting as if she had answered with sarcasm.

Cathy asked him if he had dropped his wallet on the way out of the game the other night, right before he went up the stairs. She explained that she had tried to get his attention, but guessed he didn't hear her. A strange look crept over his face, and instead of answering her, he quickly reached in his back pocket and showed a wallet to her.

"Well hello," he said, quickly changing the subject, "what a beautiful family you are. I didn't know you had such beautiful children."

"That's my Grandma," Greg said before Cathy could respond.

"Oh my, I thought this pretty lady was your Mama. What are your names?"

"I'm Greg." Greg said as he pointed his finger at himself and looked up at the stranger. "That's my brother Glenn; he will be five after school gets out." He continued as he pointed towards his brother and then moved his finger in the direction of the toddler. "That is my little sister Kimberly, but we mostly call her Kimmie. She's gunna be two real soon." Kimmie was working on getting her little mouth to break the surface of the hard candy coating on the apple. Cathy realized the children had stopped and were looking up at the stranger with their crystal red apples held at the same height as their faces. She felt Glenn lean into her and stand still. She put her hand on top of his head and slowly combed his silky brown hair with her fingers.

"I heard your Grandpa talk about your place here in the mountains. It sounded so great that I thought I would take a drive and check out your little town for myself." Mike was talking to Glenn this time, but never taking his eyes off Cathy's ring.

The sidewalk was overflowing with weekend tourists who had made the trip to the mountains to sample the flavor of the hundred-twenty year old gold rush town. It was only an hour or so drive from the big city. To miss the five of them blocking the sidewalk, people were stepping around them and spilling into the street. Mike crouched down in front of the children and had this wide grin painted on his face. His eyes looked so cold to Cathy he made this chill race up the back of her neck. She was now beginning to dislike him immensely.

"Cathy that sure is a pretty ring, do you mind if I ask what size that stone is?" He tried to sound casual but there was almost a pleading tone in his voice.

Cathy sort of shrugged, busying herself with the children and trying not to sound like the answer was important to her. "I'm not sure, it was a gift," she said, feeling uneasy giving this man any information. God knows, Tim already said too much at the game.

Mike stood upright, removed her hand from the top of the child's head, and acted as if he was going to kiss it like a gentleman. He even bent from his waist, and bowed. It was obvious to Cathy that he only wanted to look closer at the stone.

"I would say close to three karats. Better keep that beauty insured," he chirped. "Tell Tim I said Hi, and I hope to see that place of yours soon." He melted into the crowd.

She put pressure on the top of Glenn's head to move him forward and tugged on Kim's hand to direct her towards the store. Glenn stopped abruptly, turned around, and looked directly up at her.

"Grandma is that man a friend of yours?" he asked.

"No, not really, I just met him at the ballgame. Why?"

"I don't like him," the child seriously said, "he is bad." With that pronouncement, he hurried happily into the store. Out of the mouths of babes, she thought. I always knew that kid was smart!

Cathy remembered Tim had given Mike their phone number and directions to their place before they left the game. How many times had she waited while he seriously invited a stranger to their home? A couple of times people had attempted to find their place but got lost on the maze of dirt roads. Even their friends who had once found the place became lost on the second attempt. She chuckled to herself knowing how difficult it would be for Mike to find the right road, then drive down through the ruts, and dodge the rocks. Somehow, sometime, she knew he would find their house and demand their trust and friendship. Why, she thought, it didn't make much sense.

Boy, that road had been a money pit! Three years of hard work, lots of money, and it was still the Road from Hell. Cathy pulled the video out of her memory box and replayed it as she kept holding Kim's hand and guiding her in the direction of the market. It was the memory of the day she found their property when it was for sale.

She and Tim had been dating for over six months and it looked like the relationship would last. They wanted a place of their own, both of them starting out together with an open slate to create new memories together. Cathy had told Tim she always dreamed of living in the mountains. She loved the colors, the sound of the wind in the trees, the changing of the seasons. They reminded her of the family camping trips, her fondest memories as a child. They started looking for a cabin.

Each week Cathy scoured the multiple listings in the computer at work, and each weekend they drove to the mountains and looked for a suitable place to start their life together.

She had found a listing that sounded interesting and had called the listing agent for explicit directions. When they finally found the right road, Tim drove slowly and avoided the ruts, ditches and rocks. The further he drove the more he smiled. He started pointing out the sunlight, shadows, huge trees, and how green this world was.

"Look, we're here," Cathy said, "It's where the road ends. The cabin sits by its self, hidden in the forest. Look how tiny it looks compared to the size of the trees."

Tim climbed out of his Explorer, and slowly turned around with his head back, looking up at the sky through the huge trees.

"Let's buy it!" he announced to the giant pines.

Cathy was stunned, they had seen dozens of places over the last few months and there was something wrong with all of them. One had too many steps, bedrooms too small, no privacy, over priced, bad wiring, and the list went on. She was beginning to think it was more an inability to make a commitment to her than a purchase of property. Then he says, "Let's buy it" when he hadn't even been inside the house.

"You haven't even seen the inside of the house!"

"I don't care," he said, "I love the property and it has enough privacy for me to piss off my own front porch. You know that's always been a dream of mine!"

She never thought that it would be there in the forest at the end of that horrible road that they would start their life together, with their families and their possessions commingling.

Once back in the car with the kids all buckled in their seats, Cathy searched in her purse for the necessary Ziploc bag filled with baby wipes. Kim needed a good scrub to remove the remains of her candy apple. She handed each of the boys a wipe while she began washing the toddler around the thumb stuck in her mouth. Cathy knew that the thumb meant she was ready for her nap.

As she pulled out of the small parking lot, she noticed Greg waving to someone. "Who was that?" she asked

"It was that nice man. We were talking to him on the sidewalk."

"I don't like him," Glenn said.

Cathy noted Mike was driving a white van, and he was going south up the hill. She instantly turned right and went north. She figured that by going around the block she would have put herself and Mike apart, especially after she dodged all the tourists and their cars. He was the last person she wanted to follow her home on the narrow two-lane road.

Chapter Five
Surprise Encounter

As he was driving his van, dodging the tourists, and trying to learn the landmarks, he caught sight of one of Cathy's grandkids waving at him. He didn't respond, but he now knew she drove a bright red mini SUV. The three-block town took almost a half an hour to leave. Shit, so many people, he thought, and me leaving town and only taking the cash out of one wallet. He smiled to himself, as he patted his hip. His confidence restored by increasing his cash. He mentally slapped himself and remembered that he had decided, not more than one hour ago, that he was going to relax and slow down. He confessed this hard dilemma to himself with a grin. Some old habits are going to be hard to break!

He drove south on Highway 79, retracing his previous route. He was no longer relaxed, a strange feeling had come over him and he believed it was the result of the chance meeting with Cathy. That definitely didn't go well; he had to admit to himself! She had become extremely angry when he had asked her about the size of the diamond in her ring. It must have been part curiosity; because it was not often he found such a beautiful stone on such a down to earth woman. Usually the women who wore such rings would be artificially blonde, too thin, and if they were not driving their Mercedes, they would be at the end of some older man's arm. It wasn't her wedding ring; she wore the large diamond on her right hand. Who gave it to her, he wondered? Then he began to wonder how he would make Suzanne the recipient of such a gift. He almost licked his lips when he thought how much money he would receive after she sold it at a show.

He had lost his invisibility with Cathy, and that made him uneasy. He knew she was smart not to trust him. Then he remembered she had asked him if he had lost his wallet at the baseball game. He worried he might have looked guilty when she momentarily caught him off guard. She must have seen him lift the wallet from the backpack of the person in front of him as he began to climb the stairs. He began to wonder how many others saw him committing his crimes. Was he as invisible as he believed? Maybe he did need to cut back and not be so greedy.

She was going to be a tough nut to crack, he realized. She has good instincts, and he would have to work hard to get her to let him into her family. He wanted the freedom to check out their place and find out more about his Great-Grandfather. Perhaps, their property was where his Great-Grandfather had worked and was part of the stories his Grandmother had spun for him. He didn't know how accurate the stories were, or how much had been fabricated by his Grandmother, but researching the stories could give him a new goal along with some family history. He did believe the stories were based in fact, and he wanted to sort through his memories, even if only to stand on the dirt where his Great-Grandfather had worked.

He was smart enough to know that if she told Tim her feelings about him, he would be exiled. Then, on the other hand, he was smarter than the two of them combined, smarter than 99.99% of all people in the world. He would win them both over. He knew Tim would be a piece of cake, and if necessary, he would set them against each other. In that, he had years of experience.

He remembered the directions Tim gave to their property at the game. Hell yes, he remembered the directions; he remembered everything!

He turned off again at Inspiration Point and when he drove into the circle, it was lined with cars. So much for my previous privacy, he moaned, and continued around the circle and back again onto the highway. He wondered if the cat was begging from another stranger.

Around the next bend, he saw the turn-off to Tim and Cathy's place. He took it and drove up and down the roads; some so narrow that one car would have to pull over to let another pass. He saw no cars, no people, but many cabins that looked like they had been abandoned for years, some right next door to large modern houses, with chain link fences, coded gates, and dogs. The scenery was green, lush and beautiful, broken occasionally with an abandoned road going into the forest. He liked the area and tried to visualize how it must have looked a hundred years ago when his Great-Grandfather had walked these hills. He smiled when he thought, probably not much different than today.

He found the dirt road that lead to Tim and Cathy's place. He deliberately drove past and continued on the paved road until it too became dirt. At the end of the pavement, he parked the van and noted how hidden he was in the trees. In total privacy, he began to put graphics on his van. He now drove a work van for Able Plumbing & Heating with an 800 number written below the logo.

He was on foot and walking through the thick forest. He heard the birds, a horse, cattle lowing, dogs barking, and in the distance the sound of children playing. He loved the sound of children's voices, the uninhibited delight and laughter in their prattle. Their innocence amazed him. Had he ever been innocent?

He followed the sound, through the brush, through the trees until he could see them playing. They were across the creek. It was dry but the deep ravine was definitely a creek, at least in the spring. There was a large tire in a tree and they were using it as a swing. They rode it together, they rode it alone, and they shared it with their little sister, helping her climb in and out of the large ring. They made rules about sharing, whose turn it was, and he could see they were thoroughly delighted with something as simple as a tire tied in a tree. He crept closer to get a better view. He hid behind a tree and had a perfect place to observe them. Oh my God, they were Cathy's grandchildren! He had found their place by driving past it and walking back through the forest.

Their place was not where he expected it to be, but from this vantage point, he had a complete view of the creek, a large area of the property, and the deck. He could even see into the house through the large windows. He figured he was probably looking into the living room because he could see a large television screen from where he was hiding. He doubted they could see him, even if they were aware he was there, but until he had stood on that deck and looked at where he now hid, he would not take his invisibility for granted. Was it where the children were playing that his Great-Grandfather had worked?

Then he heard her. He would recognize her voice anywhere; it had both gentleness and strength. He liked her relaxed personality, the patience with the kids. He could tell she was confident with herself, open and friendly. Her body language conveyed she knew who she was and enjoyed how she had gotten there. She was the kind of woman who trusted people and loved having them around, especially her family. He figured her to be in her fifty's because of the age of her grandchildren. He remembered looking closely at her in town and noticing her face was free of makeup, her eyes clear and bright. They showed extreme intelligence, and they were the windows into her feelings. That is why he knew she did not trust him.

She was calling the kids in for dinner. They whined and wanted to stay out and swing longer. "OK. Let me know when you want to eat. We are having chicken nuggets, macaroni and cheese, and ice cream for desert. I thought you guys wanted to go look for deer after dinner?" She left the deck and went back inside, two schnauzers following her.

He watched her through the window as he hid behind the tree. She seemed much younger to him than her suspected age and noted that she was quite agile, considering her weight, and moved with ease and grace. He liked the relaxed easiness she shared with the kids. He remembered his childhood and he felt a sharp pain. He never felt special or enjoyed. He felt a pang of regret that he had not felt such a trust as a child with the people who cared for him. He often wondered if his life would have been one of family and honesty if his mother had been different.

"I cream," the toddler squealed.

"Macaroni and cheese," the oldest yelled.

"I wanna see the deer," the middle child wailed. The children scrambled off the tire and headed for the house.

He smiled to himself and felt blessed to observe this little vignette of happy children playing. They showed no fear, no motives, and total trust. He walked back to his van and continued on his tour of Cedar Grove and the surrounding area.

He knew Cathy would be a difficult challenge, but he knew he could do it. He would not push her, give her time, and if she were the kind of woman he thought she was, she would be inviting him for dinner soon. When he had a motive, he could warm the coldest of hearts, manipulate the best, and have women swoon for him. Yes madam, Cathy would get his best! When he was done with her, she wouldn't know that Mike had, had his way. He then decided he would have the whole summer to do it.

His business had been good in San Diego and it was not yet prime tourist season. He then thought of Suzanne. She definitely would not be happy they were not going to spend the summer together. He was sure she probably had a city all lined up with reservations for a whirlwind tour. He was ready to cut all ties with her, or should the term be, "sever the financial cord?"

He pulled over near the main highway under a big oak tree with a row of mailboxes. He opened the *Thomas Brothers* to the page he had just toured. He ran his fingers along the lines representing roads on the paper. Instead of memorizing them before he reached the destination, he was doing it backwards. He realized this was a new twist on his memory so he scrunched his shoulders a couple of times to loosen up the route from finger-to-brain. That's it, he believed, it had to be from the finger-to-brain. He closed his eyes and let his memory trace the route on the map. With his eyes closed, he didn't see the bright red Ford Escape filled with happy children drive past him on the way to watch the deer feed in the evening.

Chapter Six
The Phone Call

He woke up early on Monday with an overpowering feeling of dread. It was the 15th and he had to call Suzanne. Today was the day he had decided that he was going to tell her it was over between them. What could she do, he asked himself, she has no clue where I am.

He took a little mathematics test to figure how many of these calls he had made on the 15th of the month for how many years? Too many, he answered. Then he wrote a mental list of all the things about her that made him fall for her. He wrote another list of all the things that made him despise her. Then he remembered how firm and delicious her body was when they first started making love. He had to admit her body hadn't changed much at all in fifteen years; it was his feeling for her that had changed. He wasn't interested in her at all, not even when he was lonely and horny. When he wanted sex, he would pickup a woman in a bar and tell her he was in town on business. She knew from the beginning it was a one-night stand. He always feigned an early morning meeting, and left her to go to his room alone. He had made it a game he played against himself to see how quickly he could pick up a woman, get a piece of ass, and get back into his room alone. Forty-five minutes was his best time. He smiled to himself, never knowing if his pick-up line was that good or if the woman was just that easy. I think a cat would be preferable, he thought. Who needs some sniveling woman always trying to steal a piece of him?

He had scoped out a payphone with a little privacy outside a bakery. He needed a little privacy because sometimes Suzanne would give him a lot of shit, and it was hard to reason with her when people kept walking by. Today he knew she would give him mountains of shit!

Today he wished he had a cell phone. He saw everyone walking around talking, in the strangest places, with a cell phone to their ear. It would give him the freedom and the privacy he needed to get rid of Suzanne. He also knew that someone standing close wouldn't hear their conversation, but someone, somewhere with access to the satellite could hear them. How could he get a cell phone when he was invisible? What would be his name, where would he pay the bill? He felt a little paranoid having such fear over a stupid little phone, but he knew that they would soon know who he was. He knew that by watching every corner, looking over his shoulder, and keeping to himself had made him rich. But, more importantly, his continuing caution had kept him out of jail.

He did like the pre-pay phone card though. That had been one little marketing tool that had made his life, and the 15th of the month phone calls easier. He could walk into just about any store these days and pick up a card that would give him almost unlimited minutes for a call. It sure beat the hell out of trying to have a pocket full of change and waiting for the operator to announce your time was up. He hated dropping each coin into the slot, while your conversation was on hold, and hearing the loud sound of coins rolling down the chute.

Technology was running rampant in the world and it was leaving him in a time warp. Everywhere there was some new technology and he could not become a part of it. Big Brother was watching everywhere, with the cell phones, security cameras, computers and the Internet. He couldn't even fly anymore because he had to show identification. He loved to fly, and he used to give an alias and go anywhere in the United States at the drop of a hat. Now even that had changed, especially after 9-11. More and more gadgets were being used everyday, and he didn't have a clue about them. The only information he received was on the TV news, or occasionally an article in the newspaper. Just one more reason to go it on my own and give up the jewelry business, he rationalized.

He called the same number, at the same place, at the same time every month. He was calling a manicure salon. He would ask for Suzanne, and when she answered the phone, they always started their conversations with him asking how her mother was. This opening sentence, agreed upon years ago when these monthly calls began, was their secret code. She always responded with, "She is doing well, thank you for asking." That was the code to let him know that everything was safe, and no one was wise to them. He decided he would give her the lead, maybe a little out of dread, before he told her to enjoy her profession, her art, her residential and commercial buildings, and move on with her life before the battery died in her biological clock.

Today when he asked about her mother Suzanne responded, "Not well at all, she is staying with my Aunt, she needs full time care now." That response totally threw him off balance! It was also their secret code, and he was not to say anything on the phone now. He would call her back at a deli near her studio in three hours. It was a busy place and they had agreed that this was probably the safest phone to use.

After he left the phone booth, his mind was reeling. What in the hell was going on? Had she run into someone who was trying to sell her something, and she needed his advice? Was she pregnant? He asked and answered himself. It was almost seven months since they had last been together. Certainly, she would have tried to trap him long before now! Were they having trouble with the management company handling the properties? The questions kept jumping in and out of his mind. He was loosing control and fighting to maintain some sanity. His heart was racing. He made himself suck in a breath of air as he walked into a little restaurant in Seaport Village and ordered a late breakfast, Mexican style.

The eggs came drenched in a red sauce, instead of potatoes, there were refried beans, and for toast, they had substituted tortillas. It looked a little strange, but he needed the distraction. The coffee was good and hot, and as he put the fork in the red-coated eggs and took a bite, then another, and another, he begin to relax and enjoy the meal. He was back in control again, his heart rate normal. He could wait a lousy three hours to find out what was going on! He began to boil, trying to figure what the bitch might be trying to pull. "She will be sorry! I don't think this is the least bit funny," he said before he realized he was not alone. He looked around the restaurant to see if anyone had heard him.

He took his time finding a pay phone private enough for him to call, and he dialed the memorized number. Suzanne picked it up on the first ring. She began talking quietly and paused as if she must be looking from side to side, to see if anyone could overhear the conversation. Once she started to talk the details fell from her. The more she talked the more quickly she talked. He was listening to her, waiting to learn what all this cloak-and-dagger shit was all about. He could hear terror, disbelief and betrayal in the tone of her voice. This was something new for her; usually she whined at him about being gone so long, how much she loved him, when was she going to see him, and similar shit.

Finally, she spilled the whole story. She told him she had been arrested and questioned for hours because a diamond she sold in a ring proved to be stolen. The police wanted to know where she gets her stones and gold for her jewelry. They wanted receipts for her raw materials. They wanted to know if I knew you. Then the police said they knew that I knew you. They knew of our corporations and they said they were going to freeze the assets. They were going to the President of the University and I would probably lose my job. They said you were wanted for murder of a man in Jacksonville 17 years ago. Then the sobs and tears began to flow. Damn, he thought, just what I needed today! I was finally going to dump the bitch and now I have to convince her how wonderful I am so she will not turn me in!

"Yuri, did you kill someone?" she pleaded when she could talk between the sobs.

"No, don't be so stupid, you know me. I don't even use a gun; I'm not a violent man." His voice went from incongruity to sweet, sounding compassionate, and almost syrupy.

"The police said the man was strangled during a house burglary. They said that you probably didn't know the man was home when you broke into the house. You probably did it so there wouldn't be a witness."

"Suzanne, Sweetie, calm down Baby, you have to believe me! Haven't we loved each other and worked together for fifteen years? How could you believe the police? Don't you see they are trying to turn you against me? They are only trying to scare you and get you to talk." He said this in his best victim voice while he was working into his *they are trying to frame me voice*. His mind was spinning. How had they ever put it together that he was involved? I haven't even thought about that bastard in years and now he pops out at me like some fucking jack in the box!

"Suzanne, Suzanne, calm down and don't lose it. They can't prove anything! Just be cool and we'll close down the business, lay low until this all blows over. Hey, Babe, we have plenty of money, and we can get on with our lives. I promise it will all blow over and someday we will laugh about this to our grandchildren. We just have to stick together. Can I count on you Sweetie?" He stopped talking and waited for her to stop crying and answer him. He was growing more impatient with her, listening to each sob, but he had to control himself to keep her from turning on him.

"OK, Sweetheart, I knew you couldn't hurt anyone. School will be out soon and I will take a vacation. They can follow me if they want and they will never find out anything! I think I have enough money through the summer. Oh, Sweetie, I wish you could come with me; I miss you so much. I don't know what I'll do if I lose my job, and they freeze the corporations." She was crying again and the words were coming between sobs.

"Calm down, take a deep breath and just listen to me. If they had any real evidence on you, wouldn't you be sitting in jail right now?" He was trying to reason with her with his most sympathetic voice.

"I don't know, well maybe you're right. I am trying to stay calm but I'm so alone. I don't know how to reach you. I have to sit in some Vietnamese nail salon and wait for you to call. It is so hard without you. Oh, Yuri, I love you so much, and I am so scared." The tears and sobs continued with an elevated tone that became a whine. "Will we really close down the business and start a family together? Is that a promise, you won't change your mind?"

"Sure Baby, sure, I promise, I'll call here again in three months. If they are watching you we had better not talk to each other, we had better make it at least three months. In three months I'll call, OK? Just remember I love you and we will grow old together." He listened to her cry for a few minutes longer and he soothed her with his voice. He hung up quietly.

What a sniveling bitch she is, he decided. Well that bought me three months. No, that bought me the rest of my life. I am long gone by next fall! Now he had to decide what he was going to do.

First, he took inventory of his assets, making another mental list. He had sold off most of the buildings and put his money in offshore accounts. The police had obviously not shared this information with Suzanne; perhaps the police hadn't discovered he had sold off almost everything. She might soon be running on empty but he was definitely set up for life. This knowledge gave him great pleasure. Serves her right, he thought. He was tired of business babysitting the Bitch! He did have to admit she was one great jewelry artist, but that was where her talent ended. He had to hold her hand and explain each, and every business decision with her over and over. Her denseness made him crazy!

What he really hated most was that tone in her voice when she began to snivel. It always sent a chill up his spine; years ago he figured out his mother had that same tone in her voice. It must drive men crazy, he thought, because usually his mother's johns would begin being violent about the time that tone crept into her voice.

Back to the inventory, keep on track, he thought. Second, I will definitely be out of the cat burglar business. I don't need the jewelry, and playing the *Fantasy Family Game* is getting a little boring. Third, I will continue to pickpocket since it has been very lucrative. I will try to spend time where people carry cash. The baseball games have been good. Let's see, the zoo, Sea World, craft fairs. I'll use the local paper to see what events San Diego has on the weekends. I'll be a tourist, a man on vacation. I have to start learning how to enjoy my time and my money anyway. I will try to keep my expenses low so I can relax more. I think moving away from the high price hotels along the waterfront will help. A little off the beaten path is good too. All these thoughts were racing through his mind as he was working on getting back in control again. That phone call had shaken him to the core. The thought of the police figuring him as the murderer years ago in Jacksonville made his stomach nauseated! He could taste the red chili sauce that had covered his eggs.

His mind kept slipping into the memory of the murder. No matter how hard he tried taking inventory; that day kept flashing before his eyes as if it happened this morning. He began to tumble out of control and into seventeen years ago.

He was one hell of a cat burglar, one cocky good-looking stud. His lips turned up for a split second as he remembered how sure he was of himself then. He would stay in the south in the winter months and go north in the summer. He had it all planned, his technique, his skills, his route. This was before he had met Suzanne and he remembered how he was one smart B & E man. He stole for cash and a few pieces of small merchandise. He quickly gave up taking small valuables because he knew that was a quick suicide; never trust your fence! He did this in addition to his primary occupation of picking pockets. He remembered that the murder was about the time he started watching houses and began to give the occupants a fantasy life.

He had ridden through the neighborhood on the bus and he liked the way the trees lined the street and shaded the houses. He thought of the neighborhood as a suburban Mayberry. Maybe the Cleavers lived in such a house, or at least Opie. He came back to the neighborhood one evening and broke into a house that looked like the owners were away. There were newspapers on the driveway and the grass needed cutting. Once inside he saw a schedule of the family's vacation pinned to the refrigerator with a magnet. They planned to be gone an additional three weeks. He immediately settled in and used the house as his home base. He would rob the area in the night and relax during the day. The house had sheer curtains and he could sit on the sofa and watch the neighborhood undetected.

He liked the house across the street. It had a porch across the front, and two dormers in the roof. Each window had dark green shutters and the mailbox was painted the same shade of green. It had a short picket fence across the front of the yard, along the edge of the sidewalk, and there were climbing roses growing through the slats. It made him all warm just to look at the house, and wonder what kind of family could live in such a friendly looking place. He began to watch the family too. There was a woman with white hair, and another woman who probably was the white haired lady's daughter. She had three small children and she came over almost every afternoon, not always with the children. Sometimes the younger lady brought groceries and sometimes they went shopping together. Sometimes the younger lady was with a man, probably her husband and father of the kids. The man would mow the lawn on Saturday, and sweep the porch and sidewalk, as he watched from behind the curtains from across the street.

Almost every morning the white haired lady would work on her roses, she must have had fifteen bushes in addition to the plants growing on the fence. But, what mesmerized him was the way they spoke to each other, how they enjoyed each other, and how kind they were to each other. He had never seen people behaving this way toward others. It was so new to him that he would sit and watch the family, when they were in the front yard, as if he was watching some film. He would watch and wait for their voices to change pitch, their bodies to tighten, some anger to flare, or some petty grievance to raise its ugly head. He sat and watched, and waited. They remained the same, it never happened. He was jealous of such ordinary people being so obviously happy with themselves and each other.

Was the precious house across the street a façade, like some movie set? All front, and when you walked around the back it was only framing, just a prop. He would have to see the inside of the place, the last night before the travelers came home. He had planned on it. He watched and he waited, knowing that the lady and her daughter would go shopping around dusk.

When they were gone, he went across the street and slipped into the back yard. He entered the house through the back door. It was unlocked. He didn't plan on stealing anything; he had stopped that a few weeks ago. He had way more hot items than he could fence without getting caught.

He just wanted to see the inside of the place. He was wandering around on the first floor when he heard a voice, small and weak.

"Anna, Anna, is that you? Back so soon, did you forget something?" The voice went quiet and waited for an answer. "Anna, Anna, answer me! Is that you?" Now the voice was pleading, almost crying. He crept closer. Who was in the house? He knew the family; he had been watching them for weeks.

The man saw him before he saw the man. He was old, shriveled and sitting in a wheel chair. He began to cry, to plead.

"Get out of my house before I call the police! Go away!" The demands were impotent with the weak terrified tone to his voice.

He looked upon the old man with distain. Yes, the house was truly a façade. There was sickness and disability within. The old man began to cry, calling for God's mercy, and his wife to come and rescue him. The voice reminded him of his mother's when she sniveled. His mother's name was also Anna. Why did the man have to use that tone of voice? He kept looking at the old man in disgust. Slowly he walked over to the man, hit him across the face and then choked him to death.

He was surprised how hard the man fought for his life, a man so old and crippled. Why did he want to live so badly with his life confined to the wheel chair? He believed the white haired lady would be pleased that he had freed her of the old man. Now the house would be whole again. All this took less than ten minutes. He left the neighborhood and Jacksonville that same evening. He never looked back.

He was brought back into the present, but the sound of that sniveling voice still haunted him, continued to haunt him after all these years. Sometimes it was the voice of the old man and sometimes it was the voice of his mother. Today it was the voice of Suzanne. He hated the voice! He had spent most of his life trying to stop the sound of that voice in his head. Today he had failed completely. That bitch, Suzanne, he growled to himself, it is all her fault!

Chapter Seven
The New Pond

This spring had been dry and the trees and wildflowers were competing for each drop of water. It took longer but they were finally in bloom. Even with her finger on the pulse of spring, the changes in the forest, Cathy could hardly believe how fast another month had rolled by. In no time at all, another car payment was due. Of course, in spring, their lives revolved around the baseball games. Were the Padres in or out of town? How many games were they attending this week?

Cathy was looking forward to the beginning of her dream, her wedding gift from Tim. They were beginning construction on the new pond. The County finally approved the plans and the permits obtained. Predictably, it was way over budget and taking months longer to begin.

Mother Nature had taken years to silt up the natural pond behind the dam made of local stones, stacked two wide and calked with clay. Cathy tried to imagine how her property must have looked in the early 1900's when all the activity of the mill was in full swing. She had seen pictures of the mill when she had gone into the city to wade through the archives at the San Diego Historical Society. She had made it a mission to read every book on the area and question anyone that had lived on the mountain for a long time. She also wanted to verify the numerous stories she had heard from Nana telling her about the mines, the men who worked them, and life in the wild and isolated mining town. She had dug up information and learned a fire had destroyed the first mill in the late 1800's, and it was rebuilt in 1904. Then later, when new technology became available, the lumber mill became mobile and moved to the trees being felled. The dam and the stonewalls were the only remaining sign that man had milled this piece of the forest, the surrounding trees now mature again.

The terrain was steep and using heavy equipment would scar the sides of the natural ravine so it was decided the pond should be dug by hand. It was on a Friday that the men showed up to start digging. The contractor figured three men would take three days to complete the dig and undue what Mother Nature had done in one- hundred years.

A layer of heavy gage rubber would cover the area that would become the pond, and make it waterproof. The lining would be held in place with natural rocks around the edges and a layer of sand spread upon the bottom. In the winter and spring, nature would use the creek as it had been doing since the mountain was formed above Tim and Cathy's place, long before there was ever a lumber mill. The original stewards of the creek were most likely the Kumeyaay Indians who had inhabited the area long before gold was discovered. When nature made the creek run, the pump would be turned off.

The new pond would provide a place for the water to collect, a large shallow area of clear cool water, a pond that could be seen from the deck, and provide a place for the grandkids to play in the summer. The waterfall would provide the sound of water falling into the pond while it kept the water re-circulating and fresh.

It was a beautiful day and the workers had arrived by 8:00 a.m. Kathy adjusted the umbrella on the deck after she had carried out their coffee and muffins. They planned on watching the men dig from the deck. It was the perfect place to view the men while they cleared the creek. They often gave thanks to the previous owners for their foresight and energy to build such a perfect place. When the creek was running, it was breathtaking. They prayed this project would bring the pleasure of running water in the months of drought.

The men didn't need watching, Cathy and Tim were doing this for entertainment. They commented to each other earlier that it beat the hell out of watching a rerun of *Murder She Wrote,* a rerun they had seen again last week. It wasn't that they didn't love Jessica Fletcher; it was just nice to have something else to do on a beautiful spring morning. Besides, everyone Jessica meets seems to end up dead.

They settled in, Cathy with her knitting and Tim with a book. They drank their coffee and spread butter on the warm blueberry muffins that Cathy had baked earlier that morning. The dogs were sitting at their feet begging for what crumbs Tim would dole out. When it was obvious that Tim was not going to give them any more muffins they joined the men in the dry creek. This was their territory and these men were messing with it. Soon, Andy became bored and started digging the crust of the earth until he had a patch of moist dirt big enough for him to curl up and lie down; Cory just plopped down, thinking that all that digging was just a waste of time.

Before long, the men took a break and Cathy offered them muffins and coffee. The men accepted the refreshments, but refused to eat on the deck. They took the muffins and steaming mugs down the hill and sat on the rock wall with their legs hanging into the future pond. Cathy visualized her grandchildren sitting the same way, in the same place, when the pond was completed and full of water. The video in her mind gave her a contented feeling and brought a smile to her eyes.

Tim noticed her daydreaming and asked, "A penny for your thoughts."

"Oh, I'm just thinking I am the luckiest woman in the world." Cathy replied, and reached over, put her hand over Tim's, and gently gave it a squeeze.

"Really, how do you mean?" He was fishing for a compliment. Hoping he was part of what made her feel lucky. He always swelled a little when she told him how much she loved him.

"Just sitting here in this beautiful place watching one of my childhood dreams come true. You know, the waterfall and pond, let alone our place. I was seeing the kids playing in the pond and sitting on the wall just like those men are doing. I have you to thank for it all. But I am especially happy about you marrying me and making an honest woman out of me."

"What do you mean, honest?" He looked at her with a startled look on his face.

"If I ever do run into Dr. Laura I can hold up my head. We aren't 'shacking up' anymore, as Dr. Laura calls it." With that last statement, she gave him a quick pinch on the back of his hand and a wink. It was enough of a compliment to make him swell a little.

"I love you too, Babe." He picked up his book with one hand and his mug with the other. The men had resumed their digging.

It was early afternoon and Tim had gone to the post office. One of the men was knocking loudly on the back door. Cathy yelled in her bad Spanish, "Come inside, and use the bathroom." He just knocked louder and faster. She walked to the back door and opened it. One of the men seemed agitated and held what appeared to be a stick in his hand. Cathy could see the other two men hanging back on the deck. She thought Andy had been bothering the men; wanting to play and had brought the stick to them. She glanced around for the dogs. Then the man opened his other hand and it held a heavy gold ring. The ring had what appeared to be a band of leaves with berries deeply carved on it. From what Cathy could see, the design went the circumference of the ring. She leaned closer, wanting to see the details, and she noticed engraving inside with a different kind of alphabet, Russian, Greek? When she started to reach for the ring the man stiffened and withdrew his hand. He showed her the stick again and put the ring on the stick. Cathy didn't understand this little demonstration, and by the faces of the other two men it looked to Cathy like this was some kind of voodoo ritual. Then the man held up his hand and put the ring on his finger and then he pointed to his finger and then the stick. She was beginning to understand, and in disbelief was rummaging for words in Spanish to ask the digger questions. Was this stick really the bone from a finger? She couldn't recall these words in Spanish. Did she ever even know these words? She did remember the Spanish word for dead, and spoke the word with the inflection in her voice that made it a question. All three men nodded their heads up and down with their dark eyes large and fearful.

They motioned for her to follow them, and she reluctantly went with the three as she grabbed her camera off the coat rack by the backdoor. She followed them down off the deck, down the side of the hill, walking carefully so she would not fall. When was Tim going to return from the post office? Oh God, why does everything always happen when he is gone? He would know what to do. All these thoughts raced through her mind as she tried to keep her balance.

Once to the creek the men stood back and pointed to the spot where Cathy assumed they must have found the ring. She walked a little closer but all she could see was freshly turned earth. She poked the dirt with her toe, not trying to find anything but showing the men there was no reason to be afraid. Her shoe uncovered another bone! She bent down further, now in a half crouch. The bone appeared to look like the one the man had shown her, the one he was still holding in his hand. Cathy stood up quickly and handed the worker the bone she had found. She watched the men waiting for some explanation, as they watched her trying to wipe her hands on her pants as if the bone would contaminate her. The man held both bones at arm's length and slowly rotated his wrists while his partners followed the revolving bones with their eyes. They were silent, and their eyes jumped from the bones and searched the area as if they were afraid the creek had become some sacred place with some spirit watching them. They cautiously backed away from the fresh dig, forming a half circle. The first man looked directly at Cathy, nodded and stepped forward putting the ring back onto the bone and set both bones on the freshly turned dirt. They quickly picked up their tools and started up the hill. Cathy turned back, not believing what she had seen, wondering if it was all a mirage. It looked the same, freshly turned moist earth, two bones, and one ring. She leaned over and snapped a close up of the scene, knowing no one would believe her and she wanted proof to show Tim. She stepped in line, following the men up the hill not wanting to be alone by the creek.

Once back on the deck she was trying to catch her breath. The climb was steep, but she was sure her shortness of breath came with the knowledge of what she had just witnessed. How long had it been there? Was it just the bones of a hand or was there a whole skeleton hiding below the surface of the earth, hiding where her grandchildren will play? Her mind was reeling. The men were watching her with their shovels resting on their shoulders, waiting for some kind of instructions. She didn't know how to speak to them in Spanish. What could she say anyway? She was as confused as they were. The three looked at each other and again at her. They politely nodded and said "*buenas tardes.*"

"Wait a minute," she pleaded, "when are you coming back?" She realized she had asked this question in English. She wasn't sure they understood so she did her best to ask again in Spanish. They responded, and she believed they said they would return after the police had been there. Something about her husband talking to their boss when the creek was clean again. Cathy could understand more Spanish than she could speak, especially when she was upset. She was definitely becoming upset and her memory of this foreign language had flown from her brain. Did she understand the man correctly? They thought the police should come?

When Tim drove down the driveway he saw Cathy sitting on the rock wall under a giant Coulter pine.

"Hi, Babe. Catching a little sunshine?" Cathy didn't respond so he began again. "Did the men leave already, I don't see their truck?" He asked as he was collecting the pile of mail and the half-gallon of milk he had purchased while he was in town. She just sat there like she was unaware he was speaking to her. "OK," he said this time louder enunciating each word, "did they say when they are coming back?"

"They said something about when the creek is clean again. You know my Spanish is bad."

"H E L L O, Cathy, what are you talking about?" Tim had stopped in front of her, balancing the milk and the mail, as he looked directly at her. "Let's start over. When are the men coming back?"

"They found a bone, I found a bone and there is this ring they found. You've got to go look; I'm not going down there by myself."

"Look where?" Tim had this puzzled look on his face, not understanding a word his wife had said.

"Where the men were digging. They found this bone and I think it is from a hand. The ring was on the bone. They showed it to me and made me go look. Then I found a bone like their bone. Then we put everything back where we found it." Cathy was talking fast and out of breath, like she had been running but she was sitting quietly on the wall.

"They found a bone, what kind of bone? Do you really think it belonged to a human and not some animal?" Tim was frantically trying to pry the information from Cathy.

"God, Tim, I can't be sure of anything. I want to say it was an animal bone, maybe I just want to believe it, but the men were really scared. No animal would wear a ring, so it had to be from a human! The ring was really unique; gold with lots of detail that looked like leaves with berries, and it even had some foreign writing on the inside. Come with me and I'll show it to you."

"I'll take your word for it." Tim was now trying to digest what Cathy was telling him. "My knees are killing me and the last thing I want to do is climb down there. Are you serious enough about this for me to call the sheriff?"

"Yes, I am dead serious! Sorry, no pun intended." She looked at Tim with the expression of saying something clever and feeling guilty about it at the same time. "The men said to call the sheriff. I'd rather have him check it out than you."

Tim tucked the mail under his arm and helped Cathy to her feet, grabbing her under the elbow and escorting her into the house. Once inside he gave her the milk and told her to put it in the refrigerator while he looked up the sheriff's number. In the three years they had lived there they had only dialed the sheriff once, and that was when the alarm to the neighbor's house had gone off. The sheriff never did find the house, even with explicit directions. God, he thought, we don't need that again. Tim could tell this was serious by how Cathy was behaving.

Once he dialed the number, he listened to his options and pressed the appropriate numbers until he heard music. While he impatiently waited, he evaluated the situation in his mind and figured the sheriff would come out; hopefully he could follow directions and find their place, and say there was no problem. Probably just some bones had washed down stream many years ago and buried. Point out to them, as if they couldn't figure it out for themselves, that the digging crew had unburied them. It would be a simple formality and would take an hour or two. Then he thought about the way things worked up here in the small mountain community, that it would probably take a day or two to get the sheriff to find the place. He only needed to calm Cathy down. She sure was agitated! He could see her frantically removing the burners, scrubbing the stove.

"Julian Sheriff's Department," the voice answered, "how may I help you?"

Tim told them the story, beginning with their plans for the creek, the men who had come to work, and what Cathy had told him. The sheriff asked to speak directly to Cathy, sarcastically pointing out she was the actual person who had seen the bone and the ring. When she came to the phone, she began the story again including the voodoo ritual the Mexican men had given her while they were trying to communicate with her in another language. She told the deputy about following the men to the creek, and finding another bone. She explained about the ring, gave a description of it to the sheriff, and told him they had put everything back where they had found it. Except that, the ring and the bones were now uncovered, exposed.

The sheriff sort of hemmed and hawed. Cathy could tell he was sizing up the situation. Was it necessary to drive out to their place, or could this call be handled on the phone? She figured he was probably about to go off duty and had Friday night plans. The tone in his voice warned her, as he asked her to repeat her story, that all this had better check out or he was going to, at the very least, be pissed. He insinuated that if a small town classified you as a little "off" everyone would know, and you would carry that tag forever. Then he asked her if she thought he should come to their place?

"I can't answer for sure if there is a skeleton or not. I believe the two bones I saw to be human, animals don't have fingers or wear rings; at least not in San Diego, where I am from." She was slipping into her curt sarcastic voice and was trying to keep the tone from spewing all over the sheriff. "I do know it scared the living-you-know-what out of the men who were digging. They told me to call the police. I have no idea how the bones got there or how long they have been hiding there. We live where the old cedar mill once stood. The bones were found along side of the creek. Please come and check it out. Then if you think we're crazy, I can handle that."

"Lady, Lady, I never thought you were crazy," the deputy said curtly, the tone of his voice now quickly changing when Cathy had called him on his insinuations. "I am here alone now, and I'll have to send someone else out. I'm about to go off duty." He was thinking out loud now, listing off all he must do to get this call handled. "Let's see; your name is Spalding?"

Cathy could tell he was now back to official business and installing CYA, Cover Your Ass. "Yes our name is Spalding, S-p-a-l-d-i-n-g," Cathy pronouncing every letter in their name slowly. "Let me give you directions, our place is not on Cedar Grove Road, but our address is." Cathy began to give detailed directions on how to find their place, always warning that the *Thomas Brothers Map* was not accurate where they lived. She had given these directions to so many friends and family. Cathy had learned that people only listened until about the third turn and then they just went into shutdown. They could get almost to their cabin but always missed the last turn and drove around lost for at least half an hour before they could admit to themselves that they had missed an important piece in the directions.

"Mrs. Spalding, my deputy just returned from a call. I'll send him out. It will probably take him a little over thirty minutes. His name is Deputy Johnston. I have all your directions written down. He won't have any trouble finding your place; he knows your area real good. He's been a deputy up here close to twenty years."

Tim and Cathy sat down at the dining room table to wait for the deputy. It was still beautiful outside, but they wanted the security of the house. Sitting where they could not see the creek, and refusing to look through the large picture windows. They didn't say it, but they both were avoiding the deck where they could see the fresh dig.

Oh God, she was so exhausted; and the day had started so bright and promising. She wanted her pond just the way she had dreamed, with the grandkids jumping and splashing. Now it looked like some stranger was buried there for God only knows how long. Then she thought that maybe she and Tim were the intruders and maybe this skeleton belonged here, and not them. How long would it take the sheriff to arrive? Maybe the sheriff figured them right, they were more than a little "off."

It was close to one hour before Deputy Johnston arrived. He missed the last turn onto their road and it took two phone calls from the station to Tim and Cathy, and then calls to the deputy in the patrol car to redirect the deputy to their place. When the deputy finally arrived, he seemed friendly and relaxed. Getting lost and the tale of bones, maybe human, along side of the creek, certainly hadn't riled him like it had Cathy and Tim.

"Evening Mrs. Spalding, been working this area for years and wouldn't have dreamed your place was here. It sure is private." the deputy said to Cathy and nodded to Tim as a greeting. The Deputy spoke with a drawl, no regional accent, just slow and drawn.

It appeared to Cathy the Deputy thoroughly enjoyed his laid-back life here in the little mountain community and his body fit his station in life. Cathy calculated how many donuts it would take to acquire that belly. Then she remembered that the only donut shop in town never sported any deputies when she walked by. He probably has a wife that cooks great meals for him, and driving around in a squad car all day doesn't burn up too many calories. Cathy wondered what he thought about being sent on a call late Friday afternoon. His demeanor gave no hint into his thoughts or feelings. She questioned herself about why she was spending so much time on speculation of the deputy, trying to read him, giving him a fantasy life. Stop it, she said to herself, just because she was the self-appointed President of People Watchers Anonymous, didn't give her the right to let her imagination run wild. She wished she could elbow Tim and lapse into their *Fantasy Family Game*. Playing the game was a great diversion and it always lightened up her mood. She sure could use some mood lightening now! Then she understood why she was sizing him up. She wanted to feel confident he would be able to solve the mystery in the creek. Would he be able to help them? Was he even interested?

Cathy thought the deputy looked to be in his middle forties. He had merry eyes, and an upturned mouth with deep laugh lines. His tanned face looked like someone who spent time outdoors, probably cruising the back roads in his patrol car. Cathy imagined him sitting in a big chair in the Town Hall, all dressed in red with a white beard, handing out candy to the local children the weekend after Thanksgiving. She wondered if Julian did such a thing for the kids, or did the parents have to drive their children to the big city and wait in line at the mall?

Deputy Johnston asked permission to sit, and when he settled into to the big leather chair, he pulled out a pocket sized spiral notebook. He had Tim and then Cathy tell their stories again. As they spoke, he wrote notes. When he finished his writing, he snapped the cover of the notebook closed with a flip of his wrist. He stuffed the little notebook back into his left breast pocket and buttoned the flap closed. He made this gesture so automatically that it made Cathy wonder how many times a day he unbuttoned the flap of his pocket and brought out the little book. She wondered what he did with the little notebook when it was full, all the pages used? Cathy could visualize a case of these little notebooks, with their bright blue covers, sitting on a shelf back at the station. She wondered if each call got a new notebook, and if this call would somehow be labeled or classified, and the cover marked with a title. Perhaps their name or some catchy title like an author would give a novel, something with a teaser to read further before stacking it in a *full* pile on the shelf back at the station.

"Show me where you found those bones," the deputy asked Cathy. Tim walked him to the railing of the deck and pointed. It was obvious to Cathy that Deputy Johnston wanted to hike down to the creek about as much as she and Tim did. She wasn't sure if he didn't want to hike down and climb back up; or if he was also spooked by what may be buried there.

"Go with me Mr. Spalding, you too Mrs., if you feel up to it," the deputy giving the authoritative order. The men took their time before either of them moved. They seemed lost in making the decision, as if they had to mentally list all the reasons they must go, and all the reasons why it wasn't necessary to go. She could almost hear their brains humming, slowly kicking into gear.

Cathy was growing impatient and finally said, "I'll show you where the men left the bones and the ring." She wanted this to be over ASAP. They stepped off the deck and Tim held Cathy's hand as they walked down to the spot where the ring and the bones awaited inspection.

When the three of them reached the freshly turned dirt, Cathy pointed to the exact spot where the bones and the ring were placed. The slanting sun had caught the gold and it was reflecting a bright beam onto the earth. It almost looked mystical. Words weren't necessary; it was obvious they had found the exact location. Cathy stood back as the two men inched closer. They leaned over for a better view, their bodies blocking the sun and killing the beam. It seemed to Cathy that their interference had killed the ethereal aura. Now it was just two middle age men bent over inspecting something in the dirt. They stood upright again, Tim stretching by placing his hands on his hips and arching his back, and Deputy Johnston, straightening the equipment on his belt. Their activity was a stall. Both men were trying to clarify what they had seen, trying to grasp how to proceed. They looked to each other for direction, neither speaking.

Cathy was ready to scream at them. Do something, anything; this silence is making me crazy! She remained silent; trying to look patient. Now was the time to keep her opinions to herself.

Deputy Johnston broke the silence, "How long have you two lived there?" He slowly gestured with his finger towards the cabin. Oh, she wanted to scream at him about what a stupid mundane question that was! She said nothing.

"A little over three years," Tim obediently answered.

"Do you have a shovel?" The deputy asked. Tim looked around the freshly turned earth looking for the tool that had caused all the turmoil.

"Honey, what happened to the shovels?" He passed the question onto Cathy.

"When the men left they picked up all their tools and took them with them. I guess ours are still in the pump house."

It was obvious to Cathy that neither man wanted to climb back up the hill to retrieve a shovel. Tim had bad knees and didn't want to climb down here in the first place, and she knew him well enough to know that he believed that it was the job of the deputy to check out their call. She could see Tim digging in his heels and was not about to make anything easier for the deputy. Cathy was beginning to believe the deputy was trying to kill time until it was too dark to stir up more dirt. On the other hand, was he not wanting to find what he was beginning to believe may be buried there?

"I think the bones are human." The deputy looked towards the treetops speaking to the late evening sky. "I'm going to go back to my squad car and call the station. I'll ask Sergeant how he wants this handled." This statement he made directly to Tim.

"Are we to stay here or can we return to the cabin?" Tim looked to Cathy while asking the deputy.

"I guess the house is OK," the deputy answered. "Getting hold of the Sergeant, late like this on a Friday could take some time. He might tell me to come on back to the station and we'll start again tomorrow. It ain't like those bones were put there yesterday. It looks like they have been there a real long time." He started the climb back up the hill, stopping to look back at the spot, massaging his temples with both hands. Cathy couldn't tell if he was thinking or actually had acquired a headache. "If there is more to those bones, I wonder who it might have been. I just love police work. Always something different."

Cathy looked at the deputy in disbelief. His body language, his reticence, his slow nature appeared to her that he was a man who loved working in a place where nothing happened, and he didn't have to exert himself. She had formed the opinion that the most difficult decision he wanted to make was glazed or pink sprinkles. She was truly thankful she had not caught the virus of *foot in mouth disease* when she was in the throes of her impatience with the men. Maybe there was more to this man than she originally thought. She took a deep breath, and steeled herself for the climb.

"Tim, we have to make a path from the deck to the pond when this mess is over." Cathy said, pointing out the obvious to Tim as they climbed back up the hill, her breath short.

"Why couldn't we, it would only take more money. Hey, what's a little more money when we're in this deep? We definitely need one." Tim puffed as he climbed and mentally calculated the added expense.

Deputy Johnston disappeared into his car and Tim and Cathy went back into the cabin. Tim launched himself into his recliner, body back, and legs up. He hit the remote and the blinds slowly lowered and blocked the outside world from their view. Cathy started making dinner. The thought of food didn't sound the least bit appetizing, but the process of cooking, keeping busy, felt better than sitting again at the table. It was only a few minutes until the deputy was knocking at the door. Cathy invited him in, and he came in as far as the family room.

"That dinner sure smells great; makes me realize it's way past my dinner time, got to call the wife and have her put mine on hold. Just spoke with my Sergeant and told him what we'd seen down there by the creek. He said for me to hang around while he sends out a couple more deputies to relieve me. I'll go put up some tape to mark off the area."

"How long are the men going to stay out there?" Cathy questioned.

"All night, going to take shifts until the big guns from the big city show up tomorrow."

"All night? Where are they going to be?" Cathy was surprised by the response they were getting from the Sheriff's Department. Was all this really necessary?

"Watching the creek." The Deputy went back outside and off the deck.

As Cathy was cleaning up the dinner dishes she put mugs, spoons, cream, sugar, and the muffins left from breakfast on a tray. She carried the tray out to the deck with the coffee pot. She set the tray down on a table, plugged in the pot, and it started to perk. She called down to Deputy Johnston and told him there was some fresh coffee when he came up.

The dogs alerted them when the replacements arrived and they went outside onto the deck and introduced themselves. Tim told them to make themselves at home, drink all the coffee they wanted and they were welcome to use the bathroom.

When finally, they had crawled into bed, Cathy snuggled close to Tim and lie awake making a mental list of what actually had been found, and what it actually might mean. Her list didn't seem too bad, even in the dark, but somehow she knew that tomorrow was going to unfold in a way that was out of her control. She never thought of herself as someone who had to have everything her way, being a control-freak so to speak, but her life with Tim and their private piece of forest was very special and she wasn't going to let any bones or "the big city guns" mess with their status quo! All she wanted was a pond for the grandkids to splash in, and now their construction schedule was shot to hell!

Chapter Eight
Personal Circus

It was around five AM when the sun cleared the top of the pump house and the light hit Cathy in the eyes. This was nature's alarm clock and she couldn't hide from her thoughts any longer. The day promised to be gorgeous and the longer she watched the sunrise, and marveled in its splendor, the more insecure she became. She thought of gently nudging Tim but decided she wanted to be alone with her thoughts. She knew he thought she was making a mountain out of a molehill and she definitely didn't want him telling her she was being a superstitious scaredy cat! I'll let him sleep until the dog alarm gets him. Let him sleep until Andy licks him in the face!

She usually pulled herself from bed, sat in her favorite chair, and planned her day, half-asleep, half daydreaming while the coffee perked. However, today she hit the floor with a nervous energy: circling the kitchen, dining, and family room. She picked up mail, her purse, and the dog's toys off the floor. She didn't want the house to look like a couple of slobs lived there.

She mixed up a batch of banana nut muffins and filled the paper cups in the muffin pan. She set the timer on the oven and while the muffins were baking and the fresh coffee perking she stepped into the shower and let the hot water hit the back of her neck. "Ahhhh," she moaned, "my hot water therapy." She did her best thinking in the shower, but today she didn't want to think. She wanted to be busy doing things she could do with her eyes closed and her mind blank. She had a feeling it would be a long day and it had started early after a restless night.

Once dry, and dressed, Cathy poured herself a hot cup of coffee and took the remaining coffee out onto the deck with the fresh muffins. By the time Deputy Johnston and his partner arrived, Tim was up and dressed. The sun was already heating up the morning and the sky was the sweetest shade of turquoise she had ever seen. Cathy made a second pot of coffee, and while Tim talked to the deputies on the deck, she was making both chocolate chip and oatmeal raisin cookies.

Cathy put the warm cookies on a plate, placing them on the tray to replenish the eaten muffins. She remembered yesterday morning and all the joy she felt knowing the construction was beginning. Everything appeared to be the same, the deck, the tray with coffee and muffins, but her optimism about today was clouded; she couldn't believe how all their plans had been turned upside down since the men had found the bone.

Cathy made herself busy inside, dusting, vacuuming, and folding the laundry. She even wiped out the bathroom sink and scoured the toilet. She knew that today would get bigger than she wanted, and ring around the toilet was the last thing she wanted to feel uneasy about!

She called Elaine to tell her what was happening and hoped that by hearing her voice tell her daughter about the men finding the ring and the bones she could slow down and relax. She felt like a damn windup toy, spinning her wheels and running in circles.

A helicopter was hovering overhead and it was impossible to talk on the telephone. She shouted to Elaine that she would call back later when it was quiet.

Cathy crept out onto the deck to see the helicopter and she noticed how many people had arrived while she was spinning inside. There were men in uniforms, men in suits, men wearing overalls, men giving orders, men taking orders, and men just milling around. The men, who were wearing the suits in the wilderness, looked like they were from some other planet, not from the city an hour away. Cathy wondered who they could be. Who had arranged all this since yesterday evening, this morning?

Cathy went to the rail of the deck and reluctantly looked into the creek. The scene was repeated there, with men in all kinds of dress, and activity. There were men standing in the dry creek and men standing on the wall. There was a tarp spread out on the ground and Kathy could see many bags of different sizes laying on the tarp.

"What are all the bags for? They're spread out all over that tarp." She turned to Tim with a puzzled expression on her face.

He leaned forward and quietly replied, as if she was the only one who should hear, "They all have a bone in each bag. They call it tag and bag."

Cathy picked up the tray and the coffee pot and went back toward the cabin. She walked quickly, her back straight and looking directly in front, oblivious to the men on the deck who had to step aside. The sting of this knowledge made her want to flee from what she had seen. There were so many bags!

She filled a pitcher with water, grabbed a stack of plastic glasses and placed them on the tray. She put more mugs on the tray and more cookies on the plate. When the third pot of coffee finished perking, she added it to the tray and carried it outside. She was definitely not going near the rail again!

Tim motioned for Cathy to follow him, and they walked to the other end of the cabin, near the driveway. When they were alone Tim began to speak.

"The Medical Examiner has come and gone and the forensic team is now digging up the rest of the remains; the deputies are just standing there watching. God, Cathy, the skeleton had been buried under rocks and the skull has a hole in it. It was definitely murder! And, the remains of the clothes appear to be similar to what a lumberman or workman would wear. I overheard the deputy say they looked like the style from the early 1900's. They even found a leather pouch with some gold coins."

This new information almost knocked Cathy off her feet, her mouth dropped open but no sound escaped. Tim seemed charged, as if he was enjoying the activity and the mystery, being in the thick of it. She stood frozen trying to digest this new information. She hadn't allowed herself to believe it would be anything more than a few bones that had washed down stream, and she never dreamed there would be foul play. She was becoming angry about what Tim had just told her. How dare someone murder someone in her very own yard!

As she turned to stomp back into the safety of their house she noticed the driveway filled with cars. The cars near the house were blocked in by all the cars parked behind. Someone would have to move before anyone at the bottom could leave. She could visualize the mess there was going to be when someone wanted out. It brought the first wide smile to her lips. She pointed to the cars and Tim understood why she was grinning.

"Hot damn, we should sell tickets to this spectacle. It's going to be better than demolition derby." They both started laughing as they walked back onto the deck together.

"There's a van parked behind my squad car! Who's parked behind my car? Hey, I have to leave; somebody had better move that van! Anybody listening? Hey, I said; move that van!" One of the suits was impatiently yelling commands back towards the creek.

"Thank God, that's not our mess! We just live here." Tim whispered to her, with a broad smile covering his face and nuzzling her cheek.

The phone was ringing when Cathy went back inside. It was Elaine. "The boys have T-Ball and Brian is going to be with them all day. Carmen called, and I told her all the gory details. We thought it would be fun to hang around. OK with you, Mom?"

"Sure Honey, Tim just told me it was murder, poor guy had a hole in his skull."

"Wow, Mom, it's getting more exciting with each phone call. Need me to bring anything?"

"How about six tomatoes and a box of that Paradise Tropical Tea you like. We have everything else. Hamburgers sound OK?" Cathy was absently taking inventory of what she had and what she needed.

"Sure, leaving in a few." Elaine hung up and Cathy wasn't sure if she meant leaving in a few minutes or a few hours. She was glad Carmen was coming with Elaine. Cathy was beginning to think of Carmen as more of a daughter than a co-worker. She liked the feeling of Carmen in their family and was glad the two young women were becoming friends. Then she wondered if she wanted the activity of the toddler with all that was going on; she felt like a Mack Truck hit her! Maybe the toddler was just what she needed to slow herself down! Some of Carmen's comedy would cheer her up too. Cathy needed the great diversion.

She put potatoes on to boil in one pan and eggs in another. She had impulsively decided to make a big bowl of potato salad when she got off the phone.

The phone rang again and it was Carmen. "I just heard from Elaine, she said it was murder! Where was the skeleton buried?"

"Right here in my very own creek!" Cathy's voice cracked and said, "Oh God, Carmen, you wouldn't believe how many people have shown up. I have worked myself into a frenzy and I can hardly wait to have you here giving me support. Tim is out watching them dig up bones and when I talk to him, he seems to be enjoying all the drama. He looks at me like I'm crazy because this whole mess has me all wound up. You know how hyper I get when I'm upset. Just remember, you gals will probably have to hike in lugging Kim. There won't be a place to park." Cathy proceeded to give Carmen all the details, as if Carmen had never talked to Elaine, cupping her hand over the receiver like she was telling some secret gossip that no one, but her newest friend was allowed to hear. She felt like each time she told the story it became crisper, more accurate, the details lining up in some concise order of importance. This drama was becoming one of her videos that she could take out and replay. She had to be careful not to embellish the details because the images were too real to exaggerate, and they still scared her each time she thought about them.

The phone kept ringing. First, it was a radio station asking her questions, then a television station asking if she would do an interview. How in the hell did they get their name and phone number? There were a few more calls from friends who had heard it from friends. Cathy called her mother before she heard it from someone else, and then she took the phone off the hook. Her friends had her cell phone number; the rest could just get a busy signal!

Tim came in the house to tell her the neighbors were here. The people from the museum, the kid who worked in the market, and their favorite lady from the post office had just arrived. He started carrying out folding chairs. She told him about Elaine, Carmen, and the baby coming. She told him about all the phone calls, and that Channel 8 was coming, and they wanted them to do an interview. He stopped, set down the chairs and decided to change his clothes. She asked him if he thought she could lose at least ten pounds by the time News 8 found the place. "We are going to look like two round, tanned mountain people on camera."

"Hey, this mess will probably be old news by the time they find the place. That should give us plenty of time to lose weight. Maybe once they see us they will opt for a radio interview." Tim said thoughtfully. They both just shook their heads and knew this had definitely gotten out of hand and beyond their control. It was like a snowball rolling down hill, picking up speed and continuing to grow. She wondered if they ever had control. This was their place, their private place, and since the deputy had arrived yesterday evening, they had become spectators in their own lives. Who had set this investigation in motion and brought all these people to their little piece of forest?

If Tim were not sitting outside watching, he would not know about the grave, about the hole in the skull, or about the clothing and the gold coins. They had not even been given the courtesy of being informed! How had word gotten out and created this circus? How had their names, phone number, and address been thrown around like it was public information? Would it ever be their private place again?

They agreed to try to roll with it, smile and pray that it would be over soon. Tim gave her a big hug and promised her that together they should be able to see some humor in this mess. "Just remember the parking fiasco. There will be lots of idiots here that will give us ammunition to play *The Fantasy Game*." She smiled up at him, feeling better, knowing they were a team.

Cathy started peeling the skin off the potatoes. They were still hot, but she was in a hurry. She believed good potato salad needed to sit in the refrigerator overnight, and soak up all the flavors of the dressing. This salad would be lucky to get cold! After she popped the potato salad into the refrigerator, she started slicing onions, lettuce, and the tomatoes she had on hand. She artistically arranged all the slices on a large platter, and covered it with Saran Wrap. She took two giant packages of buns from the freezer and set them on the counter to thaw. She put on some water to boil so she could make a large pitcher of iced tea. She would be ready when their appetites took over.

She felt that she had been wound up like a toy, ready to spin in circles when the wheels touched the floor. The faster she spun, the less she thought about all that was happening in the creek. She didn't like how she felt, or how fast she was spinning, but she didn't know how to stop. On the other hand, maybe it was the fear of how she would feel if she stopped and allowed all her thoughts and emotions to hit her. She had this vision that the giant snowball had grown so large she was unable to escape from being run down and flattened; or maybe she had already been flattened and was trying to get up again. She hoped she could pop back into 3-D as quickly as Wile E. Coyote did after one of his fiascos with the Road Runner.

If she tried to explain all her fears and emotions to Tim, he would just try to fix it by giving her a quick hug and a glib answer. Typical man, she thought. She didn't want a quick fix, she wanted to talk about it, digest it, take it out and examine it from several different directions. Then she could begin to quiet down within. Yes, I'm glad Elaine and Carmen are coming. Women have the patience to listen to another woman and not try to fix it!

Chapter Nine
The New Celebrities

Cathy sat on the wall by the driveway acting like a tourist at her own house. It was cool under the huge pine tree and she could watch the activity and remain detached. She noticed a line of people milling around on the north end of the property. They were by the abandoned outhouse. The outhouse stood alone, hidden in trees; a shy and tiny structure isolated in the forest. Tim and Cathy assumed the little building; with the cement block foundation, was built by the previous owners. She was surprised to see people using it, they never had. They had talked of all the little creatures that might lurk there, that were impossible to see in the dark, in the hole under the toilet seat. She smiled, and yet felt guilty that all these people were using such a *facility* when they had two perfectly good modern bathrooms inside. One of the bathrooms all scrubbed and ready for visitors. She didn't want all these strangers traipsing through their house, invading their space, using the bathrooms. They came uninvited and they could use the outhouse!

"God, forgive me for my uncharitable thoughts today, I know I am not my usual self!" She spoke to the trees half-hoping God couldn't hear her but didn't believe it for a minute. She was ashamed of herself and her lame excuse. Cathy went back into the house, took out a couple rolls of toilet paper, and sent them with a woman who was walking down the hill. Cathy didn't recognize her, another lookieloo, she thought.

Cathy could hear people complaining about the deputy who was controlling admittance up on the road. She looked up and saw that the complainers were the TV news crew, the ones from Channel 8, she recognized the reporter immediately. They lugged their heavy equipment and were hot and sweaty. They stopped and asked Cathy where the skeleton was found. She pointed down the deck towards the creek. They hurriedly trotted in that direction.

Within a very short time, the TV crew returned with Tim and a deputy as an escort. When Tim saw Cathy, quietly sitting on the wall, he shrugged his shoulders and introduced Cathy to their media guests. She nodded an acknowledgement. She knew the field reporter was Carol Klein, and the cameraman was introduced as Jake Something. Cathy missed his last name and didn't want to ask. It was the first time she had relaxed in almost twenty-four hours and she wanted to guard her anonymity.

The news crew sat on the wall next to Cathy, trying to cool down from the hike, and calm down from being rejected an interview. Cathy had seen Carol cover numerous stories and liked the way she did human-interest assignments; the way she presented the details. She made Cathy feel comfortable, made he feel like they were old friends. Cathy realized that technically she had been in their home for years, in their living room every evening via TV.

Within minutes, Carol asked for a glass of water. She is good, Cathy thought, she is now setting up a situation for an interview. Tim innocently invited them into the cabin, and once inside Carol asked them to tell their story. Tim began and the incidents spilled out, Cathy finishing Tim's sentences and Tim adding details to Cathy's descriptions. The tale about their pond, the men who were digging, the ring, the gold coins, the bones, the hole in the skull, and what remained of the old style clothes.

Carol was writing in a notebook as she asked Cathy to describe the ring. Cathy was giving a detailed description when she remembered that she had taken a picture yesterday. Jake, the cameraman, asked if they could have the film and use the picture on the evening news.

"Perhaps someone would know who had worn such a ring, showing it could only help solve the mystery of who was buried by the creek." Carole was using her best tactics to try to persuade them to allow the use of the photo. She was asking for an Exclusive.

"I have it on my digital camera. Would you like me to print it on paper, or copy it to a disk for you? I could do both." Cathy helpfully informed them.

This information excited their two media guests. Jake said he would gladly download it; computers and cameras were his specialty. Cathy was relieved he had taken over the task. She knew he could do it in a fraction of the time it would take her. When she stressed, she always had trouble with her computer. She had come to believe it was some kind of techno-conspiracy, and that it only happened to people over fifty. Cathy could hear her daughter saying, "User error, user error, user error."

Jake called them to the monitor and showed them her picture of the ring. The bone through the ring was rather chilling with the second bone juxtaposed beside it. The detail of the leaves and berries carved on the gold had photographed exceptionally well. He appeared to be impressed with her photograph.

Cathy could tell Carol was getting really excited about the trip to Julian and this story. It was obvious the picture would be the grabber. Jake printed out the photograph, made a disk, and zipped it into his camera case. Carol had Cathy and Tim sign a release form, which she quickly pulled out of her media kit, so the station would have an Exclusive on the photo.

Cathy had decided she wanted to share their story. She wanted it told accurately and was confident that Carol would dramatize their story credibly, and Jake would film it. Then she worried if she'd have the time to comb her hair and put on some lipstick. Losing ten pounds was definitely out of the question! She hoped that once the story aired, and the facts presented, the dead man's identity would be revealed. Then, she prayed, their life could resume to normal!

Carol told them they would film outside, towards the creek, and away from the investigation. Cathy figured that since Carol now had the picture of the ring; she had what she had driven to the mountains for in the first place. There was no need to antagonize the *law* again by trying to get an interview.

Cathy and Tim stood on a ridge, to the north of the dig and told their story while Jake filmed, and Carol asked them questions. Asking questions to which she already had the answers. The crowd, minus law enforcement, watched the filming. After answering the last question, Jake packed up his gear and the media guests hiked back up the hill. Cathy and Tim could no longer come and go on their own property without being considered celebrities. Some claim to fame, Cathy thought!

Cathy heard her name called in some foreign accent. That must be Carmen. I wonder who she is today. Cathy smiled to herself, and knew that she now had reinforcements on her team. When she looked in the direction of the voice, she saw Carmen, Elaine, and Kim walking down the hill, Elaine lugging the diaper bag. Once on the driveway Elaine began her lament of the traffic, the deputy playing traffic cop, and the parked cars blocking the road.

"Mom, what in the hell is going on? Was that a news van just leaving, Channel 8?" Cathy just nodded her head, took Kim's hand, and walked the toddler towards the house. Her daughter and friend stepped in line, and followed.

"Hungry? Tim can start the hamburgers on the grill. I have everything almost ready. Let me slice the tomatoes you brought." Cathy absently began giving directions once inside the house. "Let's eat in the house, away from this circus. While Tim grills the patties, why don't you two go out and take a look. I'll watch Kim. Here take the meat out to Tim." Once alone Cathy pulled out the toy box from under the bed and sat down and put her feet up in her favorite chair and watched the toddler play.

"Kimmie, come sit in Grandma's lap and we'll read a book." Kimmie continued to play with the wooden train she had picked from the toy box. This was the first time she had the train to herself, no older brothers to hog it. She took the little engine and ran it on the arm of the chair, her little lips vibrating as she made engine sounds. In her other hand she held a piece of track. Cathy wanted to have her sit on her lap and kiss her sweet smelling hair, kiss her cheek. She needed to hold her youngest grandchild, to have balance back in her life, at least for one minute. Hold all that was good and innocent. Kim was playing next to Cathy, and now that she was two, she didn't want to be corralled by anyone. Each time Cathy reached for her she backed away turning up the volume on the engine sounds.

The toddler dropped the train, opened the refrigerator door, and asked for milk. Cathy got up and went to fill a Sippie cup, and noticed the hummingbirds feeding outside the kitchen window. "Look, Sweetie, want to see the tiny birds having a drink? Grandma will hold you up to see them." The toddler put up her arms so Grandma could pick her up to look at the birds. Cathy held her tight, her face in Kim's hair, holding her while she showed her the tiny birds hovering in mid air while they drank from the feeder.

Cathy could feel the tension of the day dissolve. She knew that eventually the circus would fold up their tents and move on to another town to do another show. She had to be patient, and she realized that she wanted to know all she could about who was that poor soul who was murdered and buried outside by the creek. She felt less alone now that Elaine and Carmen were here to visit. Cathy was so glad the baby was here too, it reminded her of what family was all about; the baby was what she needed. Soon Kim was squirming to be let down. She wanted to take the train outside and find her mother.

When Cathy opened the door, Carmen was coming in with the tray. The plates were empty and the pitcher dry. Cathy automatically began to refill it with the makings for the hamburgers.

"Has Tim started grilling the meat yet?" Cathy chirped and Carmen nodded yes. Carmen started helping while giving a report of the action outside. She held the catsup bottle to her mouth and went into her best newscaster voice, and then changed voices and became the interviewee. The bottle became the microphone with lots of static. Soon she had Cathy in stitches and doubling over with laughter. She could always count on Carmen to give a skewed interpretation of what was really happening with a great comedy routine thrown in. Carmen made Cathy see the humor of it all, and Cathy prayed that she and Tim didn't look as idiotic in their interview with Channel 8 as Carmen's characters did with her fantasy interview.

Tim brought in enough food for the four of them to eat, the toddler eating off her mother's plate. The rest of the lunch remained on the deck after Tim told the deputy standing closest, to tell the men to come eat. Only the officials were offered the food.

"Mom, why are you feeding all those people?"

"I'm not feeding everyone, only the men doing the investigation. There isn't anyplace for them to get food near here. I want nothing to interrupt the investigation. I want them to finish ASAP so we can return to our lives!"

"OK, but do you have to kill yourself doing it?" Elaine was starting to lecture her mother.

"I think your Mother likes to keep busy so she can keep her mind off what is going on. Besides you know how she likes to cook for company." Tim defended Cathy, hoping her daughter would drop the lecture.

"She's running around like a chicken with her head cut off. How long can she continue to do that?"

"Until I wind down, I suspect. Tim is right, keeping busy helps. Besides, cooking beats the hell out of watching them dig up more bones! Did you see all those people using the creepy outhouse?" Cathy was trying to direct the incredulity of the weekend away from her hyper behavior.

"I saw the line. Should we set up a concession stand and make a couple of bucks?" Carmen jumped into the conversation with her bright green eyes dancing. She was hoping that by involving the family in *The Fantasy Game,* the lecture would drop and the mood would lighten in the room.

"That's my girl," Tim said, "keep your entrepreneurial skills honed while you're polishing your comedy routine."

"Are you sweetly telling me not to give up my day job?" Carmen teased Tim.

"Never! Your humor is always welcome here! I really needed some of it today." Cathy chimed in.

With that encouragement, Carmen rolled into another interview. She took the serving spoon from the potato salad and held it to her mouth. She interviewed the skeleton, and presented the details of his last day above ground in a hilarious skewed light. She even made his murder into a hilarious skit. Her interview brought buckets of laughter and released the tension in the house.

Kim climbed into Elaine's lap dragging her blanket and stuck her thumb into her mouth. "That's our clue to leave. She'll sleep all the way home, besides we want to have lots of time to catch you two on the evening news."

"Oh God," Cathy groaned. "Did you need to remind me?"

"Thanks for lunch and the appreciative audience. See you next week at work?" Carmen questioned Cathy on her ability to make it to the office with all that was happening outside in the creek.

"Of course I'll be in to the office, this should blow over soon. I sure hope we get some answers. Some answers might make all this mess worth the trouble."

Chapter Ten
The Inheritance

The television was blaring. He had turned up the volume because he was tired of hearing the neighbors through the walls in this fucking motel. Fucking was all they seemed to do in this rat hole. They seemed to be having a far greater time than he had been having lately. He realized he was going through a transition in his life. He wondered if this was how men felt when they lost their job or were forced into retirement.

He was staying off the beaten track in second-rate motels. He was saving money, and believed the managers of such places were more interested in collecting his cash than asking questions about his vacation plans, or his identity. He never stayed more than ten days in any place. His neighbors often stayed less than an hour.

He spent his days acting like a tourist and picking their pockets. He was tiring of the small return on his risk. Now that he was not interested in the address of his vics, the thrill of the game was gone. There were no routes to plan, no houses to stake out, no *Fantasy Family.*

In truth, he was having a hard time finding cash in the wallets he picked. Technology was making it extremely difficult to make a living. Everyone was using either credit or ATM cards. Where has all the cash gone? He was becoming extremely frantic because he had to steal twice the wallets he once had, which made the risks more than twice as great. Was he still invisible, or was he skating on thin ice?

He was watching the 11 o'clock news and drinking a beer while eating Hostess Twinkies. He was having trouble controlling his weight for the first time in his life. He was depressed, and angry with himself, for eating such crap. Any idiot knew that beer and Twinkies did not even taste good together!

Watching the news was the one thing he did at the same time each night. It was his window into the city. He often learned about special events, their location, and the expected attendance. The weather report also gave him some indication on how early the tourist would be out on the sidewalks.

He was tearing the cellophane wrapper off another Twinkie with his teeth when he saw it; saw it on the TV. It was the ring! A ring exactly like the one his Grandmother had from her dead mother. Then he saw Tim and Cathy. He couldn't believe the interview. There had been a skeleton found on their property and it appeared it had been there for almost 100 years. It had been murder; the skull had a hole in it. The skeleton had been wearing a ring; a ring exactly like his Great-Grandmother had worn.

"Holy Shit," he yelled through the mouth full of Twinkie. He couldn't believe it had been so simple, as simple as overhearing some joker at a baseball game talking about his place in the mountains. Then seeing the joker on TV and learning about the find of the murdered skeleton on their property. It had to be his Great-Grandfather, nobody else could have had such a ring!

He remembered the story his Grandmother had told him. The details of her visit to the lumber mill when she first arrived in Julian, and went looking for her father. From the manager of the mill, and with the help of one of the workers, a friend of her father's who did the translating for her, she learned of her father's disappearance.

Her father had disappeared after the manager had confronted him about embezzling from the mill. The manager explained her father had promised to pay it all back, pleading for leniency because he wanted to send for his family. He took the money for their passage.

The manager was still angry when his Grandmother met him. He felt betrayed because he had believed his promise. He had even arranged for her father to work extra days to pay back the stolen money. The manager explained his surprise when he never returned. He had threatened him with exposure of his crime and told him how they hung thieves in a small town. He had said they called it *swift justice*. The manager explained that he could not cover for him, his ass had been on the line, and he had told the owner. Now everyone in Julian knew of the theft at the mill, and who had done the stealing. The town believed he took the money and ran.

This recent discovery at the site of the old mill made him realize that his Great-Grandfather had not abandoned his family. He was murdered! Oh, how he wished his Grandmother had known this. She had become a broken woman after learning that her father had left with the money and never sent it for their passage. Not that it would have saved her mother and baby brother, it would have arrived too late; her mother and the new baby never survived the birth. However, it possibly could have saved her. Saved her from a life of disgrace, trying to survive in a town where they hated the daughter of a thief. Each time she met someone, she knew they knew she was the daughter of a thief, and the daughter of a man who had abandoned his family.

She had survived by first going back to Guadalupe, Mexico where the women of her father's sect remained. The sect gave her ample to eat, were courteous to her, and were fair in how the chores were divided, but she knew the women distrusted her. She could often overhear them talking among themselves about her. They gossiped that she would steal from them, just as her father had stolen from his manager. Nevertheless, she knew they mostly feared her because she was young and beautiful. They feared their men would want her.

One day, one of the Mexican men from the village showed interest in her, and the women encouraged her to leave them and go with him. She could not hide from their hate any longer and left the next morning when the men returned to Julian to work in the mill. She left several hours after the men; knowing she could walk fast and join the group before dark. She knew the women would think she ran off with the man from the village.

Once back in Julian she found a job as a housekeeper for Harvey Luce. He was managing the Stonewall Mine and was trying to restore production and make it profitable again. He worked long hours at the mine and came home late every evening. Marina was to keep the house clean, do his laundry, cook his dinner, and pack a lunch for him to take the next day. She did all the things she believed a wife would do for her husband, and it wasn't long until she was doing *ALL* the things a wife does for her husband. She had fallen in love with this kind man. He was teaching her English in the evening as they ate dinner, and in bed as they made love. She could tell he loved her too.

After her housework, she spent her days alone in the forest, walking and exploring the area. She stayed mostly to herself, the women in town distrusting her because of her father and for her beauty, the men lusting for her because of her beauty. She didn't need them, she had her Harvey. Their life together was perfect. Soon her belly began to swell, and her excitement about the coming baby made Harvey smile, too. He loved to rest his hand on her growing belly as he fell asleep each night. She was so happy.

One day Marina answered the door to their small house. A woman was standing there holding a suitcase. The woman looked at her, and then at her belly. The woman began to cry, ran off the porch and down the street towards town. Harvey didn't come home for three days and when he did he told Marina she had to leave. His wife had come from Maine. He was moving her into the house. She didn't cry, when he told her this, she couldn't. She was numb, and wanted to believe she had misunderstood him. She knew he loved her and the baby. Where would she go? After two days, Harvey returned to the house. He gave Marina some gold coins and told her to pack her clothes; he would take her to the stage that was leaving for San Diego. He said he loved her, but his wife had finally come to be with him. He loved her too, she was his first love; the two of them had grown up together in the same small town. Their families were friends.

He took her to the stage and helped her inside. The baby would be coming in two months and he wanted her settled in the city before her time. He told her again he loved her and waved to her as the stage pulled away. She never returned to Julian and she never saw her Harvey again. She understood about first love, he was her first love. That was the second time her heart had been broken by a man, the first had been her father, the second the father of her coming child.

What a mess life is, he thought. People just keep fucking people over. Then the memories of people he had observed over the years kept flooding in. The families he had stolen from, the houses he had broken into. He remembered the pictures of those families sitting on the pianos, mantels, and desks. All those happy faces sharing important occasions together. The family with the crippled man he had murdered. He remembered how much they enjoyed each other, helped each other. He thought of Cathy's family, her grandkids and how she enjoyed them, how they felt safe with her. He understood that, he felt safe with his Grandmother. His mother's boyfriend had killed her and his mother had blamed him. He understood the horror of life, not the joy. Why did I get such a screwed-up family?

Snapping himself back to reality, the Twinkies gone and the beer too warm to drink, he decided he would get up early, take a little drive, and visit Tim and Cathy. After all, Tim had invited him, and with all the people that were also going to be there, he knew he would draw no attention to himself.

He wanted to be on that deck to see if he would be totally invisible from where he had observed the kids swinging in the tire. Hey, he thought, maybe Cathy would soften towards him with all the confusion. He just needed to apply a little of his charm and he would have her in the palm of his hand.

He now knew their place was where his Great-Grandfather had hidden the gold coins for the passage for his family. "I am going to find my gold," he said to his neighbors through the thin walls. After my little visit to the old lumber mill, I think I will purchase a very sophisticated, top of the line, metal detector.

"I am going to claim my inheritance!"

Chapter Eleven
The Reluctant Promise

When morning broke, Cathy had to stop and think, trying to remember what day it was. It seemed like all this mess started weeks ago, not just two days ago. She made a pot of coffee, took Pillsbury Cinnamon Rolls from a refrigerator can, popped them into the oven, and filled a pitcher with water. When the rolls finished baking, she squeezed the frosting from the plastic bag onto the tops, placed everything on the tray, and took the tray out on the deck.

Her enthusiasm was gone, or was she just plain tired and finally winding down? She called to the men by the creek, held up the coffee pot, and pointed. She went back into the house and sat in her chair with a cup of coffee. She hit the button on the remote and turned on the TV. Oh God, there they were! Coming into their own living room and answering Carol's questions about the skeleton found on their property. They had seen it last night, but somehow the interview looked different today.

There was their property, shown as virgin forest. It all tied together, the huge trees, the isolation, the creek where the lumber mill once stood. Her photo was next, the camera closed in, and the screen filled with the image of the ring with the bone. There was no sound, just the picture over-enlarged for several seconds. It looked chilling, like some Stephen King jacket cover for a new book. Then the footage was of the present, showing the forensic team in their white overalls, the tarp covered with plastic bags, and the interview with the two of them. Cathy had to admit that Carol and Jake had done a good job. The piece gave more mystery than answers about the skeleton. Cathy surmised that since there was no interview with the sheriff's department, Carol had to take this approach. It worked; Cathy would have loved the news piece even if they were not part of it. It said a lot, and yet it answered no questions. Maybe that was why it worked; designed to create curiosity.

Cathy went outside to have Tim help her with lunch. Today would be hot dogs. He was talking with someone on the deck. When she recognized who it was, she got a knot in her stomach. It was that Mike from the baseball game and in Julian, the day she had the grandkids. Instinctively she turned her hand so her ring wouldn't show. What in the hell was he doing here? Dumb question, she said to herself. Tim had given him an invitation, directions; and he had probably seen them on TV. He stood up when she approached, and gave her his best plastic smile. Cathy barely nodded and pulled Tim into the house feigning she needed his help with lunch.

"Honey, you were rude to Mike. What's wrong, it's not like you?"

"I can't stand that guy, and I certainly don't trust him!"

"Whew, Babe, that's really strong for you. What did he do?" Tim acted hurt, like she had just kicked his best friend in the shins.

"Call it instinct, sixth sense, voodoo, or any name you want to call it. That man is not to be trusted! He has some motive for his phony friendliness; I just don't know yet what it is. Just seeing him gives me the willies! Promise me, you will never let him in the house!"

"Jesus, Cathy, I was just talking to him and you take this flying leap that he has some motive. Aren't you overreacting?"

"Be friendly all you want. Just don't include me or I'll show you what truly rude is! Even Glenny could see he was bad."

"Now you're listening to some five year old? Where in the hell did Glenn see him anyway?"

"When I had the kids, Elaine was doing her 60 mile walk, and I took them into town. The day I promised them candy apples. Mike was there, in front of Jack's Grocery. Glenny didn't like him either."

"This is the first I heard about you seeing him in town. What did he do to set you off?"

"Oh, nothing really, just the way he tries to con me with his smile, and his eyes look like he has no soul. He can't take his eyes off my diamond. He even asked me how many karats it is."

"Give me a break, I know this weekend has been hard on you, but if you could hear how you are going on over nothing. You'll have to agree with me that you are totally overreacting. You are judging this guy with no facts, only with your feelings."

"Now I am pissed!" Cathy forced her words through clenched teeth. "You don't have to believe me; you can even think I'm crazy. I don't know yet why he keeps after us, showing up at the games and now here, but I believe he has some hidden motive. Mark my words; this man will make this weekend seem like a picnic! I don't ask you for much, so will you promise me...promise me that man will never come into our home!" She reached out and touched Tim on the shoulder, trying to get eye contact with him as she forced out her words so as not to be overheard. Her eyes danced with anger, as she looked Tim in the eye.

"OK, OK, can I at least talk to him? I will talk to him outside on the deck. He's real interesting and I like talking to him. He loves baseball and wants to sit by us at another game."

"I don't care, outside is all right, just not inside. Promise me you won't let him inside our home?"

"OK, I promise." Tim said with a pout. Cathy thrust the tray at him, turned around, and went back into the kitchen. Tim opened his mouth to say something but snapped it shut and walked outside shaking his head.

When Cathy looked out, Tim was grilling the hot dogs and chatting with Mike. She watched the two men from inside the house. She stood motionless and watched as she tried to sort out all that had happened this weekend and her distrust of this man. In her fear and uneasiness, she couldn't separate one from the other. She watched the man she loved, generously cooking hot dogs for the visitors to their property, as he visited with Mike. She watched Mike visit with Tim while his eyes scanned the officials, the creek and the forest. He was talking to Tim as he continually smiled, but she was sure he didn't see him. Why did he make her feel so uneasy? She knew Tim would keep his promise and keep Mike from their home. She relaxed a little in the comfort of Tim's promise.

In the early afternoon, Cathy heard a knock on the door. She was afraid it might be Mike. She instantly became angry with Tim, thinking he left her to deal with Mike on her own. When she opened the door, she saw the deputy standing there. It was Deputy Johnston. She had to release her anger before she unleashed it on the deputy.

"Hello, Deputy, you working the whole weekend?" With each word, she relaxed a little.

"Not usually, Mrs. Spalding, I asked for this assignment. I have learned a lot helping with the forensic team. Don't get too many opportunities like this up here."

"Any new information on how long the skeleton has been there?" Cathy was fishing for any new information she might pry from the deputy.

"Not my department to figure out forensic evidence. Just wanted to tell you we have finished and we all are leaving. The Department wanted to say thank you for your cooperation, and your hospitality. All your food was greatly appreciated. You can now get back to your routine, and the Donut Chalet will be back in business again. I'm personally going to miss those muffins of yours." The deputy said contently patting his belly.

Cathy said good-bye, and thanks for the thank you. After she closed the door, she leaned against the wall in the small laundry room and took a deep breath letting the air escape through her closed lips, puffing out her cheeks. She dropped her chin to her chest, stretching the back of her neck to release the tension she had been holding for days. It was finally over.

Chapter Twelve
Caught on Tape

Life seemed to be settling down again. The dig, a.k.a. the grave, remained an open hole and every time Cathy and Tim looked over the deck, they remembered that poor man that had been murdered and buried there. No one seemed to know who he had been.

Although they had a contract with a completion date for the pond, the contractor was doing his best to try to cancel that clause in their contract. He pointed out that he had his men there on time, and due to no fault of his, they had to stop and wait for the investigation to conclude. Now the men were busy on other jobs that were scheduled when theirs was to be complete.

"We are willing to move our July 3rd date to September 3rd. Can you promise us that?" Cathy pleaded with the contractor.

"Everyone wants their pools and water features completed by summer. I am totally booked up. To be honest with you, Mrs. Spalding, the men really don't want to work where that man was buried. Let alone all the questions they had to answer for the police. Men from that part of the world don't trust the police; they were terrified they were going to be deported. Of course they're legal; I hire only legals, but try and convince them they won't be shipped off!" He cheerfully chirped on, not answering her question about a completion date.

"Then what guarantee can you give us?" Cathy was fighting that *foot in mouth* virus again. Her anger was growing by the moment. Not only did the contractor have 50% of their money, they had done about 1% of the work. Now he expected them to go to the end of the line. She could still visualize the grandkids jumping and splashing in the pond. She wanted it to happen this season before it got too cold.

"Let me talk to the men, see if I can get them to work extra days. They will want more money for giving up their days off, overtime you know. Overtime wasn't figured into your contract."

"Well, putting us at the end of all your other projects wasn't figured into our contract either." She was trying to control her rage; she knew she had to keep calm, sound sweet and feminine. "You have done so little on the project, perhaps you could return our money, we would pay the men for the half day they worked, and find someone who isn't so busy." She said this in her most innocent voice.

"No need to do that, I didn't say we wouldn't complete the project. I just don't know when I can get the men back up there. You realize it is a long way out from our yard."

"I know it is far for your men, but you knew that when you bid the job. I'm sure you factored that into your price." She hoped she didn't sound too knowledgeable about business, she wanted to sound like a pouting woman whose grandchildren wouldn't get to play in the water if he didn't finish. She was not going to let this man off, to do the work when he felt like it, especially since he had their money.

"We would be willing to pay the extra for the overtime if you would give us the September date. If it would make your men happy, they could leave the wall alone and only work on the pond and waterfall. We could deduct that part off the contract. We are willing to put a cross on the spot where the skeleton was found. I know that's important with men from their culture." Cathy hoped her appearance of cooperation would make him keep his end of the bargain, at least pencil them in on this summer's calendar.

He didn't answer her immediately. She could tell he was sizing up his options, calculating how long he could keep them as customers before he had to return their money. How he could fit them back into his busy schedule.

"Let me get back to you, Mrs. Spalding. Your proposal sounds reasonable to me. I will have to talk it over with my men, of course, before I can promise you any dates. That idea of yours about the cross might just work. My men sure are superstitious; you should have seen them the day they returned from your place. It took me over an hour to get them to tell me why they had returned here early. Funniest damn thing I have ever seen."

"Good, when can I expect to hear from you?" She kept her thoughts to herself; she didn't think that man who had been murdered and buried in her yard was funny at all.

"I'll call you tomorrow morning after I have talked to my men."

When Cathy hung up, she relayed her conversation to Tim. He had turned over dealing with the contractor to her. Tim had previously made several phone calls to the contractor and got no promise of a date to return. With each call, the two men had dug their heels in deeper, the distance between a solution becoming greater.

The idea of placing the cross on the spot where the skeleton was found had come to her while she was talking on the phone. She hoped that by convincing the men the earth was somehow special they would feel relaxed and return to work. A cross, marking the spot where the lumberman had been buried, reminded her of all the little shrines that were placed as roadside markers where people had lost their lives. She saw many along the curving narrow roads as she drove to and from San Diego, some looking abandoned, some with fresh flowers, some with personal belonging hanging from the cross. Who installed these shrines? Was it family, friends, or the Angel of Death? It was within the last few years that this tradition of marking the location of a death was taking hold. She didn't know if she liked the new tradition or not. Some days, the last thing she wanted was a reminder of a death on the road she drove daily. She hated seeing a cross on an otherwise unspoiled landscape: a beautiful spot that proved God's ability to give simple joys. The cross standing alongside the road, laden with flowers of garish plastic in half buried Mason jars, reminding her how fragile life is as she drives to and from her daily routines. Did people drive safer when they see such a shrine? Or, was it as simple as a marker placed where a life was lost? Cathy believed it was a personal message from God, reminding her that the evolution of the seasons and the force of nature are constantly marching forward. Reminding her she is just a short-timer here on earth. She had better mind her Ps and Qs!

As she waited for the pond to be finished, or construction to begin again, Cathy promised herself she would not spend a millisecond worrying over something about which she had no control. She would slow down and enjoy everything around her. There was beginning to be an ebb and flow of the days, months and seasons. She especially loved the changing of the seasons, and spring was slowly evolving into summer.

She loved spending hours on the deck, under the umbrella watching the birds. She loved daydreaming while she watched the wind blow through the trees, and listened to the sounds as the trees bent and swayed, directed by some invisible conductor manipulating the forest. She loved it when the trees lost their golden leaves and shimmered on their way to earth, riding slowly on the wind. These same leaves had somehow survived the winter snow and rain, and now in the glory of spring, decided to let go for one final ride.

She spent many hours talking and playing with the *boys*, the two Schnauzers that had become their substitute children. Oh, how those two dogs brought them joy. The boys' favorite game was to sneak out the back door and then scratch at the front door so Tim would have to get up and open it for them. They knew better than to try to sucker Cathy into that game.

The boys would hear something in the forest and take off running and barking. If Cathy felt ambitious, she would follow them and look for what they thought they had heard. They enjoyed protecting their territory and tried to inform her of what the danger had been. They would give her eye contact and jump merrily at her feet as she talked to them. It was usually nothing, perhaps a squirrel too far away for Cathy to see, and of course, it was gone long before the dogs could come near. The barking scaring off any quarry long before they arrived. She wondered what the boys would do if they did catch something?

The boys took guarding the driveway very seriously. They would warn them of any visitors that were coming by barking and running to greet the stranger. Lately they had taken to barking at the oddest times and running in the oddest directions. Now they ran and barked towards the creek or the outhouse. They never ran to these locations, only in the direction and stopped short, and rummaged with something on the ground. Then they would abruptly turn around and return to the house. Always coming to find either Tim or Cathy, their short tails wagging until their hindquarters vibrated.

Sometimes they would howl like wolves; they had learned this warning from the penned wolves that lived up the mountain. Once they began their howl it was hard to make them stop, with each verse their pitch rose and the chorus lasted longer. It usually took a rolled-up paper that

Cathy would strike against her hand to make them stop this primal song. They hated the sound of the slapping paper, and immediately stopped their howling. They would crouch and hang their heads, trying to get Cathy to apologize for threatening them with corporal punishment. Tim would call to them and they would run and jump into his lap. He would always hug and kiss them and apologize for having such a mean old mom.

"Some behavior reinforcement," Cathy would growl at him. She loved him for his soft heart; but sometimes she wanted to hit him with the paper. His heart was so soft that they bought Andy to keep Cory company when they had to leave them at home. Tim didn't want him to be lonely, so now they had each other. It was hard to believe this was the man who didn't have any animals and didn't want any pets when they first met.

Cathy always had a pet, and when she first began dating Tim, she had a little Poodle, and one cat. Her little dog had gone out one night to lift his leg and never returned home. Cathy looked for days, and put up posters everywhere. She knew what had happened; a neighbor's cat was snatched from his porch the week before and the owners had witnessed the horrible catnapping and kill. It was coyotes and she thanked God she didn't hear it. She hoped it was quick. Her little dog had been very old and she knew she would have to make the decision in the next couple of months on how to deal with his age and recent deafness. The coyotes had taken her choice from her. After a couple of months, she was over the loss of her long-time friend. She didn't mourn for him anymore, but she missed having a dog to love. She wanted a dog!

She had been talking to Tim about buying a dog, and she would tell him of her lunchtime trips to the pound in search of a face that would melt her heart. He had a habit of either ignoring her or changing the subject. They had only been dating a few months and neither had the right to give very strong objections to each other on much of anything. A strong opinion might mean that the relationship was taking a more serious turn than either was ready to admit.

Cathy ached for a dog, and one day she realized she didn't want a man in her life who didn't want a dog in his. This clarity scared her because she was becoming extremely fond of Tim. By making an ultimatum, she might risk losing him. She chewed on this new revelation for several days and finally realized that a dog was more important to her than a man who didn't want a dog!

After all, she had written she was an animal lover in the Bio she had submitted on the Internet. She had written a brief description of what she was looking for in a mate and threw in a paragraph about herself. Tim had read it in cyber-space and that is how they met, first on the Internet, then on the telephone, then at a restaurant. They had hit it off right away and had been dating ever since. Both of them had changed their lives to include each other. Could he include a dog? She finally got up the nerve to put it clearly to him. She told him under no uncertain circumstances can I have a man in my life that doesn't want a dog!

"What's so important about a dog anyway? Every time you want to go somewhere, you have to board him in a kennel. Then there is the flea problem. I am not going to have fleas in my house!" He couldn't believe she would throw him away over a stupid animal. God, he thought, I am really falling for this woman. Am I clueless? I thought our new relationship was going great. She always seems happy when I call and says yes when I invite her out. His heart had started beating faster and now there was a knot in his stomach.

Cathy felt so horrible seeing the look on his face. She wanted to take him into her arms and smooth his hair, nuzzle his cheek. She wanted to tell him he was better than any damn dog she could ever have. But, this dog thing was too important to her, it was more than the dog, it was an attitude about a life style; a warm relaxed, fuzzy kind of life style. It was something she couldn't explain to anyone, it was a feeling she had that she was not going to throw away. If he didn't want a dog he was not the right man for her!

"Let me make two promises to you," she negotiated. "One, I have been watching Elaine and Brian's dog while they went out of town long before they gave me grandchildren, now it is payback time. They can and will watch any dog I own when I leave town! Two, with all the new flea medication I promise no dog of mine will have fleas! Deal?"

She could tell he was thinking over what she had offered. The time was slowly passing as he was deciding. He didn't say a word; just looked at the floor in front of him, and the silence seemed to last an eternity, each second making her feel more guilty by drawing a line and putting this demand on their relationship. Tim's head rose and he looked at Cathy; he opened his arms and invited her in. There was room in his heart for both her and a dog! Their relationship had just taken one giant leap!

Recently there had been little peace in the forest. The howling was getting out of hand; the boys were doing it more and more often. Some days they would bark incessantly, and then there would be a week or more without one outburst. They were beginning to believe the dogs were crying wolf so much that they would not go and look when there really was some danger approaching. When Cathy told Tim about her fear of the dogs crying wolf, they both instantly broke into laughter. Wolf is exactly what they had been crying; they had learned it from the real thing, the real wolves living up the mountain.

They had even discussed one of those electronic dog collars that shocked them each time they barked. Tim would hear of no such gadget zapping his boys to scare them into submission. He reminded Cathy that a dog was necessary when they lived so isolated, it was a warning system. Everyone on the mountain had at least one dog. It was also necessary for a dog to leave a scent so the wildlife would stay away. They missed seeing the deer so close to the house as they had when they first moved on the mountain, but they didn't miss the mountain lion in the yard. Cathy had caught him in the beam of her flashlight when she heard their cat screaming one night. The cat came down out of the tree when she called and the mountain lion ambled away after he sat and watched her from near the pump house. She prayed she scared him more than he scared her. She also prayed she continued to have the good sense to stay close to a door of the cabin when she went in search of a scream armed only with a flashlight.

This was the ebb and flow of the days and weeks, the passing of time, the evolution of spring, the progression of the baseball season. The days' temperatures increasing, the heater quiet, all the signs that summer was near. Their life had returned to normal, the acres in the forest theirs.

They were watching the news at 11 PM, each with a dog on their lap, when a new news feature filled the living room. It was Carol interviewing victims of a pickpocket. She interviewed at least five people who had their wallets stolen, and then almost immediately found, minus the cash, on the same day at the ballpark. The segment also talked about similar thefts at the zoo, the embarcadero, and the boardwalk. Carol also interviewed a detective from the San Diego Police Department. He spoke of a rash of home burglaries. These victims also had their wallets stolen at the stadium, always with only the cash missing. The police were trying to make a connection between the burglaries and the pickpocket.

Cathy watched the feature with extreme interest. She tried to catch all of Carol's assignments since their own personal circus. They showed footage from a security camera of the man they suspected. They showed him lifting a wallet from a backpack at the stadium and dropping it several feet ahead. His motions were smooth, he never changed his rhythm; he never looked around. There was the thief, caught on tape!

The tape showed the pickpocket wearing a Padre hat, a Tony Gwynn baseball shirt with a huge number 19 printed on the back, Levis and running shoes. As the camera continued to roll more men filled the screen with a big 19 printed on their backs. Probably, fifteen thousand men were dressed the same at the Padre game and the pickpocket had melted into the crowd. As Cathy watched the feature, something clicked in her brain. There was something familiar about the pickpocket. It was the way he moved, his gait, the shape of his body. She leaned closer for a better view. She was ready to climb into the television to get a better look, to follow him through the crowd.

"LOOK," she said to Tim, getting his attention. "Look, that guy stealing the wallet is Mike. I can tell it's him by the way he moves."

"Here we go again, always seeing something that makes you think Mike is the bad guy. Give me a break; that guy looks like every Tony Gwynn fan at the game. Look at all those big 19's on the backs of all those men. I saw the video too, and from what I just saw you took one hell of a flying leap."

"I recognized the way he leaned into the lady he took the wallet from, the way he dropped it. I saw him do that the day we first met him. That was on Opening Day and I was waiting in line at the bathroom. I even tried calling to him. I just thought he had dropped his wallet. I didn't know he was dumping someone else's wallet."

"Shit, Cathy, I'm too tired to go through this again tonight. This is just another one of Carol's features to create curiosity and stir-up viewers when the city is quiet. You should thank God that we aren't watching footage of some murder, or drive-by shooting of a teenager."

"Did she make up shit when she did our feature?" Cathy threw the word *shit* back at him. She was beginning to be angry with Tim because he had a habit of discounting her intuition. She knew she was right, she could feel it in her gut. He would do almost anything not to have to admit that she was always right when she had such strong feelings.

"No, but you will have to admit she leads the viewer where she wanted them to go, gives them an E-Ticket ride."

"You're lucky I'm old enough to remember when Disneyland had separate tickets for rides, your kids wouldn't even know what you are talking about, E-Ticket rides, my ass!"

"Don't get hung up on some technicality, I was referring to Carol and her subtle persuasion she works on her viewers."

"Sure, I will admit that she is good at that, but I am referring to ten to fifteen seconds of a video tape of a man lifting a wallet, not Carol's feature. I saw Mike doing the same thing at the same place on Opening Day. I even asked him if he had lost his wallet at the game and he had the strangest look wash over his face!"

"When did you ask him that? Every time you are around him you instantly turn into truly rude."

"I asked him that time I saw him in Julian, when I was with Elaine's kids. I told you about seeing him before. The time I told you Glenn didn't like him either."

"Oh yeah, now I remember, the kid who can see into the soul of a stranger." Tim spoke in his most sarcastic tone. Cathy shot him back a look that could have killed.

"OK, sorry. What did he say?" Tim was now trying to defuse her anger. He was at least pretending to give her side of the story some interest. He hated going to bed all angry. It made it hard to fall asleep. He was not willing to believe the man in the video was Mike.

"He didn't answer my question. He just reached into his back pocket and held up a wallet. Then he changed the subject. I know it was a deliberate ruse."

"So, what does that have to do with seeing him in Julian?"

"Nothing really, I'm telling you I saw him on Opening Day dropping a wallet, and when I saw him the next weekend I asked him if he had lost his. His reaction to my question was not typical. It was too plastic, too planned. Now I see a video that was duplicating what I witnessed. Don't tell me I'm accusing Mike because Glenny doesn't like him! I know it is Mike!"

Tim just looked at her from across the room, deciding if he should just agree with her to end the argument. He wondered why every time they mentioned Mike's name they had an argument. It was late and he was going to bed.

"Should I call the police?" she asked Tim.

"Do whatever you want, just leave me out of this one. Why not call the police. The deputies up here think we're half crazy anyway. Soon, all of San Diego County will know who we are. Good thing you make a hell of a muffin, makes 'em feel guilty when they think they have been eating the food from a crazy!" Tim walked into the bedroom, spilling Cory off his lap and the dog fell into line.

His attitude infuriated her. He could just get up and leave the room, leave everything hanging. He hadn't helped her by pretending to listen; he had only dumped it back on her. She didn't want him to make a decision for her; or even agree with her. She just wanted to process it with him, go over the details. Definitely, she thought, when you want someone to listen and not try to fix it you call a girlfriend! Men, they are definitely from Mars!

She knew she had gone about it wrong. She had behaved like a woman; he had reacted like a man. Some things were always the same. Why couldn't she take solace in that?

Chapter Thirteen
Searching For Gold

A new purpose in life is just what I need, he thought. He was trying to think of himself as Mike while he spent so much time in Julian. Yuri was a name of his past. Maybe he would use it again when he had his Great-Grandfather's gold in his hot little hands. After all, he had the same name as his Great-Grandfather.

He was close, so close, and he was enjoying the search. He was actually experiencing an adrenalin rush as he wore the headphones to his Super-White's Metal Detector and scanned the ground for treasure. So far, he had only found some old tools, nails, bottle caps, a fork, and some unrecognizable rusted junk. He was having fun but this was not what his search was all about!

It had almost become a full time job looking for the buried gold. It wasn't that he was spending so many hours using his new metal detector. It was finding the hours he could use it undiscovered by either Tim or Cathy.

His biggest problem was those damn dogs; they were making the search extremely slow. About the time he turned on the metal detector, those insane mutts would come running at him with their mouths yapping.

He had to run for cover behind a tree or the outhouse. Luckily, Cathy never ventured too close when she came to see why the dogs were barking.

He hated the way she talked to those mongrels. The way she carried on you would think those imbeciles where her precious babies. She carried on complete conversations with them and praised them for guarding the property. If they were so goddamn smart, why was he still able to hang around? Those dogs hadn't eliminated him, only slowed him down. He knew when that infernal barking began she was coming out of the house. Those dogs had become his early warning system.

He hated dogs, especially those two, and sometimes to get even with them he would blow his sleek nickel-plated silent dog whistle and really drive them crazy. Those two would begin to howl, and they sounded just like wolves. They would keep up the howling until Cathy came after them with a rolled up newspaper. He knew she had a newspaper, he had seen her threaten them one time when she came out in the forest. The brats acted scared but they knew she wouldn't spank them. Thank God, it did make them stop that horrible howling.

Progress was so slow that he started throwing out chocolate candy, and when they ran towards him, they would gobble up their treats. He had heard chocolate was deadly for dogs, but he hadn't seen any ill effects, and it was obvious they loved it. It wasn't a perfect solution but it was giving him more time to search. After their treats, they would return to the cabin all happy. The barking had almost stopped. Well, it stopped after they ate their candy.

When using the metal detector was impossible, he would sit on a small folding camping chair, watch, and listen to Tim and Cathy from across the creek. He sat in the shade hidden behind the trees. When they were in view, he could look closely at them with binoculars. He had also purchased a night vision monocular and could watch them after dark. They became one-dimensional and almost unrecognizable. He could easily play his *Fantasy Family Game* with them while they were green.

While he was shopping for his night vision monocular, he saw a listening device he just had to have. With this new toy, a small dish, he could listen to them from almost anywhere in the house, and their voices from the yard and deck were especially clear. He wore headphones while he listened to their amplified conversations, and was amazed what one 9-volt battery and $99.99 gave him. He loved his new toys. Little pieces of technology that he was able to use, something invented that helped him learn more about people, their schedules, their lives, and their fears. When he folded up camp, he just collapsed the telescoping legs, and folded the dish closed and slipped his Bionic Ear back into its carrying case. He stashed it back into a cupboard in his van, along with his camping chair.

Soon he was bored of listening to the middle age couple. What a boring life they had and what boring conversations! The conversations were so trivial. They talked about what was for dinner, did the boys need a drink, did they need more ice cubes, what television program to watch, and all the other bullshit of daily life. It was more than boring; it made him want to puke! He reminded himself of the importance of listening. He needed to know what they were doing and planning. When were they going to town, when was the next Padre game. When he knew, he could adjust his schedule so he could search for his buried gold. It appeared their boring life was full of family, baseball, and those two damn dogs.

He found himself listening not to what they were saying but how they were saying it. Their conversations were full of kindness, patience and genuine love. This went way beyond his comprehension. He wondered if they still had sex. He hadn't been able to pick up conversations in the other end of the house where the bedrooms were, and he didn't know if he wanted to hear that or not. He thought their sounds would most likely be too funny, TMI he told himself. Too Much Information, and two old farts getting it on was definitely TMI!

They also had discussions that quickly flared into loud arguments. Tim would stomp off and Cathy would follow him and read him the riot act. They were stupid arguments. Tim usually accused her of always telling him whatever he did was wrong. He would take this tact when she questioned him. Cathy would flare, and tell him he was a self-centered old fart, and she wasn't going to be conned into believing what he said as true just because he had yelled it at her. She was not going to buy into his manipulation just because he threw a tantrum! This was the common thread of their arguments. He had heard the same flair-up on numerous occasions.

That old buzzard ought to deck her, he thought. Then he realized he liked Cathy because she never cried or sniveled when she argued with Tim, she always held her ground. He hated a woman who would snivel! Not that any of these stupid arguments ever changed anything, because within five minutes, or the next sentence spoken, the love and concern was back in their voices. I just don't get it, he thought. The only time he had even come close to this tenderness was when Suzanne was new in his life. Then he remembered how quickly he had gotten over that feeling! He had continued to speak kindly with her because he needed to do business with her, and some easy sex thrown in was generally worth controlling his rage towards her. Thank God, she was now a thing in his past, just like his name Yuri.

Listening to conversations was a new dimension to his *Fantasy Family Game*. He liked it, and it bored him. He had to adjust how he played the game because he no longer could make up the dialogue. He considered not using the Bionic Ear, but then that created the problem of missing any information about their schedule. He was smart, damn smart, so he would adjust. This was just a new game and the winner came away with a pot of gold! He had already discovered the search was half the fun. He just needed to be able to search without those yapping mutts!

He had discovered the cabin next to Tim and Cathy's place was vacant. It was obvious the owners had not visited the little hideaway in a long time; the leaves against the door had become quite deep. It had a long driveway, and he could see someone coming far enough in advance to slip out the sliding glass door long before the owners had their key in the lock of the front door.

He parked his van on the west side of Tim and Cathy's property, totally hidden in the manzanitas, under the huge umbrella of oak and pine trees. He had to pass two houses on the road to the other end of their property, and he prayed no one would see him driving into the overgrown dirt road. Once he was spotted on the road by the neighbor. He was feeding his chickens, so he nodded, waved to the man and acted as if he was lost. He turned around and drove back up the hill as the man was approaching his van. He knew the man was unaware of his intentions because he had graphics on his van that advertised a landscape company. Weren't the Spaldings doing all that work on the pond before the skeleton was found?

He didn't need to be spotted again on the road. It could signal the neighbor to make a report to the sheriff, or at least a call to the Spaldings. He began driving down the road after dark with his lights off. When he stayed in the cabin next door, he began his search for gold at daybreak, long before the Spaldings were awake and the dogs let out for their morning leg lifting.

He used the house next door sparingly. He didn't want to become comfortable like he had years ago. That was the only explanation he could accept. He must have left some hair or fingerprint in the house across the street from where he killed that man in the wheelchair. He believed he must learn from a mistake, never repeat it or risk arrest. He would die before he would ever spend time again in prison. He had done fifteen months in Juvenile Hall, and he sure as hell was not doing prison!

What good were all those years of working, building wealth, perfecting invisibility, to throw it all away with one stupid move? He wasn't stupid! He would find his gold, collect his fortune and retire in some obscure location. Begin a new life with respectability, or at least the allusion of it. Maybe even a wife and family were in his future. Definitely, there would be a cat in his plans! He could taste success; it's buried across the creek in some can, right under his nose. It's mine! My Great-Grandfather left it for me!

When he was not working on the Spalding's property he was working in San Diego and staying in another cheap motel. He was counting the days until his gold was discovered, and counting the days until it was safe to pull his money out of his off shore accounts. School was now out and the tourist trade was flourishing in the city. He was in full swing, mingling with the crowds. The County Fair was opening and he had big plans for the Midway. He was watching the television from his motel, and the local news was showing footage of the Fair from last year. The crowds warmed his heart. He could almost smell the cash he would collect. How many motels and restaurant meals would that buy? He smiled as he visualized his new wealth.

He was sitting on the bed, Indian style, in the motel. He was drinking a Corona from the bottle and he had squeezed a sliver of lime into the neck. This had become his favorite beer and he loved what a hint of lime did to the flavor. After he took a sip he watched how the beer foamed from passing through the neck of the bottle as it snuck past the lime. He loved to dip tortilla chips into salsa and snack on them while he drank the beer. The beer, chips and salsa were a great combination of flavors. They made a great snack, or quick meal, and it was easy to find in any liquor store or quick mart, and reasonably priced. Well, not the Corona, but the beer was worth the price, and he never drank that many anyway. He marveled how he had come to love the food of Southern California; he loved the Mexican flair to everything. Mexico was sounding better all the time as his final destination.

After the feature on the San Diego County Fair, that Carol What's-Her-Name was doing a new feature. They had promoted the teaser as Personal Safety in Public Areas. The TV Station cut away for a commercial, then another commercial, and yadda, yadda, yadda. Were they going to show the piece on Personal Safety or not?

He had started watching Carol's features because of the one she had done on the Spalding's property, the feature on his Great-Grandfather's grave. When the news began, Carol was interviewing people who had their wallet lifted at the baseball game. Reality hit him slowly.

"SHIT," he yelled at the television and threw the beer against the open door to the bathroom. It sprayed everywhere as it landed in the shower enclosure making a large crashing sound. When the bottle exploded on the tile, the lime further activated the foam, the beer spraying everywhere. The temporary resident next door hit the wall and yelled,

"What the hell is going on over there? Want me to come over there and show you quiet?"

Reality then hit him quickly. They were warning everyone about him. How was he going to work and support himself until he could get hold of his money? The real threat was that people were now aware, now on guard to anyone crossing into their private space. He couldn't remain invisible while he worked his craft. That would screw him up; cut him off at the wallet! How could that plastic face Carol deny him the right to make a living? I just bet that bitch has had a facelift, definitely a boob job!

He popped open a fresh beer and took a swig as footage of him lifting a wallet at the game was being shown. A few frames later, it showed him calmly dropping the wallet. He was fighting to control his fear, his breath now shallow and quick. He sat frozen watching the footage, angry with himself for being so stupid to get caught by a security camera. He finally began to relax when he became aware that he looked like half the men at the game. The Tony Gwynn baseball shirt had given him great cover. Most of the men had a big number 19 emblazed on their back. No one could identify him as being the pickpocket.

"S h i t," he said again, drawing out his anger with each letter of the four-letter word. This time he said the word quietly. He mentally began making a list of what he must do, and when. He began to weigh his options and the risks of staying in San Diego.

"Thanks, Carol, for the heads up. Sorry, I won't see your phony face at the Fair this year." He calmly spoke to the television, his fear abated and his rage now under control.

"I guess I will be heading east, and search for my gold. You know the place." Calm settled over him and he leaned back against the pillows on the bed. He punched the remote, turned off the TV, and set the empty bottle on the nightstand. Soon he was in a deep sleep dreaming of Mexico with warm sand beneath his feet as he walked on a deserted beach. He carried six tall frosty golden bottles of Corona in a cardboard carrier.

Chapter Fourteen
Girls Night Out

As Cathy slid off the passenger seat of Tim's truck, she blew him a kiss. He was on the way to the baseball game and she was meeting her friends at a restaurant. She had arrived a good hour early because Tim was worried about a parking space at the stadium.

Cathy didn't mind arriving early. She had a full hour to peruse the bookstore next door to the restaurant. She knew she was entering dangerous territory because she could not ever remember leaving a bookstore without carrying a heavy bag. Books were a weakness with her. It was all those hidden characters waiting to jump into life when she opened the cover and read the pages. She had to admit she was addicted to fiction, and being in the throes of a good book would totally consume her life. When she finished the book, she was both relieved and depressed. She was relieved because her life could resume, and depressed because she would never be with those people she had come to know. Now they were gone to her forever because the author had ended the story.

On her short walk to the bookstore, she spotted one of her friends. They waved and started walking towards each other. When they met, Cathy hugged her long time friend and they sat on a bench, near the restaurant, and waited for the remainder of the group.

"I hope I didn't ruin your plans? It looked like you were on a mission to explore the Barnes and Noble." Sally questioned.

"Actually I think you saved me before I fell into a financial abyss. I can't resist a book with a great jacket cover." Cathy explained apologetically. "How come you are here so early?"

"My car is in the shop. I'll need to bum a ride off one of you tonight. One of the women from work dropped me off on her way home. Why are you here so early? Julian is a little far to bum a ride home."

"Tim is at the baseball game and will pick me up after. Let's all pray they don't go into extra innings and I have to hang around here all night." Cathy held the palms of her hands together and bowed her head in the gesture of praying.

"God, I have missed the glass group. How long has it been since we last got together?" Sally was referring to a small group of friends who loved art glass and belonged to the local Association.

"Too long! Remember when we used to meet about once a month. Now we are lucky to meet once a year. Where does the time go?" Cathy flashed back on the handful of friends she was looking forward to being with this evening.

The two sat outside on the park bench and visited, watched the people and delighted in the found time they could spend together. The group decided to meet where they had met the last time. The location was central and they made a killer pizza. Cathy had put in a reservation when she first climbed out of the truck.

As the two friends visited, Cathy watched hundreds of people climbing aboard the trolley to go to the baseball game; the station was swarming with fans. She was watching all the large 19's on the backs' of the commuters. Cathy's memories snapped on to a similar scene she had witnessed at the stadium and replayed on the television. She wondered if her memory was playing funny tricks on her. She saw him. It was the way he moved, the shape of his body. It was Mike, and he was climbing aboard the trolley with all the other number 19s going to the game. She guessed he had not seen the Channel 8 feature on pickpockets. Only a fool would return to the scene of the crime! Cathy also guessed he was going to scope out Tim, work on the friendship, or whatever agenda Mike had planned. She dreaded the conversation and the long drive home with Tim after the game. Every time they spoke of Mike, they had an argument.

"You OK? You left me for a while. It looked like some dark cloud swallowed you." Sally was tapping her on the shoulder drawing Cathy back into the present.

"Yeah, sorry about that. I saw someone I know getting on the trolley."

"By the look on your face, it isn't a friend of yours. Sure you're OK?" Sally asked again.

"It's a long story, a thorn in my marriage. This guy introduced himself to Tim and me one day at the baseball game. He keeps popping up in our life, and in our face where you least expect it. He seems so plastic. You know the kind of man, the kind who doesn't give you eye contact while he has this obscene smile on his face. I just don't trust this guy!" Cathy said all this as she was slipping back into the dark cloud.

"He sure got you all stirred up. I hope I get to hear all the gory details. Will you share it with us at dinner?"

"Are you sure you want to hear it? When I say it out loud it all sounds so stupid." She absently said this to Sally, willing her thoughts to the present as she stared at the vanishing trolley. Cathy started to tell her friend about the dark feelings, and her suspicions about Mike. She told it all as if she had some compulsions to get it off her chest, in the safety of their friendship. She hadn't waited for Sally to say that she had wanted to hear it.

Sally patiently listened to Cathy explain about the dropped wallet at the stadium, the feature on the news about San Diego's pickpocket, meeting this man at Opening Day, seeing him again in Julian, and then at her house when the skeleton was found. She told Sally that every time the man's name came up she had an argument with Tim. Tim liked him, and she felt angry and impotent that she could not get Tim to feel her fear. Mike made her all anxious and uneasy, just like he had done when she saw him get on the trolley. She explained how she got mad at herself because she couldn't shake the feeling once he was gone again.

Sally didn't say anything after Cathy spilled her guts. She knew that she was a sounding board and an evaluation or a fix-it theory was not appropriate now.

"I am sure Jean and Margie would love to hear it all, but let's wait until after dinner when we can brainstorm. I would love to hear what they have to say. Remember all the world problems we have solved in the past. Collectively we can evaluate if you are crazy or just weird." With this advice, Cathy nodded in agreement. Her friend's suggestion brightened her mood.

Cathy heard her name called on the loud speaker at the restaurant. "That's us, our reservation must be ready." She looked at her watch and realized she had lost almost an hour of her life again, stuck in that damn dark cloud she was beginning to refer as *Mike*. She and Sally rose and saw the rest of their friends looking for them.

As they entered the restaurant, Margie asked Cathy, "What were you two talking about? We kept trying to get your attention."

"If you've got the time after dinner I will spill my guts with you too. I would like your evaluation. I know you will give it to me straight. I really need you guys tonight but it isn't fair, this was to be a fun get-together."

"Damn, do I have to wait until after dinner? Now you've got my curiosity up and you're going to make me wait?" Margie said with impatience and teasing in her voice.

This is just what I needed, Cathy thought, and she started to relax. I need these dear friends who will keep a perspective on my sanity. Or, should I call it my insanity?

Dinner was fun and full of news of each friend's life. It was always interesting to hear about their relationships, kids, professions, and the news about the Glass Association. The familiar teasing began almost immediately, and a familiarity shared by these friends in Cathy's life made her feel relaxed and special. This group had always been so important to her and she was glad she had not gone to the game tonight with Tim. Then she realized if she had gone to the game, she would have run into Mike again. That thought made a chill run up her spine.

Elliott was the first to ask Cathy, "What on God's Green Earth is wrong with you? Come on lets hear it!" Leave it to the one man in the group to cut to the chase. He had been allowed into the women's group because he was not only fun but also they loved his slant on an issue. He also had the ability to make the evening end at a respectable hour. Without him, they were unable to cut off the talk, usually creeping home in the wee hours. Cathy loved having Elliott in their group, even if he pointed out their weaknesses. She respected him so much she decided to hang her Real Estate license with him, making him her boss.

Cathy looked at Sally and then to Margie. Her eyes asked permission to ruin the mood by stealing everyone's time. They both just shrugged. "Just get it over with. Ignoring your cloud is raining on all of us anyway. Besides, I'm dying of curiosity." Margie said.

Cathy felt guilty, and silly, as she took a deep breath and began again to tell her friends what Mike was doing to her life. She pulled out the video in her mind and played it for them. She gave them the unabridged version with all the out-takes. When it ended, she looked to her friends for some reaction, she hoped for some validation. She could tell by their expressions that her feelings were controlling her. She had stopped breathing. It was all in her mind, just like Tim had said. She knew she had no real information only *feelings*. God, she was glad she hadn't called Dr. Laura and asked for her advice! *Feelings* were a flash point with Dr. Laura, and Cathy couldn't take that kind of criticism now. She hoped her friends would be gentle.

They sat silent, and then looked at each other and then at Cathy. Their silence was undermining any confidence she had left. Was sharing this with them emotional suicide?

Elliot began to speak and asked a few questions. He wanted to get a couple of details straight. Margie tried to put a chronology of meetings with Mike straight in her mind. Sally put her hand on Cathy's to relax her. Cathy felt like she was on the operating table under bright lights and they were all examining her, examining her ability to discern between reality and *feelings*. Sweet Jesus, she thought, and this was elective surgery. I pray the diagnosis isn't terminal!

"Remember when you were all obsessed about your missing brother and your Mother believed he was dead? You had that dream, and one of the men in the dream said he was on an Indian Reservation in Tucson. It took you three months to get there but when you showed the flier you had made with his picture to the homeless, there were over ten people who had seen him in the last two weeks. You didn't find him, but you knew he was alive. Then when he finally shows up six years later and you ask him if he was ever on the streets in Tucson, he said yes. The time he was there coincided with your dream and your trip." Jean reminded Cathy of this, remembering another time in Cathy's life, another one of her dilemmas.

"Remember when you were taking care of all those foster kids and the Welfare Department was placing the worst kids with you? When you asked the Social Worker why they were giving you the most psychotic, they told you they were giving them to you because you were the only one who could figure out what they had experienced. They told you that you had some kind of sixth sense. They needed your insight into their damaged souls to help them help the kids. Don't you remember that?" Sally said with a pleading tone to her voice. It was her lawyer voice, a tone as if she was trying to convince a jury in her closing arguments.

"God, Cathy, I love the way a client walks into the office and within ten minutes you know what kind of a house will meet his needs. It takes most of my agents two weeks of showing houses to come to the same place as you do in ten minutes. You have to have some kind of intuition to do that." Elliott was giving Cathy praise for her Real Estate skills and this made her feel good. She loved working in his office and being treated equally with the more experienced agents.

"I was always jealous when you were first starting your glass business. I hated the way you could walk into a shop or a gallery, and then go back to your studio and design what you thought they wanted to stock. You always got instant orders because you designed for them. You could design what they wanted without them even knowing it." Lindsey spoke for almost the first time during dinner.

Lindsey's honesty surprised Cathy. She had been quiet this evening and Cathy had the *feeling*, (there is that word again) she wanted the time to share her dilemma *du jour*. Cathy thought she had something going on in her life she wanted to share with the group and now Cathy was taking center stage.

"Cathy you are the most intuitive person I have ever met. Actually, you have had dreams or insights that have made my hair stand on end. I would be scared to death to have such premonitions run through my head.

You just seem to take it in your stride, as if it is an everyday thing. I'm glad I don't have the *gift*, you can have it!" Jean bemoaned.

"That's just it. I haven't had any premonitions in over five years. Maybe it's my HRT." The women just nodded in complete agreement.

"What's this HRT shit? Hocus-pocus Rescue Training?" Elliott looked from face to face for some explanation, he felt left out of the group.

The women busted-up laughing and it was Lindsey who patiently put her hand on Elliott's and calmly explained that HRT meant Hormone Replacement Therapy.

"No shit? Now I understand. Was I expected to know that?"

"We will forgive your ignorance this time," Margie explained. "Just one more reason we need to meet more often. Poor Elliott, being in the dark about such terminology is a sad thing. Hasn't your wife explained the facts of life to you?"

"Not about HRT. I do know about PMS and the really scary acronym recently referred to as ED. Talk to me about all the real estate acronyms and I can hold my head up with the pros."

"ED?" Sally asked.

"Haven't you seen the commercials with Bob Dole and Viagra?" Cathy quipped back. Sally smiled bashfully. She had caught on about Elliott's fears.

"OK everyone, let's get back on track with Cathy so she can finish." Lindsey announced like the third grade teacher she was.

"Where was I? Oh yeah, now I remember. Then this man starts talking to Tim at the baseball game. Something as innocent as that, but I get an overpowering uneasy feeling. This guy just doesn't sit right with me. I can't put my finger on what he does or doesn't do, but when I see him I feel like some evil is going to harm me or my family. When I get this feeling, I can't shake it. I am spending too much time in a semi-anxiety attack, waiting for some metaphoric shoe to drop. Not being able to control it is really pissing me off! Then Tim gets all pissed at me and says quit overreacting. Sometimes I think I must be, but I sure don't want him telling me that!"

"But thanks, all of you. It sure was sweet of you all to remember all those things in my past, back when I was young, thin, and ambitious. So what do you think I should do?" Cathy pleaded with her friends, she now felt safe with them. She now could handle any advice they could hand out.

"Go home, shut up, and love your new husband. You have to remember he has known you for a short time in your life. We have known you for an eternity! To believe and understand how you know something is amongst the unexplainable. It takes a lot of history to know you are always pretty much right on track. Shit, Cathy we don't understand it, we just accept it. It is just part of you. Cut the poor guy a little slack!" Margie was giving her best advice to her dear friend.

"You wouldn't just feed my ego would you Margie? You know how angry I was with you when Pond Scum and I broke up, and then you told me you never liked him. I made you promise from that day forward to tell me what you thought even if I didn't like what you said. Remember?"

"Sure I remember, I still feel guilty about that. I guess I thought you wouldn't listen to me. It was hard seeing you so happy and I felt he was just *too* nice, *too* perfect. I sure hated being right on that one!"

"Who says I am the only one in this group with intuition," quipped Cathy.

"Get real, Cathy, that wasn't intuition. That was just plain and simple experience! Don't be too hard on yourself. You had just hit the dating market after twenty-seven years of marriage. He saw you coming with your divorce settlement, and girl, you looked good to him!"

"Yeah, and as my money disappeared so did his love for me. I was mostly angry with myself because I was totally blind to him. I thought I had done everything right. Known him from work for a long time, met his family, kept him at arms length, and yadda, yadda, yadda. I still wear the engagement ring. I look at it three times a day and remind myself: *all that glitters is not gold.* Mike loves the ring too; he can't take his eyes off of it. He even had the balls to ask me how many karats it was."

"Tell me, I have been wondering myself for years. It's one big hunk of a rock." Elliott spoke with a teasing grin on his face

"Getting back on track here…you are saying to just sit back and see how this Mike shows himself?" Cathy resumed the discussion, deliberately ignoring Elliott's question.

"I was just suggesting, keep your mouth shut on your feelings about him to Tim. Mike hasn't done anything you can prove. You are probably right; trust your instincts. They have generally been accurate, excluding Pond Scum of course. Mike probably does have some agenda, like you feel, and can't be trusted. But what can you do without any real proof?" Lindsey said. Cathy felt she was trying to close this matter and hope there was time to move on to her.

"Advice will be taken. Just one more thing, I made Tim promise that he won't let Mike into our house. Is that being too unreasonable?"

Her friends went silent, looked at each other, did an exaggerated eye-roll in unison, and looked at the ceiling. Their crazy faces signaling Cathy she was totally from another planet on this one.

"How did you ever get a grown man to promise anything like that? Promise that he can't invite anyone he wants into his own house?" Sally questioned.

"I guess it does sound kind of bitchy. I got him to promise when the skeleton was found by the creek and hundreds of people showed up unannounced. I was feeling like our private little retreat was being violated, and someone had the nerve to murder someone and bury the body right under our nose. Then I look out and I see Mike with his big plastic grin all over his face faking friendly, not giving Tim eye contact but skimming the deputies and the crime scene. Tim is totally oblivious to how this guy keeps asking him personal questions, and he just loves to continue spilling his guts. I demanded that Tim entertain him outside, but not inside. Thinking back on it, he probably only promised me because everyone was walking on eggs and we were just trying to survive the circus."

"Did you ever find out anymore on the guy who was murdered?" Margie asked.

"Not really, they said it was probably about a hundred years ago. By his clothes, he was probably a lumberman. I think they jumped to that conclusion because the mill was right there. Too long ago to do any real investigation and no one has come forth and given any information about the ring." Cathy explained.

"I saw you on the news and felt so excited because I know you." Lindsey said.

"Yeah, I thought all the exciting stuff happens to you. Here I was out showing houses and I saw you on the TV in a strange family room. I decided not to say that you were one of my agents."

"Thanks for the endorsement, Elliott."

The mood had changed and the group was back to the casualness that made them all close friends. Lindsey refused the opportunity to talk and her conversation remained generic.

Elliott remained true to form; he looked at his watch and quickly rose. He announced he was buying all the "girls" dinner because he had a big escrow close today and he was feeling rich. He grabbed the check, quickly went around, gave each of the women a kiss on the cheek, and went to pay the bill.

"Who was that masked man?" teased Sally.

As Cathy watched Elliott pay the bill she saw Tim enter the restaurant, and the two men shook hands and began to visit. Cathy signaled Tim to come and say hello to her friends. Greetings, good byes, and hugs were shared. Sally bummed a ride from Lindsey and the group left the restaurant together and parted for their cars. They promised to meet again soon.

Back in the truck, Cathy settled against the door for the long ride home. She was full, relaxed and glad to be with Tim and going home.

"Did you have fun with the girls tonight?" Tim absently asked as he pulled out of the parking lot.

"I sure did. I am always sorry we get together so seldom. How did the Padres do?"

"Same old shit, lost again. The crowd was in high spirits though, true Padre Fans."

"I saw Mike taking the trolley to the game. Did you see him?" Cathy wasn't following her friends' advice to the letter but she wasn't going to sound negative to Tim either.

"Yeah, he came to sit in one of Joe's seats about the sixth inning. He sure loves to ask me questions about our place, said he fell in love with it when he was there. He was asking if we found out anything from the sheriff."

"What did you tell him?" Cathy was dying to point out that she thought it a little strange to look Tim up at the ballgame and ask about the skeleton. She bit her tongue and took her friends advice. She wasn't going to have an argument with Tim on the long ride home.

"I told him we were still in the dark." Tim answered.

"Hum," Cathy murmured. She relaxed and thought this was definitely better than an argument about a creep that keeps popping back into their life without a reason.

Chapter Fifteen
A Change in Lifestyle

He never could understand why grown men would dress up in baseball shirts. Wear some big number on their back and go somewhere where ten thousand other men where dressed the same.

He had always feared that numbers on your back were for instant identification, and separation from others, not sameness. He only knew he never wanted to wear any uniform that gave him a number. Maybe if he had played a sport as a kid, actually been on a team, he might think differently. Team sports had never been his thing! Team was a term for which he had no concept.

He smiled reluctantly as he donned his Number 19 baseball shirt and caught a glimpse of his reflection in the mirror as he stepped out the door on his way to the game. Tonight he wanted to look like all the other idiots, blend in with the others, be a robot; look like a fan. Now that the damn shirt had been through the wash at the Laundromat several times, he was beginning to look like a true Padre fan. Best investment I ever made he chuckled to himself.

Working the stadium had taken on a whole new meaning since he saw the clip of himself on TV. He had no idea how many people actually saw the feature on pickpockets, or how many of those people who saw the feature would be at the game. They were not the people who concerned him; he was too good at his profession for them to know when he struck. They were just the vics who had what he needed, the money to support himself until he could slip into Mexico and retire. He needed money until he found his gold, the gold his Great-Grandfather had left for him.

Security at the Stadium made him leery, and he knew the police were scanning the videos looking for him. All those men in the red windbreakers with the name *Elite* emblazed on the left breast, who roamed around trying to look like they had sixty-five thousand people under control. The *Elite* were trying to look like they were able to stop some drunk from fighting when an umpire made a bad call. The *Elite* walking around with walkie-talkies on their belts and earplugs in their ears, acting like they were in on some secret language. As if their presence could control wild fans, and keep them from using four letter words in front of small children. Some security, they were no more than a bunch of baseball fans paid to watch the game! The cameras scared the shit out of him. They created a documentary of his crimes. He had been caught on tape once, filmed twice was not going to happen!

This semi retirement made him feel like lightning had split him down the middle, one foot in his old life waiting to place the other foot in his new life. Until he was ready to leave the good old USA forever, he was stuck in San Diego working at trying to remain invisible. The cost of living in a tourist town was about killing him. Well, actually the cost of living and everyone's use of plastic for money was what was killing him. Where had all the goddamn cash gone?

He had to keep using different locations so no one would begin to recognize him, which made buying his groceries and gas a major hassle. They all had cameras too. Those damn security camera were everywhere and he was tired of always wearing a hat, looking down, keeping his guard up, being friendly, and using his ever shrinking supply of cash.

In a small town, it was definitely easier to lose your invisibility. The residents paid more attention to strangers because they saw so few. In a large city everyone was a stranger, no one gave you a second glance. He felt truly nervous for the first time he could remember. He wasn't able to schmooze the clerk, the waitress, or the gas station attendant. He was amazed at how he missed these superficial exchanges of human contact. Maybe I just need a piece of ass, he thought. He knew he couldn't play the *One-Night Stand Game* in Julian. The whole town shut down at six in the evening, only a couple of restaurants stayed open later. Besides, Julian was so small that the town prostitute was still a virgin! He laughed at himself for remembering the old joke and using it to describe the social life in the tiny mountain community. Pretty accurate, he thought to himself.

He hoped life had been more exciting for his Great-Grandfather when he was working at the mill. If he believed his Grandmother's stories, his life had been pure. She had told him how much he loved his wife, his family, and how hard he was working to bring his family to America. I bet she believed that shit because no daughter can visualize her parents getting it on. Shit, everyman needs a little booze and sex throughout his life. A man needs to kick up his heels when he is feeling randy.

Then everything he had seen about Julian was how they were boasting its past as a mining town. It looked like they were working damn hard to keep that old wild frontier gold rush feeling alive. Even the Fourth of July Parade had a shoot 'em-up, drop dead street fight in front of all the spectators, in full cowboy regalia no less. The kids loved it anyway. He even had to admit he enjoyed watching the funky little parade, something right out of Mayberry, North Carolina. God, I am getting desperate for entertainment, he thought.

He began to now choose his vics at the stadium by where he did not see a camera. He was lifting the wallets between innings when the crowds were the thickest around a concession stand. He liked the beer stands the best. Actually, he didn't like being pinned in and having to dodge the rush. He was becoming afraid he couldn't melt into the crowd undetected. He actually had one vic turn around while he was lifting his wallet and told him to back off and give him some space. He melted into the restroom and lifted his next wallet by standing next to a man at the urinal. What could he do?

He was in a slump; all this security shit had made him lose his rhythm. It was too risky to be off his game. This slump was beginning to erode his feelings of confidence. This was the first lesson his mother's boyfriend had taught him when he was first learning his trade. He taught him that to succeed you had to know you were smarter and better than your mark. He had warned him that if he ever doubted that to be true, his days of freedom were numbered. Dear God, he thought, he had that feeling a lot lately, feeling that his days of freedom were numbered. He hadn't been able to completely shake that feeling since he had last talked to Suzanne, since he knew the police knew he had murdered that useless cripple.

Why were they so worried about him killing the old man? They hadn't been too concerned when he had killed his mother's boyfriend. He actually overheard a cop telling his sergeant that the kid had done them all a favor, saved the county big bucks for a trial. Two pieces of scum eliminated from society, the boyfriend beating to death that old whore and the kid killing the boyfriend. The cop had called the boyfriend a worthless piece of shit.

His punishment for beating the boyfriend to death was being free from them at last. He had been placed with a foster family, the *Leave it to Beaver* kind of family. The kind of family where the mother gets up early every morning and fixes the kids their lunches for school while she serves them a hot breakfast, eggs or oatmeal with stinking raisins. All that attention made his skin crawl. On the third night, he had quietly slipped out and run away.

He had a skill, and he had to support himself. So what if he was only twelve! He liked being on his own, not having to give his earnings to the boyfriend. But best, was not hearing the fights and the fucking through the thin walls. He loved killing the boyfriend, he loved seeing the life finally ooze from him. He loved the act of killing him so much that it scared him. He had read about serial killers, their need to kill for the thrill of it, sometimes becoming sexual. He didn't know if he was into murder for the excitement of it but that son of a bitch had made it personal with him. The cops were dead on right! He was a worthless piece of shit and he had killed his Grandmother! She was the only person who had ever made him feel loved and safe.

The cops had informed Suzanne correctly, he only killed the cripple because he didn't want a witness. He was still pleased to remember he had no thrill in that killing. It was just a job that had to be done. Ever since that night he knew he wasn't the serial killer type.

Only once was he busted and spent time inside. Luckily, he had still been a minor and he had learned there was no way in hell he was ever doing time as an adult! He wasn't going to do time for the old man! He knew that his confidence was down right now. He had better back off and relax.

It was the sixth inning and he slipped down to the field level, it looked like Cathy wasn't at the game today. Good, he only wanted to visit with Tim anyway. Joe's extra seat was empty and he slid in and gave them his friendly greeting, acted interested in the game and thanked Joe for the use of his great seat. With all the social bullshit out of the way, he began to watch Tim for an opportunity to pump him about his property, the skeleton, and work on making Cathy look like some crazy bitch. Tim was easy prey; he was friendly, trusting and open; the best personality type to become his mark. Then there was the unknown fact to Tim that he had been able to hear about seventy-five percent of everything said in his own home. He knew Tim's weaknesses and his strengths; he was going to start working on his weaknesses.

He opened his conversation with a couple of baseball questions. Both Joe and Tim dug deep in their databases to give him not only the correct information; they also gave him the history of why the rule stood. Good start, he thought.

He asked the next question during a play, a non-baseball question and knew that Tim would be the only one to answer. Joe ignored all non-baseball questions during plays. Bingo, he had Tim's total attention.

Slowly he worked Tim for information about the investigation on the skeleton, the ring the skeleton was wearing, and the estimated year the murder had been committed. Tim lit up when he talked with him about his place. Unfortunately, Tim didn't have any more information than he did the day he sat on the Spalding's deck.

Then he started asking questions about his recent marriage to Cathy. Tim gave him a run down on their romance and wedding. Then he asked why Cathy didn't like him, why he had not been invited back to their place? Tim became quiet and evasive, and he could tell Tim didn't want to answer him. The schmuck was so totally honest he just can't lie. This idiot must be best friends with Ward Cleaver! Where has he been living the last fifty years? Doesn't he see what a screwed up world he lives in?

Tim stiffly turned around in his seat and looked Mike directly in the eye. "Look, I'm sorry, Mike, for some reason Cathy just doesn't like you. I apologize but I can't make her into someone she is not. I love her in spite of all her little quirks. She is a good woman, very loving and kind. Sometimes she makes me crazy one minute, and the next minute she is making me laugh or spoiling me rotten. She also doesn't tolerate any crap from me, there is good and bad to that. I promised her that I would never let you into our home. I will honor any promise I ever make, especially a promise to my wife. I guess it is just easier for us all to keep it on a baseball level." Tim turned back around and started watching the game again. He caught Joe from the corner of his eye turning ever so slightly away from him, as if touching his arm as they sat next to each other would give him some disease.

Rage for what this bumpkin had said to him was a word that did not encompass the emotions that were now engulfing him. Revenge was an idea that was starting to take shape and bring him pleasure. That husband of a bitch was going to wonder what had hit him! Not here, not now, but soon!

Chapter Sixteen
The Golden Dinner

He had overheard they were leaving for a long weekend. He hoped the dogs would be gone, not cared for by a neighbor. With or without the dogs, having them gone would give him all the time he needed. He would be able to use his metal detector until he heard the sound of found gold. He could feel his excitement, the thrill when he dug up his inheritance.

Then he would be gone, gone from Julian, gone from San Diego County, gone from the USA. He would be free of the Spalding's, Suzanne, and the threat of prison. Retirement was looking so good!

Of course, he still had some work to do in addition to finding his gold. There was the little matter of revenge. He still didn't have all his plans formulated, but when he did he would sit back and watch the dominoes fall, one by one, knocking each other down. He would sit across the creek, and listen to their anger, their fear, and their accusations. They would call the Sheriff and he would listen to their story, and then drive away shaking his head. Those crazy hermits, living in the middle of nowhere, making up crimes. This was going to be better than any *Fantasy Family Game*. He thought he would call it *Reality Robbed the Spaldings* or perhaps *Finders Keepers, Losers, Weepers!*

Once Tim and Cathy had driven up the driveway, all packed with the dogs in the truck, he began his search in earnest. He crossed the creek and headed for the outhouse. He had stored his White's DFX Spectrum E-Series metal detector there. His pockets were full with the eight AA batteries that would replace the ones he would run down. With his headphones in place, he turned on the machine. Back and forth, back and forth, he swung the wand; listening for the beeps that would distinguish metal buried underground. He had already dug up enough junk to recognize the sounds on the machine that would signal him when he had struck gold. One pull on the trigger and it would show him how deep he had to dig. His heart was pounding; he had all weekend to find his treasure, and two nights to come up with a plan of revenge.

Back and forth, back and forth the machine hung from his arm, listening to the beeps: waiting for the exact sound of his treasure. Within a short time, he had to stop and rub his arm. The DFX Spectrum weighed only four pounds but it felt like twenty-five pounds on his outstretched arm. His head was hurting, the beeps were all running together. He wasn't sure he could distinguish the correct sound anymore. He took off the earphones and stuck his fingers in his ears, shaking his head as if he had to free some evil that had gained entrance through the headphones. He sat down in the dirt leaning the machine against the trunk of a tree. He was pissed! He finally had all the time he needed to search for the gold and within a short time he was exhausted. Here he was blaming the lack of privacy for his inability to find his inheritance and now that he had the privacy, he realized he would have to work in short shifts. This wasn't going to be easy!

He spent most of the day swinging his metal detector in twenty-minute shifts. He had dug up a 1985 dime, a couple of square nails, an old tin pan, and a coffee can. He was sure by the sound the machine had made when he found the can that he had finally struck gold. God, finding that rusty old can had about broken his spirit.

He was hungry, but too full of purpose to walk to the cabin for some food. He saw the vacant house and decided he wanted her to know someone had been inside, he knew she would be aware. He also knew Tim would think she was paranoid, overreacting again. The thought made him smile.

He circled the house and tried the doors; they were locked. He made a mental note of the makes of the locks and knew they were easy to open with the help of his handy little tool kit he had hidden in his van. He spotted the doggie door next to the slider. One kick on the flap and he knew how he would enter the house. Wouldn't this set those two yawpers wild? His scent on their door would have them sniffing and howling for hours. He squeezed through, first one shoulder then the other.

Once inside he looked around. It was pretty much how he thought it would be. There was so much stuff sitting on glass shelves. Shit that would always need dusting. It looked like they collect eagles. Upon closer inspection, he noted that some of this shit must have cost a fortune. He didn't think they would spring for anything more expensive than their season tickets to the baseball games.

He slowly perused the house, entering each room, and opening each door and drawer. The drawers in the master bedroom were stuffed with clothes; and there was jewelry in a box on top of the dresser. He looked inside and saw some costume jewelry mixed with gold necklaces and earrings. Nothing unique or expensive stashed here. He still wondered how Cathy had come to own the large diamond. He closed the lid. Now that he and Suzanne were no longer doing business, this shit wasn't worth stuffing into his pockets or melting down. That crappy little collection was not the gold he was looking for.

The refrigerator didn't hold any surprises. It looked like Cathy had used most of the fresh food in planning for their trip, but the freezer was stocked full. He decided to heat the family size lasagna. What he couldn't eat for lunch he would have later. He would take it back to the cabin. He turned on the oven and slid the large frozen casserole inside. He opened a bag of salad, poured it into a bowl, found an assortment of salad dressings on the door of the refrigerator, and chose one. He set the timer and began to eat his salad. His eyes wandered around the room while he contemplated his revenge. He hadn't formulated any ideas yet that would excite him enough to call it even. He felt confident he would know it when he found it. He was scanning the room when he noticed a closet with a deadbolt on the door. He took another bite and visualized where the key might be placed. He had seen a set of keys on a hook in the laundry room. He relaxed again, and continued chewing the crisp greens. He knew there would be a key on the ring that would open the door. People with such trust in their souls were never suspicious or devious. He had built his career on just these kinds of people.

With the salad eaten, he took the keys, opened the door to the closet, and began an inventory of the contents. There were shelves across the back half of the closet about one foot apart from floor to ceiling. Stacked on the shelves were small thin paper boxes set on edge, two deep and two rows high. Standing in front of the shelves were several rifles in leather cases, and sitting on the floor were several large coffee cans full of coins. Each can sorted by denomination. He noticed that there were two cans filled with silver dollars, one sitting on top of the other. He had lifted the top can to see the contents of the bottom can and could not help but notice the weight. He bent down for closer inspection and saw that the other cans contained half dollars, quarters, dimes, and pennies. He couldn't begin to count how much money was just sitting there.

He took the guns from their secure compartment and leaned them against the buffet. He slid out the cans of coins and placed them in the open floor space of the living room. The shelves were now unobstructed for easy appraisal. Slowly and methodically, he opened box after box. Inside each box was another box or velvet folder, and inside the interior container was a set of U.S. Proof gold coins. He couldn't believe his eyes, his find. Sitting right under his nose was a fortune!

As he rotated his wrist to work out the soreness, he realized he had been scanning the dirt for a reported old rusty can that his Great-Grandfather had buried. He had been hanging around waiting for a shot at finding his inheritance, dodging those barking animals and all the time it was sitting right here. As he recovered from his fatigue and reflected on his pursuit of treasure, he realized that finding this golden treasure left him emotionally deflated. It was like playing *The Fantasy Family Game* and when he finally entered the house, it held nothing like he anticipated. It was like opening a present you thought was a model train and discovering the contents held a flannel shirt. He backed up looking past the open door, into the closet. Why wasn't he thrilled?

He now understood the significance of finding the lost buried can left by his Great-Grandfather. The rusty old can filled with gold would verify all the family history his Grandmother had shared with him. He needed to believe that families really loved each other, worked together, shared their successes, and stayed together during their failures. He needed to know that his Great-Grandfather had not lied to his wife in his letter, had not abandoned his family. He needed to know that his Great-Grandfather had been saving the gold for the passage of his family to a new land. Was being with his family worth becoming a thief? Had he been murdered because of it?

The discovery of the remains of his Great-Grandfather buried by the creek had opened an old wound, a wound that had been festering for years. A wound slashed deep the night his Grandmother died. He had lived with a mother who had no love and a Grandmother who had loved but carried a broken heart. What about his Great-Grandfather, had he loved his wife, and taken great risks to come to a new country to give his family a better life? Why murder, who had killed him? Did the manager pull the trigger or some supposed friend? Was there a fight, or was he murdered unaware he was being stalked? For almost a hundred years, his family history was buried. Only the skeleton and the ring survived. He was angry that he had come so close to learning about his family, and now he believed he would never have his questions answered.

What had happened to the can of money his Great-Grandfather had buried in a secret place? He had seen the letter himself when he was a child. Was the can still buried out there and he just couldn't find it, or was the money stolen from his Great-Grandfather the night he was murdered? Shit, too many unanswered questions! He was beginning to believe the answers were buried with the gold. Believing they were never to be found and never to be answered.

Life was strange. Coming to San Diego, going to the game, overhearing the name Julian, and seeing the feature about the skeleton on the TV, the phone call with Suzanne, seeing himself caught on tape, and a million other trivial incidences that change the direction you take. Life is kind of like some board game, he thought. Roll the dice and see how many squares you can move. Move past Go and collect two hundred. Hold onto your Stay Out of Jail Card until you need it. God, how he wished he had a Stay Out Of Jail card now. Maybe Julian and the cabin next door was his Stay Out of Jail Card. He was biding his time until he could slip out of the country and collect his stash. He bet, in a hundred years, when they discovered his remains all that he had done would leave a hundred unanswered questions, too. Just like his Great-Grandfather. He smiled at that thought. Families go full circle.

His thoughts were back on revenge but the timer was making an annoying sound that brought him back to the present. He turned it off and removed the large disposable aluminum pan from the oven. He decided to leave the oven on. From overhearing Tim and Cathy, he knew such forgetfulness would give them at least a five-minute go-round. Leaving it on for the whole weekend would become a major squabble. He smiled and loaded a plate with a large serving of lasagna and carried it to the dining room table. He put a place mat under his plate and sat down to eat.

He noticed the dishes, the placemats; the kitchen décor was all apples. How apropos he sarcastically thought, apples and Julian. When the gold had run out the residents had planted orchards. Now they promoted apples. What a come down for the town! He liked the historical connection of Julian and gold better, and here he was sitting in front of a closet that had become the Mother Lode! The gold all minted and boxed!

Then the idea came to him. He would empty the closet and lock it up again. He would sit across the creek and wait for the gold discovery. Well, maybe discovery of lost gold would be a better term to use. He had jumped their claim! That would serve that arrogant husband of a bitch right. Telling him that he can't come inside their house because of some stupid promise, he made to his wench. Here he was sitting inside the very house where he had been denied admittance!

What fools they all were, playing by some rules that another bunch of simpletons established. They liked to use words like honor, promise, love, and commitment. They were just stupid sentimental words that people throw out into the wind. If those promises were so goddamn great, why did people get divorced and finally end up shitting on each other? Thank God, he was too smart to get sucked into that trap!

He still had work to do. He began wondering how many dinners he would be eating here before he left the good ole U. S. of A.

Chapter Seventeen
The Empty Closet

Cathy surmised they must be old when going home looked so damn good. Maybe we are barn sour, she mused. Once out of the barn they were always looking back over their shoulders as they headed away from home, and took the quickest and most direct route back.

It had been a wonderful three-day weekend and they were now on the way home. Three days filled with hugging and kissing Tim's two-year old granddaughter, staying with his daughter and husband, a lot of driving, and sleeping in a strange bed.

Cathy was glad they went; the trips north were too far apart. Tim has only the one granddaughter, the light of his life. She knew that seeing his daughter and granddaughter would brighten his life for months. Cathy always became the photographer and once the film is developed, the trip relived, and the photos added to the gallery displayed around the house. A duplicate set of pictures would be sent north to his daughter and placed in a special "Grandpa Album" for little Angela to view between visits.

Cathy felt so blessed. She was able to be with Elaine's kids weekly, and the constant time together with them had enabled her to build a relationship with each child, a bond that filled her life with love. She prayed Tim could develop such a strong bond with little Angela, but the distance made it so difficult. She could tell that he and his daughter were both working very hard to make it happen. Cathy would be flexible, even change her life to facilitate trips, and phone calls, or do anything so that Angela could develop memories with Grandpa.

They had been driving for hours and Cathy's back was getting stiff. Her discomfort brought her back to the present. As she squirmed and twisted to regain some circulation in her legs, she looked into the back and noted the boys sprawled out on the seat sleeping. Cathy knew they were ready to return home too. This had been their first trip north and they had to obey many new rules. They especially hated the rule about sleeping in the garage! She was thinking that dropping them off at Elaine's would have made everyone's weekend much easier.

"You OK, ready for a break?" Tim asked when he noticed she was twisting in her seat.

"I'm getting stiff. How are you doing?"

"OK, but stiff too. We'll buy gas up about another twenty miles and I can stretch there and give the boys a leg lift and a drink. Do you want to stop for an early dinner or drive straight through?"

"In this heat I worry about the boys in the car. Let's just get home. I can pop that lasagna in the oven and I have a bag of salad that will still be good. We could eat in an hour and by then the car will be unloaded." Cathy was actually thinking out loud, taking inventory of her refrigerator by memory, and calculating how hungry they would be when they arrived home. "I could break out the cheese and crackers from the cooler and hand you a snack as you drive."

"Sounds good, pop me a Diet Pepsi too." Tim was happy that they would be home an hour earlier because of no meal break. He was mentally counting the money they had just saved. He knew he spent too much on that play set for Angela. He wanted it desperately for her, before her other grandparents bought her one. He knew that Denise would tell her the swings were from Grandpa every time she went out to play. He wanted her to remember how much he loves her. It is so damn hard living five hundred miles away! Now that she was talking, the phone calls helped a little. He loved hearing her sweet little voice and coaxing words from her and into the telephone.

He envied the relationship Cathy had with the kids. He wasn't jealous because she was able to spend so much time with her grandkids; he only wanted to do the same with Angela. He enjoyed Cathy's grandkids too and fell in love with them just as easily as he had fallen for Cathy. It was weird though, the way you felt about your own. He guessed it was that blood thing, that generational thing. Was it because you knew that the continuation of your own genes would flow on long after you are gone? Why did they have to move so damn far away?

Cathy leaned against the doorframe and relived the trip in her mind. She remembered the pictures they had shared with Denise. The roll of film was taken in April when Cathy had the kids for the weekend and they had hung an old tire in a tree. She had shot the pictures from the deck with the zoom lens on her little Nikon. The first half of the roll was taken without the knowledge of the children while they played. The second half of the roll the children saw their grandmother with her camera. The pictures were precious and always brought a smile to her when she shuffled through the stack. There was a picture of each child separately and pictures with the kids swinging together from the tire. They arched their backs and stretched for the sky as they clung to the rope, wide smiles covering their faces. There were pictures of their precious faces with their tongues sticking out in defiance of the photographer, and pictures with fingers making horns behind the head of a brother or little sister. In the last picture on the roll, the picture with the kids making faces, there was also someone else in the photo. This picture showed someone hiding behind a tree on the other side of the creek. Only an elbow covered with a plaid shirt and the toe of a shoe were visible, but in all the times Cathy and Tim had looked at the pictures, they had never noticed the intruder. They had been too preoccupied viewing the precious faces and the projected tongues to see someone in the background. It was Denise who had asked, "Who was hiding behind the tree?" She had thought it was Brian, the children's father.

As Cathy looked closer at the intruder in the picture she knew immediately it was Mike, she remembered the shirt. He was wearing the same shirt that day in Julian. How long after seeing him in Julian, did she take the pictures of the kids? So many questions bombarded her mind. The horrible cloud instantly surrounded her and she wanted to be home. Home where she would have the privacy to sort it all out, control her anger for his invasion, and suck back her tears. Denise noticed immediately how Cathy's mood and body language had changed.

"What's wrong? If that isn't Brian who could it be?" Denise asked innocently.

Tim looked from his wife to his daughter. He was trying to calculate how far these two women would take this new mystery in the photograph and run with it. Given his interpretation of the situation by the look on their faces, he was ready to run, leave the room before he had to explain to his daughter about Mike. He just didn't have the answer, and having to explain how Cathy kept harping about Mike was the last thing he wanted to do, especially on this trip.

"It is an ongoing disagreement your Dad and I keep having about this man we met at the baseball game." Cathy didn't want any conflicts in front of Tim's daughter, and the last thing she wanted to do was ruin their short trip north with her dark cloud hanging about. She was trying her best to sound light and casual and shake off that damn feeling that something horrible was about to change their lives.

Tim picked up the conversation when Cathy stopped talking. She just became silent. He began to tell Denise about Cathy's *feelings* about this man. Cathy tried hard to be objective as she listened to Tim's rendition of how their life was changing since they had met him. It was hard to admit, but it did sound more like hocus-pocus when she heard how Tim told their story. This was Tim's version, of course, but she needed to hear it as he told it to his daughter. Oh God, he makes is all seem so simple and harmless. She had to bite her tongue to keep from interjecting her thoughts, fears, feelings, interpretations, and their chronology of events with Mike. She so desperately wanted Denise to have all the information so she would have a clue into how her Dad's new wife was spinning out of control by fear of this man. Why couldn't she let it go and relax as he could? She decided she didn't want Denise to hear how she really felt. It was sort of a cross between sounding like an idiot worrier, and creating fear in Tim's daughter that something horrid might happen to her father. She chose to remain silent and look casual and unaffected by Tim's story, no easy task she realized.

Cathy started reading a book to Angela as she ignored Tim's epilogue. Slowly, very slowly, and with great effort she lifted the cloud surrounding her. Not for one minute was she going to forget the evidence in the picture of the man hiding behind the tree! It was only an elbow and a toe, just a tiny piece of evidence, but why was he was hiding? Why would someone be out in the middle of nowhere in the first place, let alone hiding behind a tree? They might all think she was crazy, but she knew who it was. Repeatedly, she had tried to find the answer to this simple question, the answer still eluded her.

Cathy was still spreading cheese on the crackers and handing them to Tim when they turned down their driveway. She was counting on the snack to stave off their hunger until the lasagna was hot. The boys recognized the road, jumped up, and started pacing and whining.

"What's a matter guys?" Tim said to the dogs, "You glad to be home too?" He pushed the button and the back windows slid down in the grooves. The dogs leaned out until it looked as if they were going to fall. They had caught the scent of home and their excitement increased. Each dog ran from window to window sniffing the air, back and forth, back and forth, missing each other in the middle as they passed.

Cathy caught her breath when their house came into view. It still happened to her even after living here for over three years. She couldn't help it; her body automatically responded to the pristine beauty of the tall trees, and the dappled shadows they cast across the cabin. It was always the surprise of finding a little piece of serenity tucked between the trees, waiting to welcome them home. Only three hundred feet of paved driveway until you were home, the last little bit of distance until the cabin and the forest swallowed you. It was all smooth and downhill from here. It was like the last swoop on a roller coaster ride, once past the rough spots you just glided to a smooth stop. Ah, home at last!

The boys jumped free of the truck in wild enthusiasm. They ran to their favorite tree and lifted their leg. The tree was so huge there was no waiting in line, each using one side of the trunk, hidden from each other. Then as if some silent whistle were blown, the legs went down and the patrol of the property began. What had violated their space while they were removed from guard duty? Run, run, run, sniff, sniff; sniff. They ran shoulder to shoulder circling the house and deck. Faster and faster, they circled until they disappeared. They had entered the house through the doggie door.

Tim and Cathy were still unloading the truck when they heard the dogs begin to howl from inside the house. It was that wolf howl. They knew it would continue and become more frantic until they called it off. They looked at each other and hurried inside to see if the boys had cornered a small animal. An animal intruder had always been a possibility, but luckily, to date, it had never happened. The consequences of an intruder could soon end their peaceful return. They were tired and didn't want any problems with intruders, leaky faucets, or disturbing phone messages. All they wanted was a hot meal followed by relaxing reruns on TV, and a good night's sleep in their own bed!

Once they were inside the house, the dogs continued to howl. Tim searched the east end of the house while Cathy searched the west. They could find nothing but two dogs sitting by the doggie door with their heads thrown back howling. Cathy thought they were throwing a major doggie temper tantrum. She rolled up a magazine and started hitting her other hand, making loud smacking noises. The howling stopped immediately, but it was obvious the boys were unhappy with the threat of a spanking, and unhappy with their inability to warn their masters that their house had harbored an intruder.

The silence felt gorgeous. Cathy began to start dinner and walked to the oven to preheat it. She felt the warmth as she faced it with her hand raised to turn the dial. It was on! How could that be? Cathy stood facing the hot oven trying to remember when she had last used it. She recalled last week's schedule and remembered she had worked late on Thursday night and had not cooked. They left early Friday morning after a bowl of Cheerios. She was sure the oven was off when they left, wouldn't they have felt the heat a dozen times when they walked by? She couldn't remember when she had last used the oven this summer. She elected to omit this piece of information about the oven to Tim, no use stirring trouble. Now, she was standing in front of the freezer with the door open looking for the lasagna. She pulled out a few items and placed them on the counter to dig under some packages of frozen meat. Where had it gone? She removed everything from the basket at the bottom to be certain that the lasagna was not there before she unloaded the counter back into the freezer. Still shaking her head she opened the refrigerator door and checked to see if the bag of salad was there. It was gone too. She puzzled over the missing food and decided this had gone way beyond weird. She looked at the boys and shrugged her shoulders. She was in a silent conversation with them as she moved around the kitchen. Their eyes followed her, still wary about the threat of the spanking. She knew they would be willing to forgive her if she issued them a handout.

"There is no food here boys. You were right. Some creep used your private and special doggie door to come inside and eat our food." Cathy used her most sympathetic voice as she spoke to the boys. "I guess a doggie biscuit wouldn't hurt before dinner. I know the intruder was the two legged kind, he left your treats alone." The dogs came alive as she reached for the cookie jar that held their treats.

"Tim," she called in a loud voice to get his attention.

"Yeah?"

"Did you eat that lasagna and salad while I was in town last week?"

"No way Babe, I have learned to ask before I raid the freezer. I only eat the leftovers without permission. Thank God, you still cook as if you are feeding all your kids. It gives me mountains of leftovers." Tim shouted this to Cathy from the bedroom as he unpacked his suitcase.

"It's gone; I can't find the lasagna or the bag of salad." She yelled towards the bedroom.

"You sure you didn't take it out to the freezer in the pump house to make more room for something else?" Tim was trying to find a solution for the missing lasagna. This solution making, always made Cathy angry. She knew he was throwing out ideas and taking them for facts. Tim was good at just thinking up an answer and then believing his solution would make it happen. He was tired too and he didn't want any friction, only dinner. This solution was simple, no friction and the lasagna would instantly reappear.

"No, but I'll sure as hell will go look and see if it mysteriously reappears. Please let me find one lonely rectangle of lasagna in a disposable aluminum pan, just sitting there on a shelf all frosty and frozen hard as a brick." She had answered him much frostier than she meant. The crisp sarcastic tone of her voice just slid out before she could take it back or hear how it sounded. She realized how tired she was. How did she ever think dinner at home would be as simple as popping the casserole into the oven and dumping a bag of salad into the bowl?

It was too late, but that meal at a restaurant was sounding good. Oh, how she wanted a restaurant where a waitress brings the food to your table and cleans up the dishes when you leave. The more tired she felt, as she walked to the freezer, the more she wished she had voted for a sit-down-air-conditioned restaurant. Now she was tromping one hundred fifty feet to the pump house to look inside the freezer to see if the lasagna was in there. She wasn't doing this to prove to Tim she didn't have a bad case of lost memory, she was doing this to prove to herself that someone had been in the house while they were gone, and had either taken or eaten the lasagna!

She stood looking into the frosty box while the frozen air escaped making a fog as it hit the warm air. There was lots of food waiting to be rotated into the small space above the refrigerator in the house, but this freezer didn't hide any lasagna. This discovery gave Cathy a strange dilemma. The dilemma of what were they going to eat for dinner and how to present the missing lasagna to Tim. God, she was growing wearier by the minute.

"Hey Babe, how long will the lasagna take?" Tim quipped as he stashed his empty suitcase under the bed in the guest room.

"I guess forever; or in no time at all since it don't exist." She was now angry with Tim. Usually, calling her Babe didn't bother her. She actually had grown to cherish the way he called her that. It was his way, his endearing way, to let her know how special she was to him. Let any strange man call her Babe and just watch out! She would most likely verbally cut him to shreds. Then it hit her; she had just realized he was certain she would find the lasagna in the freezer in the pump house!

"What do you mean it doesn't exist?" He questioned, "I sure as hell didn't eat it."

"Well somebody did, and I believe it wasn't you. I saw it myself in the freezer in the house when we left Friday morning. I was taking out the Blue Ice for the cooler. I had planned on us eating it tonight or tomorrow night along with the salad." She was working very hard on a calm explanation for Tim. She hoped she could bring him to realize that their private space was violated while they were gone. This time the violation was from inside their home! The dogs knew it; so that left only Tim to realize someone had been inside.

"The salad is also gone and the oven had been left on."

"You mean to tell me the oven has been on all weekend. Why didn't you check before we left to see if you had left it on?" Tim jumped on this new information and was now blaming her for any extra expense of propane used unnecessarily.

"I did not leave it on!" Cathy snapped back trying to control her anger. "When did I last use the oven in this heat? Wouldn't we have felt the heat when we walked by?"

"Hum," Tim murmured under his breath as he thought out loud. He was also trying to control what he said so there would be no argument with Cathy. He could tell the lost lasagna had pushed her to the edge. He was tired and hungry and wanted a good night's sleep.

"I can't remember when I used it last either. I was happily cleaning out the leftovers, and you know I only use the microwave when I don't eat 'em right out of the fridge. The oven takes too long."

"What about the missing lasagna and salad." Cathy reminding him the issue was larger than forgetting to turn off an oven.

"Beats me."

"It doesn't bother you to know that someone has been in our house and eaten our food? He probably squeezed through the doggie door, cooked in our kitchen, sat at our table, and left again, leaving us to question the missing food and hot oven?" Cathy was trying to get Tim to make the giant leap and admit they had a visitor.

"Shit, Cathy, what is the big deal? You and I both know we would have invited him in if he would have showed up on the doorstep, and you would have served him on our best china. What's a little lasagna and a bag of wilted lettuce? We should thank God it was the store bought lasagna and not your secret-recipe-homemade lasagna. One bite of that and he would be moving in and waiting for more of your great home cooking." Tim was now smiling and starting to play hurt. "I am a bit hurt the stranger didn't leave a thank you note. I would hate to think we fed an ungrateful son of a bitch."

"Come on Tim, get a grip," she was pleading now but enjoying the hurt act Tim was dishing out. She loved the way he was praising her creative cooking. "It is not what was taken but how it was taken!" She was not going to fall for a change in subject by falling for his lightheartedness or compliments. "How about believing me when I say it was Mike who came in here and ate the food? You told him you had promised me that you would never let him in. Don't you think this is his clever little fuck you? I will come into your house anytime I want, with or without your permission!"

Tim rolled her questions over in his mind. He still couldn't agree with Cathy on her total all-out-war against this guy. It just didn't make sense to him. Why would he drive that entire distance, squeeze through the doggie door, and eat their food? That was a lot of trouble just to show them he could do what he wanted. No, Tim thought, it was just some homeless mountain man that was hungry, no big deal.

"Next time I promise to lock the doggie door to keep out intruders, both the two legged kind and the four legged kind. We should thank God the intruder didn't spray the house because he was pissed because he didn't know how to cook the lasagna."

Cathy finally smiled at the vision floating around in her mind of one pissed-off skunk throwing a temper tantrum in their house. The skunk was hungry and the only food in the house was frozen. She was definitely glad they had not returned home to the inside of their house smelling of skunk!

"Do you want to go to the restaurant at the Lake for dinner or do you want me to open a can of soup?" Cathy hoped that by pointing out indirectly that the food was missing, and reminding him that his hunger would soon again raise its ugly head; that it would gradually sink in that they had indeed had an intruder.

"You want me to choose between a sit down dinner with a view of the lake and a can of soup?" Tim questioned her with a grin on his face.

"I want you to decide between getting in the truck again, driving to the restaurant and paying for a meal, or eating canned soup at home and not spending any money." She was now playing with him, knowing they would go nowhere and he would not complain about a lousy meal.

"I just want to stay home and get unpacked."

"I will even serve our best, no water added, gourmet canned soup with crackers and cheese. You just have to sweet talk me a little," she teased.

"If I call you Sweetie, will you spread a little peanut butter on some of those crackers? I'm about all cheezed out after the snack on the drive home."

"It's a deal if you totally unload the truck." Cathy would have promised him anything so she wouldn't have to make several trips outside to haul it all in. She was promising herself that she would not pound him with the obvious. To her it was obvious that Mike had been into their house while they were gone. She knew it to be a fact. She was beginning to fear that Tim would never accept that this man had some agenda against them. Tonight she was too tired to try to point out anything to him but the pan of hot soup.

Before Cathy dropped the empty soup can into the trash she lifted the lid to the trashcan and looked for the remains of the lasagna. The disposable aluminum pan was not there but the Ziploc bag that had held the salad was.

"Look Tim," she pointed, "here's the bag the salad was in. Remember you replaced the liner in the trashcan the very last thing before we left?"

"Yeah, I remember. OK, I agree someone was here after we left. Find any clues about the missing lasagna?"

Cathy shook her head and resumed preparing a dinner that she knew would leave them both disappointed. Tim continued unloading the cooler, replacing the Blue Ice in the freezer, and putting the unopened cans of Cokes back into the refrigerator. He was in her way in the kitchen, oblivious to the fact he was stepping in and using the very counter space she was using to spread the peanut butter on the crackers. She stepped aside and held her tongue. The last thing she had the energy for this evening was pointing out how obtuse he was.

Once finished unloading, Tim picked up the coins his daughter had given him for Father's Day. She had kept her gift for him until she could give them to him personally. She wanted to see the look on his face when he opened her rare and special collection. A gift she had obviously spent time researching and acquiring for him.

Tim stopped in front of the closet and opened the top folder. He was staring at a proof set of coins minted the year he was born. A second folder held a proof set of coins minted the year his daughter was born, and a third folder contained a set of coins minted the year his precious baby Angela was born. Cathy could see the tears of joy in the corner of Tim's eyes as he stood there gazing upon his very special and expensive gift. He seemed lost in time, and so touched by this special gift from his daughter and her husband. Somehow, she knew how he felt, knew that this special gift signified some concrete validation of all that family was all about. He held it close to his heart as he opened the closet door with a key he kept on a ring with his truck keys. He would place his special gift in his closet with all the other rare coins he had been collecting for the past thirty-five years.

Cathy was watching him because she felt proud to love a man who had the ability to show emotion. She felt a little guilty stealing a peek into his private tears of joy. She knew he was oblivious to her voyeurism, and she knew he would not be angry if he spotted her watching him. She also knew of the dilemma he would face in choosing the appropriate shelf in the closet to place his prized gift. The closet was already crammed full of folders containing coins, and the floor covered with large cans containing loose coins. Tim just stood there peering into the closet as Cathy watched. He stood motionless pressing the coin folders he was holding tighter against his chest. This emotional gesture warmed her heart and she began to form a smart quip, wanting to point out the problem he was facing. Where was he going to put these three new folders?

An audible moan escaped from deep inside Tim's soul. Cathy couldn't recognize the sound or why the sound had escaped; so she came close to see why. She stood next to Tim and looked through the open door. The closet was empty! He had the most devastated expression on his face, his color gone, and his shoulders were sagging. The three new folders unconsciously protected against his heart and held there by the pressure from his left arm. She spoke to him, he was lost and trying to process what had happened to his prized coin collection. He didn't hear what she had said, he had shut out the world.

There was nothing to do but try to process his loss. Tears were again forming in the corners of his eyes, and any fool could tell that these were the tears of a broken man. She led him to his chair and pushed on his shoulders to get him to sit. He folded at the knees still clutching the folders, still oblivious to how he had come to his chair. Cathy left him sitting in his chair as she quietly walked to the phone and called the Sheriff.

Cathy picked up the remote and put the blinds down. Somehow, it seemed appropriate to share this heart wrenching moment with the man you love in private. Yet the whole gesture seemed so ridiculous because of their isolation, but shutting out the outside, putting blinds between them and the world made her feel safer.

Tim didn't notice the blinds lowering or the noise the small battery-powered motor made as they descended. He only heard the pounding of his heart, the thumping in his brain. His most precious collection was gone. Gone was the reward of tracking down a rare coin and spending his hard-earned money for its acquisition. Gone were the hours of overtime he had worked to support his addiction to coin collecting. Gone was the reward of bidding against another collector who could probably buy the coin without a blink of the eye or a personal sacrifice. Gone was the ability to show your friends your latest prize when he slowly opened the dark government folder and explained about its significance and how many were stamped. Gone was the ability to open, view, stack, and rearrange each and every folder that contained his beloved coins. His idle time would be spent doing what? Start what new hobby his age? This thought broke his heart; he knew he was too old and too poor, since his retirement, to begin collecting coins again. He sat in silence as his arm continued to press his Father's Day present against his chest.

Chapter Eighteen
Final Indignation

Around and around she stirred the soup with a flat bottom wooden spoon. The liquid swirled as the spoon pushed it in a counter clockwise direction. She looked in to the vortex and believed that somewhere within, the clues would be revealed. She believed it was as simple as finding Mike, and then finding the coin collection. It was just a matter of concentrating hard, seeing beyond the bottom of the pan. She needed to believe this because she knew intellectually Tim would most likely never see his prized coin collection again and that Mike was somewhere gloating. She was afraid that the *Law* would think she was as crazy as Tim thought she was about Mike. She needed to believe they would find the coins because Tim needed to believe. She loved Tim completely and she wanted to fix his broken heart.

When Cathy heard a knock on the door she looked up and wondered where she was, and how long had she been standing there. She looked for the dogs to see why they hadn't warned them someone was coming. They were asleep on the couch. The trip must have worn them out. Some early warning system, she thought, as she dropped the spoon into the pan and hurried to the door. It was Deputy Johnston. He smiled and nodded his head when she opened the door.

"Good to see you again, Mrs. Spalding. Heard you had a burglary?" He took the door into his hand and swung it back and forth, as he looked at the lock. He then looked at the doorframe before he entered.

"Yes, we were gone over the weekend and when we got back this afternoon we realized someone had been inside the house and ate some of our food. Tim went to put away his Father's Day gift, and when he opened the closet his coin collection was gone." Cathy was walking to the open closet as she was explaining their loss.

"What did you say was stolen?" Deputy Johnston asked as he looked at the lock on the closet door.

"My coin collection that I have been working on for over thirty-five years!" Tim seemed to come out of his trance and spoke to the Deputy. "Also some rifles, four of them and two pistols."

"Are they registered?" the deputy jumped in and questioned.

"The two pistols are registered with the El Cajon Police Department. I had the rifles before it was required to register them. One of them is a Revolutionary War Rifle that was my great, great; I don't know how many great-grandfathers'. It is not only a collector's item, it is our family's history. It has been handed down to the oldest male for generations. I got it because I am two minutes older than my twin brother." Tim's voice was becoming strained and desperate.

"I'd love to see that." The deputy said changing the tone of his voice now that he was interested in Tim's old rifle. "I sort of collect guns myself. I've never even seen one of those old rifles except in a picture once. What kind of guns were the others?"

"The pistols were both Smith & Wesson. One was a 38 and the other a 357 Magnum. One was a 12 gage shotgun, one a 410 single shot, one a 30-06. All three were Remington's." Tim listed them off quickly from his memory. Cathy didn't know any of this, just that there were guns in the closet. She hated guns and was afraid of them.

"Anything else in that closet?"

"Big coffee cans full of loose coins." Cathy added. She knew about the loose coins because she had often pointed out to Tim that several thousand dollars was sitting on the floor of the closet doing nothing and he was complaining about being short of money. He wouldn't spend a penny of it. He just kept adding loose change to the cans.

Deputy Johnston reached up, unbuttoned the flap on his left chest pocket, and pulled out a small blue spiral notebook. He began to list the missing items on a blank page. The familiar motion of him removing the notebook made Cathy flash back to the previous time she had witnessed the same scene when had come to their house the day the skeleton was uncovered. The strangest sensation washed over Cathy. Was some premonition being revealed to her or was it *déjà vu*, one of her mental videos in replay? Cathy blinked and stood a little straighter trying to shake off the feeling. Tim was slowly getting to his feet and standing by the two of them in front of the empty closet.

"Anything else missing?" Deputy Johnston stood ready to write again in his little notebook.

"A pan of lasagna, a bag of salad, and the propane from leaving the oven on since the thief came in here and ate our food. He probably sat at that very table and then unlocked the closet door and saw that he had struck gold." Cathy was talking too fast and too loud. She was getting over being the victim and getting angry. She was getting over being sweet and sympathetic to Tim. She was now enraged that Mike had come into their house! She had been violated too!

Deputy Johnston moved away from the empty closet and slowly sat down on a dining room chair. His motions were so slow and relaxed that it made Cathy crazy. He moved so deliberately it slowed her down. She instantly recognized his skill in defusing a situation. She took a deep breath and began to speak again in a normal tone.

"When we came in the house the dogs were going crazy, howling like wolves. At first, we figured an animal had used the doggie door. Then, when we noticed the missing food, we realized the thief had entered though the little door. Tim believed it was some hungry homeless guy, but I am sure it is this guy we met at the Stadium. I have seen him in town and he came here the day the skeleton was found. You probably saw him yourself when you were still here that day."

"Who is this guy? Why would he hang around here?" the Deputy asked.

"I know it doesn't make a whole lot of sense but he always asks Tim a thousand personal questions when he is with him, mostly at the baseball game. He comes and sits by us late in the game. He is always looking at me or scanning the crowd. Then, I saw him one night after the game and he dropped his wallet. Anyway, I thought it was his wallet. I asked him about it when I saw him in front of Jack's Market. He had the funniest look on his face and didn't answer me. He just reached into his back pocket and held up a wallet." Cathy was talking too fast again. She was becoming frantic and feared that either Tim or the deputy would cut her off before she could explain how she knew that Mike had been their thief. She looked at Tim and he had a patient look on his face. She prayed she had read him right. If she had, he had finally believed that Mike was their thief. Maybe that was only wishful thinking, he was probably too tired and too crushed to even react to her animated story about the *Enemy Mike*.

"Hum," was the only sound from the deputy as he scribbled into his notebook.

"Did you see that news feature on Channel 8 about the pickpocket and burglaries in San Diego?" Cathy asked and waited for an answer.

"I don't see much TV. Don't get the local stations on my satellite dish." He answered her when he had written down everything he wanted first. The silence seemed like an eternity to Cathy.

"Well, we did. We try to catch all the features that Carol Klein does. Especially since she did that one on our skeleton. You did see that one didn't you?" The deputy looked up from his notebook and looked directly at Cathy like it was the first time he had ever seen her. He shook his head no, very slowly. Cathy was sure she had read a look on his face that showed he wasn't going to be sucked into any media frenzy. He was a trained law enforcement officer and the media was a Royal Pain in the Ass! Moreover, being the trained professional that he was, he was not going to voice his opinion on her frantic questions either.

"Well," she continued. "They did this whole feature on a pickpocket and they showed a tape taken at the Stadium of this guy lifting a wallet. I recognized him! It was the same guy that sits behind us and asks Tim a thousand questions. It is the same guy I saw dropping a wallet. He said his name is Mike Jenkins."

"OK," said the deputy. "How does that put him in your house, by way of the doggie door, eating your food and stealing everything from the closet?"

"I know it sounds unbelievable but I know it's him." Cathy heard how dumb and hollow her explanation sounded. She knew where this investigation was going by his replies to her information. This whole investigation was going quickly down the toilet. The vision of the toilet flushing reminded her of the swirling soup on the stove. She remembered that the soup was still heating on the stove; she had left it on. She quickly stepped into the kitchen and saw that the pan was glowing red and the liquid was now dry and had become a blackened mass on the bottom of the pan. No more swirling vortex here she thought, as she flipped the knob on the stove to the off position. She couldn't understand why she had not smelled it burning. Was she that far out of it, that frantic to get the deputy to believe her? Yes, she was, she had to admit, even to herself.

"Do you keep the closet locked?" the deputy asked.

"Yes, always. Cathy demands I do because of the guns. The grandkids are never to know what is inside the closet." Tim answered.

"I don't see any signs of forced entry on the door or frame. Where do you keep the key?" The deputy kept writing as he asked the questions.

"On my key chain with my truck keys. Where is the key I gave you Sweetie?" Tim now looked to Cathy like she had the answer to find the contents of the closet.

"I keep it on my key chain too." She replied. There she thought; how could he open the door when they had the only two keys.

"Can I see your keys now?" Deputy Johnston asked.

Tim pulled his keys from his pocket and handed them to the deputy and Cathy began a mad search to the bottom of her purse. She finally began to pull each item out and set it on the table. She became so embarrassed as she set her wallet, makeup purse, address book, calculator, Kleenex, Lifesavers, pens, a wad of receipts, empty prescription bottle, coupons, camera, a Ziploc bag filled with baby wipes, and finally two checkbooks. The keys were not in the bottom of her purse or in one of the pockets. The deputy very patiently had sat in the chair and watched her frantically search for her keys.

"Did I leave them at Denise's house?" she asked Tim in desperation.

"Why would you take them with you? We had my truck." Tim spoke as if her keys were the least of their problems.

Deputy Johnston seemed stuck until she produced them or at least had an explanation of where they were. Cathy quickly looked on the kitchen counter, the buffet and then stepped into the laundry room. They were hanging on the key holder on the wall. She very sheepishly picked them off the hook and gingerly carried them as if they might explode. The dogs heard them jingle and they got all excited as if they were going somewhere again. The nap seemed to have restored their hearing.

"Ah, that explains why there was no forced entry." A simple calm statement uttered from the trained law enforcement professional. "Describe to me what was in your coin collection."

Tim began to describe his collection as Cathy had heard him do for their friends and relatives. Actually, he loved to show it to most everyone who came to visit. Their friends got a lesson in coin collecting 101, whether they wanted it or not, often reminding her of having friends forced to watch vacation slides. He told the deputy of his lucky purchases, of the auctions he had bid in, and he told of his addiction with ordering directly from the Mint. Cathy watched as the deputy continued to write in the notebook, casually turning a page when one was full.

"Do you have an inventory of your coins?" the deputy asked, not looking up from the notebook.

"Yes, well sort of. When I had the shelves built in the closet and the steel door and steel lining installed, I wrote down everything I had. I have added a lot to the collection since then. I try to keep up with it but I'm afraid sometimes I forget to add on my new purchases to my list."

"That's good. May I see the list?" the deputy asked in his patient, calm voice.

Tim got up from the dining room table and withdrew a red book from his desk. He returned to the deputy and handed him the book.

"This is a book. I thought you had a list?" The deputy questioned, not understanding.

"It's in the book. This is the *Whitman Official Red Book, Guide Book of United States Coins*. Look, I marked each coin I have in the margin of the book. I also coded the book with the grade of each coin I have. That way, you can get the value of each coin as you look to see what I have, and how many." Tim very enthusiastically explained his inventory system to the deputy.

Cathy's heart fell as she noted that Tim was still talking of his coins in the present tense. The deputy held the *Red Book* and flipped through the pages. He flipped through as if he was expecting the images to move in some animated sequence or line up in some graph. He flipped like a dealer would flip a stack of coins or chips in the casino. He closed the book, turned it over, and set it on the table.

"I'm sorry, Mr. Spalding. This could be your wish book. As an inventory it doesn't hold much water."

Cathy could hear the air escape from Tim's lungs. He reacted as if he had been kicked in the gut. That simple sentence had knocked the wind right out of him. She wanted to tell the deputy to get his you-know-what out of their house. If he was not going to help, or believe them, they would just go it on their own. Give them a couple of days to regroup, get back on their feet, and they would come up with a plan to find Mike! That is a low thing to say to a man when he is down, she thought. She was now directing her anger at the deputy and away from Mike. She decided to keep her rage to herself.

"What do you mean?" Tim pleaded. "It's far more accurate. It has all the years each coin was struck, the grade, value and, how many were stamped. It contains all the pertinent information to value the coin."

"Do you have any proof that you had a coin collection?" The deputy asked as Tim's head came up and snapped level. He gave the deputy a look that could have killed! After a few seconds, Tim visibly took a large breath, and filled his lungs before he spoke.

"I have a lot of receipts. I have many friends who can vouch that I have such a coin collection. And, I want you to understand one thing, here and now! I DO NOT LIE! Now please look around, ask what questions you must, and leave us alone to understand why decent people are robbed and then treated like they are liars!"

"I'm sorry you misunderstood. I never said you weren't telling the truth. You just have to understand how little information you have given me and what you have isn't much." The deputy calmly tried to defuse the electricity in the dining room. "Let me understand. Were all the coins in coffee cans?"

"Jesus, no, there were only about eight or nine coffee cans filled with coins on the floor. Look at all those shelves, each shelf was packed full of folders containing coins. Look, like these my daughter just gave me for Father's Day." Tim pushed the gift folders into the hands of the deputy. The deputy opened a U.S. Mint Folder and looked at the coins placed in the cutouts. The folder from the year Tim was born was fuzzy, like it was velvet. The deputy absently rubbed his finger across the smooth fuzzy surface. He opened the other two folders.

"All the coins were packaged like this?"

"Most of them were in similar folders. Some were in plastic coin boxes. The ones I bought from private parties or a coin shop."

"How many of these folders do you think you had?" The deputy was trying to imagine how many small folders it would take to fill the closet.

"I never counted them in one day, a total, I mean. I took my inventory by writing in the margin of the book. I had two rows deep and two rows high on each shelf. The shelves were jammed full. I never even took the book and totaled up what my collection was worth. I didn't care because I wasn't going sell them. I was going to leave my collection to my kids when I die." Tim said all this as if he didn't even have the desire to go on now that he didn't have his collection to leave to his children.

"What about the coffee cans on the floor? What kind of coins were in there."

"That was just loose coins. I had two big coffee cans filled with silver dollars. The real silver dollars, not the ones sandwiched with another metal. There was one can with half dollars, another with quarters, two cans of dimes and four cans with pennies. Don't forget the guns that were stolen, too." Tim desperately gave a verbal inventory of the stolen items and the deputy continued to write in the notebook.

"Did you say two dimes and four pennies? What about nickels?"

"No nickels, I just never started saving nickels. I guess I never liked them enough. Most of the proof sets of coins contained nickels though. If the mint stamped nickels that year they were in the folder." Tim was now lapsing into his adult course on coin collecting. He had showed and explained the collection to her when they had first began dating. It had been in a different closet in another house. He was no longer giving the deputy an inventory of his stolen coin collection; he was giving the deputy a lesson on the love of coins and their value, Numismatology 101.

"About what value would you place on the collection? Understand I don't mean what you would want because it means so much to you but what you could actually sell it for?" The deputy was holding his pen still, in the writing position, as he looked again into the empty closet. Poised and ready to write when Tim gave him more information.

"Whew," Tim let air escape as he ran his finger through his beard. He was seriously trying to place an actual value on the collection. "Want that to include the guns and the coins on the floor?"

"No, just the coins on the shelves."

"Hard to tell, want me to have Cathy add up the totals from each page in the *Red Book*?" He was thinking hard, trying to be accurate, not inflate the value, and not cheat himself.

Cathy was annoyed that he was giving her the job of finding the inventory value from the book. She knew it would take most of a day to come up with a total. She would have to set up a spreadsheet. She hated using Excel. She hated using it so much that she had to relearn it each time she used it. If asked she would certainly do the spreadsheet, it would be the quickest and easiest way to inventory and total the value of the collection. Hating Excel had kept her from doing the inventory from the *Red Book* in the first place. She was going to do it someday anyway, just not today, maybe tomorrow. She had been saying that to herself for the last two years. Now she felt so guilty. Poor Tim, he would have his stinking inventory to give to the deputy if she had just done it!

"I would have to give a pretty close estimate at around forty to fifty thousand dollars. Cathy could give you an exact amount tomorrow."

"Whew," the deputy said half under his breath. "That much, you're not putting me on are you?"

"I said I don't lie! I would never do that! I told you Cathy could give you an accurate total tomorrow. Accurate to two years ago when I moved my coin collection into this closet." Tim was trying to control his anger again. When would the deputy figure out that if he wanted calm he didn't insinuate that Tim, the victim, would lie or cheat?

"Calm down, Mr. Spalding. You have to understand that this is the first time I have ever answered a call where the resident says fifty thousand dollars is stolen from his closet. You have to understand people just don't have that kind of money sitting around in the first place, when it should be secure in some bank or something."

"How can you enjoy something when it is stashed away where you can't get at it? I love to do research, touch, and catalogue my coins. I have to have them in front of me to enjoy them."

"I see your point, but people can't just leave valuables lying around in their house and expect them to remain there for long." Deputy Johnston was now trying to give Tim a lesson in the decline of the morals in the United States.

"That is just *my* point!" Tim lectured. "A man should have his house safe and sacred. He shouldn't worry about some thief out to get him or anybody else. Until a couple of months ago, only a handful of our friends and family even knew our place existed. Our cabin has sat here for over twenty-five years totally hidden in the forest. It was safe until the skeleton was found and all the law enforcement and the media showed the world we were living here."

"That's just *my* point," the deputy repeated. "Now the world knows you are here. Not only living here, but also isolated. How long do you think it took the thief to carry all those cans of coins, guns, and folders full of coins out of here? Could he have done it in the city under everyone's nose?"

"It would have taken hours of hard work." Cathy interjected.

Tim leaned back in the chair. His head was back, looking at the ceiling as if it had written on it the formula to calculate how long the thief had worked. Did that include the time he took to cook and eat dinner, he thought.

"It would have more than filled up a trunk of a car, maybe a van. He would have had to have parked near, maybe in our driveway." Tim was now thinking of how the thief had hauled off his possessions. He had given up on the answer to how long it took to unload the closet.

"Mike drives a white van." Cathy said. "I have seen it in Julian."

"Anything more you can tell me about the van besides the color?" The deputy turned to a fresh page and poised his pen.

"I remember it didn't have any windows except in the back doors. It looked like the back windows were tinted dark so no one could see in. I think it was a Chevy or a GMC. Definitely not a Ford or Chrysler product and it had fancy aluminum wheels. Not standard equipment."

Cathy gazed out the dining room window as if she could see the van in the neighbor's driveway.

"Pretty good description, where did you say you saw it?"

"I had the grandkids in my car in the parking lot at Jack's Market. That was in April sometime. I know; it was the weekend after the Opening Day of the baseball season. We had first met him there at the game." Cathy wanted to tell him all about the questions Mike asked Tim, the dropped wallet, the phony bow in front of Jack's Market while he eyed her diamond, and her premonitions and her fears. She knew he wasn't the least bit interested. He was taking down answers to simple questions, while filling his little notebook. Oh God, she was exhausted and she felt like she had been banging her head against a stone wall. Now it was not only Tim not believing her about Mike it was the deputy too!

"Why do you think the burglar used the doggie door? He definitely didn't haul all the items out through there. He would have had to have a vehicle. He would have used the door to the house to empty the closet into a vehicle."

"We only know that the dogs were sure someone had used their door and that someone had been into the house. When we got home, they ran into the house and started howling. You know, just like wolves. We came in and looked for a trapped animal. Then when Cathy started dinner, our food was missing. She found the oven on and the bag that held the salad in the trash. As I said earlier, we then knew our intruder was the two-legged kind. It wasn't until I unlocked the closet that I realized we had been robbed." Tim was now telling the incident like Cathy remembered it. Were they finally getting on the same page about Mike being the thief?

"Why don't you check with the neighbors to see if any of them saw his van? Aren't you going to check with the coin shops to see if anyone is trying to sell the collection? How about watching the classifieds in the paper and looking for great coin sales on the Internet. Are you going to dust the house for prints? He must have been in here a long time; I'll bet he left some print, hair or something. In addition, your department should check out Mike Jenkins. I know he is the one in the tape from the Stadium. I know he is the pickpocket." As Cathy pleaded for cooperation from the deputy, she could see his mood change. She knew she had gone too far by telling him what she wanted him to do.

"Please Mrs. Spalding, let us do our job. We'll check all this out. I'm afraid that the statistics of retrieving your items are slim to none. I hope you had that collection insured." With that comment, the deputy stuffed his notebook back into his chest pocket, rose and left the house.

His exit reminded Cathy of that day with the grandkids and Mike in Julian. The day the kids had the candy apples and he called to her in front of Jack's Market and asked her, "How large is that stone in your ring? Better keep that beauty insured." He just slipped into the crowd on the street and disappeared. The deputy's remark about the insurance reminded her of Mike's quick quip. They both had just slipped away after the same kind of remark.

"You're not mad at me for giving him suggestions on finding Mike are you?" She was almost apologizing to Tim. Tim looked like he had just returned from a war and was shell-shocked.

"No, I am roaring pissed at him, trying very hard to control my temper. Good thing he just got up and left. I was ready to shoot him. Fortunately for him, I no longer have any guns. I got the impression that he will do the minimum to find our thief. He will do just enough to cover his ass. He made it clear that he thought we were either lying about the value of the collection or extremely stupid for having such a thing in the closet. He made you look stupid when you couldn't find your keys in your purse and then found them where the thief could. As if it is our responsibility to live in a house with nothing of value, because when someone steals from you it is work for the Department. I am sick and tired of people taking from people who have worked hard all their life! I hate people who think the world owes them something for nothing and are too lazy to work!"

"I'm not totally convinced Mike was the thief. I want to believe you, but when you tell someone about him, it all sounds so far fetched. Why would some guy we met at a baseball game do this to us?" Tim continued before Cathy could answer. "Don't get mad at me; I wish I could believe you, knowing it was him would make it all so simple." Tim leaned towards her and held her tight. He nuzzled her neck and kissed her on the cheek before he let her go.

"I love you, Babe. I am sure glad I found you in my old age. God, I feel so old right now, but it sure is easier with you here beside me."

"Hungry?" she asked. "I turned the soup into a charred brick. I even killed the pan. I could find something else if you're still hungry."

"Got some ice cream in the freezer? That sounds good right now. Maybe it will even help cool my temper."

Chapter Nineteen
The Predator

If he learned one thing from sitting for hours in his camp chair, he had learned the stiff canvas made your ass go to sleep along with your legs. When he had felt the tingling, he pushed himself up out of the chair, and realized how stiff he had become from his immobility. Once on his feet his legs gave out and he fell and landed on a rock. The pain soared through his body as it tore a gash in his knee.

"Oh F U C K," he yelled into the forest. "That goddamn rock killed my knee." He could hear the sound of his misery fill the valley and roll up the mountain.

"Shit," he whispered as he tried to see the damage the rock had caused. He was scared Cathy and Tim, or a neighbor would have heard his cry for help, might believe a hiker had fallen and come in search of his cry. He lay there quietly holding his wounded knee against his chest, the blood seeping onto his shirt. He rolled slowly from his back to his side quietly moaning, waiting for the pain to subside.

He had patiently waited for the Spaldings to return from their trip. He wanted to observe how Cathy reacted when she discovered the oven was on and the food was missing, and he had bet against himself that Tim would be mad as hell for her forgetfulness. Mad at the cost of the squandered propane. Now he lay here in the dirt bleeding all over the forest when he wanted to listen to their discovery with the Bionic Ear. He was now filled more with his disappointment and anger, than pain.

"Just what I needed," he spit in a whisper. His knee was bleeding like a geyser. He began to calculate how he would get to his van or the cabin and clean the wound, and stop this infernal bleeding. Leaving his camp, just when they came home, really pissed him off! He decided against going to the cabin. His first reason was the distance, and his second reason was the fear of dropping any blood, one tiny drop of blood somewhere in the cabin. Had he cut his face shaving; stubbed his toe in that house across the street from where he killed the old cripple?

His van would have to be the place to clean up his leg. He thought he would lie here a few more minutes, just wait a few minutes for the searing pain to go away. He heard something move in the forest. Did someone hear him, and had come to look for him? Wouldn't they call out to find him? He now lay in fear bringing his other leg up making his body into a ball, hopefully small and impenetrable. Or, could the movement be from the mountain lion? Had she been so near, watching him and now smelling his blood? He had seen her once. She had been watching him, crouched and ready to spring. He had jumped to his feet and swung his camp chair in a large arc making him look large and angry. She had slunk away, turning as she went. He had taken to pissing on the trees to leave his scent, marking his territory. He had not seen her again.

His heart was pounding and a sticky sweat escaped from every pore of his body. He knew she could smell his fear in addition to his blood. He was lying perfectly still, pretending to be dead. Do lions eat what they don't kill, or would she kill him and then eat him?

Slowly he forced his legs straight again, rolled into the sitting position, and pushed up until he was standing. The blood was now soaking his shoe. He silently tried to walk to where his van was hidden, the pain pulsating through his body with each step. With each step, he stopped and listened for any sound. He only heard his own faltering footsteps. The thought of being mauled by the lion frightened him almost as much as being incarcerated by the police. At least it would be over soon if the cat got him. Rotting for years in jail plain scared the shit out of him.

Once to the van he climbed inside and locked the doors. His gesture of locking out a mountain lion amused him. He had begun to give her human like characteristics since he had seen her. He quietly talked to the forest believing she could hear and understand him. He thought of her as a scruffy stray cat, but admittedly, the scariest fucking cat he had ever seen! Cats had always intrigued him. It was their independence, their quiet strength and their sensuality. Sometimes they were affectionate, sometimes aloof, and sometimes striking out without warning. They harnessed a power that could lash out without provocation and open up a wound so deep it may never heal. A wound so deep it could even kill. He had come to fear the lion as he had feared his mother.

The gash to his knee continued to bleed uncontrollably. The tissue was mashed from the fall and was both swollen and jagged. He knew he needed stitches and the wound professionally cleaned or risk infection. He had seen a doctor's office in town behind the Town Hall. He thought he could pull off a visit by feigning a hiking fall. He would give a fictitious name and whip out his cash. Shit, he thought, I have pulled off far greater deceptions than this. He had better hurry before the doctor left for the evening.

He was in and out of the doctor's office in a little less than an hour. When they saw him covered in blood, flashing his cash and giving them his story, they worked on his leg immediately and asked no questions. He had an appointment to have his stitches removed in ten days, an appointment he had no intention of keeping. The pharmacy across the street was closed, so they gave him samples of pain relievers, some extra bandages and an antibiotic cream. He knew he would sleep great tonight in the cabin. He might even have the dream about the warm sand and cold beer again. That sure beat the hell out of the dream he had been having lately about being tapped on the shoulder and when he looked around, he was being handcuffed and arrested by the San Diego Police. That bitch, Carol from the TV station, was pointing her finger at him.

This was the second time today he had used the road into the forest on the west side of the Spalding's place. He prayed those nosy neighbors didn't spot him. He could tell they tried to give the illusion of being prominent and upstanding citizens of the small town. He had seen the fancy sign with their name on the rock walled entrance to the driveway. The rock entrance was far more elegant than the house that hid behind the wall. It reminded him of the hovels in Mexico, ostentatious walls with rotting houses hiding from view. The smell of pot from the property drifted into the cabin several times a week, he could almost get high from the smoke floating across the forest. He didn't care what people did. Just don't act like they were innocent to him. He knew better. People like that were always hiding something and trying to get the community to think they were so gracious, involved, committed. They are no more than the self-appointed Mountain Police looking for flaws in their neighbors. If they continued to harass him, he would have to add an egg to his omelet each morning. He would be up to three a day. Maybe he could catch fresh chicken for dinner, and eat fresh corn from the garden. Let the nosy bastard think a fox had been in his hen house! He knew that today his threat was pure fantasy. He would have to wait for his leg to quiet down, it was throbbing and the pain was as if a drum beat in every vein of his body.

Once out of the van he limped back into his chair, vowing to move more frequently so he wouldn't flirt with the same disaster again. He had carried a shovel from the van. He used it as a crutch, but he had brought it with him to bury his puddle of blood. He wondered how deep he would have to dig to be safe from the lion?

It was almost dark when he heard a car come down the Spalding's driveway. He quickly put on the headphones to listen to the Spaldings and their visitor. He was surprised when he learned it was the deputy. He could see his face in his memory from the time he sat on the deck across the creek. He recognized the voice. It was Deputy Johnston.

He couldn't believe his luck! They had called the Sheriff's Department because the oven was left on and food was missing. This was going to be good. He cranked the up volume on his Bionic Ear until his ears were almost ringing. He could hardly wait to hear them tell the deputy about their burglar. He knew the deputy would see there were no signs of forced entry. He knew Cathy would probably go on and accuse him, the phantom Mike Jenkins, for being the thief. By the end of the call Tim would be trying to quiet her down, apologizing to the deputy for his wife being upset and emotional. He was dying to hear what went on after the deputy left. The fight they would have.

He knew this visit from the sheriff's department was just the first act. He certainly didn't want to miss the final act. That would be when the deputy came back, and they told him the coin collection, and guns were missing. By then, he knew, they would have no credibility with the Sheriff's Station. Half of Julian would think they were either delusional or liars. He wanted to be right here listening, wait it out. Wait until they discovered the closet was empty. His biggest fear was making too much noise laughing when he heard how they tried to convince the deputy of what had been in the closet.

He stretched his sore leg and gave it a shake. He didn't want it to fall asleep again as he quietly listened. He wanted to catch every word. Then he heard it, heard the whole story; heard the final act. It wasn't until Tim had described the gift from his daughter that he put the pieces together.

Tim had opened the closet door and discovered it was empty! He didn't know if he was happy it all happened today, or if he had wanted it drawn out, prolonged like a weekly serial. He was beginning to feel that having it all discovered today was somewhat anti-climatic. Very disappointing, and he hated it when the fantasy up-staged the reality.

"Shit," he said quietly to himself as he continued to listen. Then a smile spread across his face as Cathy told the deputy about the dogs howling, the missing food, and the oven being on. All true, he thought. He could almost feel his shoulders twisting through the doggie door as she told the story. He could hear her voice rise and become more desperate. Then she began to rant on about Mike Jenkins, how they met him, what he looked like; the kind of car he drove. His head jerked up, the earphones falling back. He never knew she had seen him in his van before. It was probably when that little brat waved to him! Fear ran through him. It wasn't that he was afraid that Cathy's story about him being the thief frightened him; he was safe because Mike Jenkins didn't exist. It was that fear, any fear invaded his confidence, broke his stride. He depended upon that confidence to remain invisible, to remain a free man.

He listened, and became relaxed again. Oh, this was good, he thought. The reaction from the deputy was priceless. He had to place his hand over his mouth to keep from busting up. Then he heard the value of the collection. He choked on the amount so hard that the air that escaped his lips blew his hand away. "Whew, fifty thousand fucking bucks!" He never dreamed it had such value! All he could remember was how much work it took to empty the closet. Shit, he hadn't even taken a real close look at the coins.

He loved how the deputy reprimanded the Spaldings for being so stupid to have so much cash in their house. He treated Cathy like she was retarded, made her feel stupid to have a key to the closet hanging in the laundry room. He made fun of their inventory of the coins. Man, he had them going, crushed! He had to give Cathy credit; she didn't come unglued or snivel like most women would. She just pointed out what the deputy needed to do to catch him. Her telling the deputy what to do sure pissed him off! He could hear the tone in the deputy's voice all the way across the creek. Now the deputy was going to drive away, shake his head, and laugh all the way up the driveway, all the way back to town.

Somehow, the whole final act left him disappointed. He wanted to feel the excitement of his revenge. He felt no joy in the knowledge of their loss. They weren't even fighting. They are even closer now, more kind and loving. What is it with these idiots? Steal something from him that he had been working on for thirty-five years, worth almost fifty thousand dollars and they hug each other and say they are thankful they have everything that's important. They have each other, their health and their wonderful family. He stuck his finger in his throat as if he was going to puke.

The whole point of stealing from the Spaldings had been to cause friction. His theft had missed the target. This put him back to square one, figuring out a fitting revenge. Thank God, Tim still didn't believe that ole Mike had done it. The door was still open for him to pound a wedge between them. He was going to reflect on it for a while; give the old leg time to heal.

The freebie pain medication was helping, but it was making him nauseated. He needed to get some food into his stomach. He had forgotten to eat since his snatched eggs this morning. A bowl of soup and a piece of bread is what would make him feel better. He would take two more pills, elevate his leg, and sleep like a baby.

He had taken to eating from the larder in the cabin. It was obvious the cans had been sitting there unused and collecting dust for years. He was sure what he had taken would never be missed. When the presence of a freeloader was noted, he would be long gone. His only concern would be if the owners were to arrive while he was inside. Today he couldn't run quickly but he was sure he could leave by the sliding door in enough time to hobble to his van.

With the soup bowl empty, and two beers consumed, he was beginning to feel like he could sleep until morning. This thought filled him with contentment. He had been sleeping horribly lately in the cabin.

The nosy neighbors had been having frequent parties on the warm summer nights. They cavorted around the hot tub until early morning. He had often come outside and watched from the deck of the cabin with his night vision glass. The longer they sat in the hot water the more they glowed a bright green through his monocular when they climbed out. He had the best of times putting the couples together as they climbed from the hot tub. One night he had become totally confused before he realized he hadn't dozed off, they had swapped partners. His night vision monocular made standing watch fun. Watching all those swingers, had turned his watch into a deluxe edition of *Fantasy Family Game.*

Tonight he wanted no parties, only sleep. He prayed for a deep sleep to restore his mind and heal his leg. He had a lot to do tomorrow. He planned to leave early, before the neighbors came alive. He knew he must be away from the Spalding's property and the cabin in case the deputy did more than a little CYA, Cover Your Ass. In case the deputy actually drove out and checked the property.

He would stay in a motel for a few days, let his leg heal while he mulled over the best revenge. He knew he could not work while he still limped. A man with a limp was not invisible. That little trip to the doctor had cost him the equivalent of two days stay in the city. He would have to decide how to recoup the money he spent. He was also looking forward to looking more closely at some of the coins in Tim's collection. He was still in disbelief at their value. Was Tim telling the deputy the truth or was he inflating his collection for insurance purposes? He must try and remember the name of that book that Tim had written his inventory in. He knew the name would come to him when he felt better, and his mind was clearer. He would buy the book so he could recognize a valuable coin when he saw one. Did the title use a color in part of the name? So many thoughts flooded through his brain as he leaned back and put his leg up on a pillow. He took one more pill and tried to remember what time it was and what time he had taken the last two pills. As the medication began to blur his thoughts, he fell into the long awaited sleep. Whizzing and whirling, he began to fall.

His leg was impaled on a branch; he was unable to move, to free himself. He looked down and could see the raw flesh, the open wound. Then he could hear her: hear her breathing. At first the breathing was soft and shallow, relaxed. As he tried to free himself, crawl away he could hear her become more excited. As he became more terrified he could hear her breath quicken, it was now a sound deep in her throat, almost a purr. He was scratching at the dirt, trying to pull himself free of the limb. He kept clawing at his world, trying to run in fear, going nowhere. His hands were now bloody. He screamed for help. The sound shook the forest, yet no one heard. He was totally alone, no help to fight off the animal. She was so near. He could hear the sound of her footsteps crunching the leaves; hear her breath deep in her throat. Could he smell her, smell her hot felinity? Oh God, he pleaded, keep me safe from her. His terror was coursing through his veins and pounding in his temples, pounding with his heart. She was on top of him, pinning him down. He was thrashing, screaming, trying to free himself, pleading for God to intercede. He had her by the throat, squeezing, pulling, gouging deep in her flesh with his fingers, chocking off her breath. An eternity had passed and finally she rolled over and lay still by his side. Had he killed her? His shoulders finally relaxed, as he lay next to her, free of her weight at last, spent yet totally exhilarated. In this afterglow, his eyes sprung open and he noticed he was wiping his hands on his shirt. He looked down and saw his clothes covered in blood. Was this fresh blood from the kill or blood from his knee bleeding earlier? He looked to each side, looking for the body. He was alone in the cabin. He must have fallen asleep. Had he had a dream, it seemed so real. Whom had he killed? Was he fighting with the mountain lion, Suzanne, Cathy, or his Mother?

Oh, thank you God, you have kept me safe. He laid back and tried to slow his breathing. Once in control again he tried to remember his dream, each of the details. He could remember his terror but more strongly, he remembered the thrill, the exhilaration of his kill. He compared his excitement, this experience with the best orgasm he could ever remember. He smiled and he now knew he would strangle Cathy.

His dreams and fantasies were so entwined that he was having a hard time separating what was giving him his excitement. It reminded him of his youth when he walked around with a constant hard-on, trying to conceal his excitement from the world. He remembered that was the best time of his life; when his whole life lie ahead and he could do anything. God, he was cocky then. It was good to have that feeling again. Was it his impending retirement and the new life that lay ahead in Mexico that was exciting him, or the anticipation of the kill? That was a hard question to answer; he admitted to himself. Both goals awakened his senses. The anticipation gave him hope, squelched the depression he had been carrying around for months. He was only deeply disappointed that he had not found his Great-Grandfather's hidden gold. Tim's gold would give him money out of the country, but no big thrill.

Then he smiled to himself as he fanaticized his hands around her throat, felt her fight for her life. She was a big woman with lots of pluck. She would fight like the mountain lion. That thought excited him more. He was looking forward to her death. He had given Tim the chance to become his friend, but he had chosen his bitch instead. It served him right! Oh how sweet the revenge! After all, she had made it personal with him.

Chapter Twenty
The Storm

Cathy sat down in Tim's big leather recliner and reached for the remote. She flicked it on and punched on the local station out of San Diego for the news. She thought she could catch fifteen to twenty minutes of uninterrupted time to relax and find out what was going on in the *big city*.

The grandkids were here enjoying the end of summer vacation. Actually only the two boys; their sister was at home. Elaine hated parting with the baby and Cathy had felt relieved when she wasn't coming this time. She was such a joy, but watching a two year old who insisted on being outside kept her old grandma hopping. The boys played so well together, and in this weather, Cathy had hardly seen them. They hadn't come to visit much this summer. It seemed that lately Glenn was having lots of stomach problems. Her daughter had chalked it up to pre-school jitters. Glenn was going to start kindergarten soon. The big disappointment was that the pond and waterfall were not yet complete.

Cathy's mind flashed back to that fateful day when the crew clearing out the creek had found a skeleton. She remembered their fifteen minutes of fame. It seemed like half the county found their isolated place after they were seen on television. The sheriffs, medical examiner, news crews and the locals had arrived and it looked like a feeding frenzy. She smiled at remembering all the walking she had done giving everyone either iced tea, coffee, or water. She had even baked muffins and cookies to distribute. She remembered how upset she was and felt their life was out of control when the investigation was going on, and all the spectators were hanging around. Thank God, it seemed like another lifetime ago. Then she remembered that was the first day that Mike Jenkins had darkened their door with his presence.

Her mind still was wondering, and with her feet up and her head back, she could have slipped into a nap. That was dangerous territory when the two young ones were outside playing, she must always keep alert. It was mandatory that they stayed together so one could run for help if the other got hurt. Sound was tricky on the mountain and you could not count on hearing someone calling. Some days when the wind was just right, they could hear someone talking from the other side of the ranch almost a mile away. Another time it was hard to hear Tim call to her from the pump house. Then if the wind was really blowing, your words traveled only a few short feet. Cathy was pleased that they obeyed the safety rules for Grandma's place, and smiled at the memory of them recanting the rules back to her and Tim.

Cathy was called back to the present when a news flash interrupted the local broadcast. There was an unstable weather front moving in and they expected lightening and thunder with flash flood warnings. The news anchor came back on and began discussing the storm with the weatherman before the scheduled weather forecast. They slipped into a conversation that was relaxed and cute. It bored Cathy, but she could agree that San Diego had been in a drought, and rain was desperately needed. Her mind began to whirl and she tried to calculate what the forecast would mean to the weather in the mountains, specifically at the foot of her mountain. Would the storm hit here earlier than San Diego, later, or not at all? Was it coming from the north with cold air, or up from Mexico as a tropical storm? The word storm had a much different meaning in the mountains; in San Diego, it meant that the city *might* experience some rain.

She smiled to herself as she remembered the summer storms in the mountains when she was a child, camping at Green Valley Falls. When there were thunderheads in the sky the kids were kept from going to the swimming hole. The dangers of lightning were told to the children in much the same way an older child might tell a scary ghost story when they had a captive audience. She remembered the stories, and she remembered running through the trees trying to catch big fat raindrops in her mouth on a hot summer day as the lightning and thunder crashed about.

Cathy was now sitting upright in the recliner as she tried to squeeze information out of a disinterested news team. If there was anything she had learned from living on this mountain in the last three and a half years, she had learned that the weather here was nothing like the weather in San Diego. Watching the news would give her only a morsel of weather information applicable to where she lived.

Cathy decided she better get off her butt and plan for the storm. She would fill a few empty plastic gallon bottles with water. Just in case, the electricity went out and they were unable to pump water from the well.

After the bottles were full, she stepped outside on the deck to check the weather. She hated filling those damn water jugs, especially when she could see that the day was beautiful with not a cloud in the sky. She loved the view from the deck, actually, she could not see that far because the trees were so thick, but the pines, cedars, and oaks were like a painting. She loved the smell of the clean air, the sound of the wind through the trees, and the sounds of the insects, birds, and wildlife. Whenever she felt lonely, she would step outside and remember she was surrounded with life. She noted that the forest was still. There was not a sound from the wind, not a sound from a bird. These creatures know something is up and it is going to be big. They have the sense to run and hide for cover. She had better take their lead and get the kids inside.

She could see Greg on a flat spot below the deck playing with the wooden train she had purchased at a discount store the year before. He had a little city set up in the dirt. Cathy called to him and asked him where his brother was. She had to repeat herself, and the only response she got was a shrug of his shoulders. That kid could infuriate her with his tunnel vision and selective deafness if he was into what he loved doing.

"HELLO," she said louder than her original question. In her tone was annoyance. She often used this tone with Greg to announce to him that he had better come out of his fog and listen to his grandmother. He looked up at her as if she had just stepped onto the deck, and with an innocent look of pleasure, pointed for her to look at his mini city. He kept crooking his finger for her to come there.

"Hello," she said again. "Where is Glenn?" He looked around his mini city and shrugged his shoulders as if he expected to see him sitting next to him.

Cathy calculated that it had been about ½ hour since she had last seen Glenn. She started calling his name and she felt a cold wind begin to blow. She looked to the north and could see black clouds forming. "Here it comes," she said to the sky, "and it's coming fast!"

"Hey, Greg, pick up the train. A storm is coming in and it looks like it is going to be big enough to wash the train pieces into the creek." Greg looked straight up at her and then the sky and went back to pushing the train on the track.

"I said pick it up! I need you to help me find Glenn. NOW!" He started to get up with a very displeased look on his face. She resumed calling for Glenn and decided to call in the other direction. Cathy walked around the deck to the other side of the house. As she rounded the corner, she caught sight of the back of a van going out of view on the neighbor's driveway. A stab of fear hit her. She would know that van anywhere! Mike was on the Miller's driveway. Why had he come here? Oh, my God, where was Glenn?

The wind had definitely picked up and it was cold. She ran back to find Greg and had a hard time getting his attention. He was slowly picking up the pieces to the train set and looking unhappy. Greg was becoming aware of the wind because it was blowing over pieces of his tiny city. He would set the pieces upright before he reluctantly put them into the box.

Cathy was frantically calling him in her loudest voice. Between the wind, being breathless from running around the deck, and fear; her voice had lost all authority and most of its volume. He finally looked up and saw her. She motioned with her arm in strong gestures to get into the house. "NOW", she yelled. Greg went back to slowly picking up the pieces to the train.

"Shit," Cathy blurted out. The increasing wind blew that word away without a sound. Good, she said to herself, he didn't hear Grandma using words he wasn't allowed to say. She hated herself when she started lapsing into profanity. It seemed like every time she got stressed those unlady-like words just floated up and slipped out.

She descended the steps and started picking up pieces of the train set and throwing them into the box. Greg looked at her as if she were some crazy woman. He was right; she was scared to death, and definitely going mad. Where was Glenny?

She figured out it was not the storm that had her scared; it was the sight of Mike's van. If she had Glenny at her side, she would be only angry because Mike was back. Why did he keep coming back when Tim had told to stay away? Why wasn't he at the game pumping Tim with his million questions? Why was he here today of all days?

She had to find Glenn and soon! It was more than just the fear for his safety. It was that Elaine had trusted her with her children. It was a bond of trust between family members. A bond that couldn't be broken if the family was to survive. To let a child be harmed, a child you loved as if he was your own was unthinkable. It was so unthinkable it made Cathy's breath shallow and her knees weak. Her biggest heartbreak would be telling her own daughter, her flesh and blood, that something horrible had happened to her child while she was in charge. Tears started to roll down her cheeks and she wiped them away with her sleeve as she continued to pick up those damn train pieces. Greg just watched her, sitting motionless.

She threw the last train piece into the box, picked up the large box and stashed it under her arm. She grabbed Greg's arm and started to drag him back up to the house. He started to pull away but decided that this was not the time to push his grandmother. He wanted to play with the train but the wind was ruining everything anyway. Boy, her mood sure had changed; what had he done to make her so mad! Where had Glenn gone? Greg thought of punching Glenn in the arm when he found him.

Once inside the house, Cathy grabbed the remote and lowered the blinds. She clasped her fingers around Greg's arm as she sat down on the edge of the chair. Now they were eye to eye.

"Do you know where Glenn is?" she asked. He shrugged again.

"Listen to me, Greg," she demanded, "this is serious!"

"No, Grandma," he said with a soft voice he often used when he believed he was in trouble.

"Where do you think he might go?" she pleaded. "I am afraid he might be hurt, or scared. You have to think hard and answer me. Did you see that man Mike and his van today?"

Greg's face lit up as if he finally was on the same page as his Grandmother. "Well," Greg said, deciding just how much to tell her, "Glenny said he saw Mike camping."

"Camping, Camping where?" Cathy demanded.

"Across the creek," Greg calmly remarked

"How could he see across the creek through the trees?" Cathy cried. "Did Glenny go across the creek?" She realized her voice was starting to rise and show hysteria. Greg was getting reluctant to answer her. Calm down and don't show the child how scared you are, she told herself.

"No, Grandma, Glenn would not go across the creek. It is one of your safety rules."

"Then how did he know Mike was camping?" she demanded. This interrogation of a seven year old was taking up valuable time. She should be spending time looking for Glenny before the storm hit full force. She could now hear the wind through the double glazed windows and the living room was getting dark. With the blinds down, she couldn't get an immediate check on the weather.

"He saw him from his hiding tree," Greg said.

"His what?" She prayed that Glenn was up in some tree watching the world and would soon climb down. "Where is this hiding tree?" she pleaded.

"Oh, you know, down by the creek." Greg just shrugged his shoulders and hoped his grandmother would leave him alone.

"If there was ever a time to tell the *whole* story to Grandma it is now! No more secrets or keeping a promise to Glenn! Glenny might be in great danger from Mike, or at least from the storm. You have to tell Grandma everything so I can find Glenny!" Cathy applied stronger pressure to his arm and drew him a little closer. Gregg took a deep breath and pulled back, trying to break the hold she had on his arm. Cathy couldn't tell if he was going to give her any more information or not. Just then, a loud clap of lightning and thunder hit almost simultaneously, and the television went dead. She hadn't even remembered leaving it on after the weather report. It scared them both. Cathy used this start as an opening to get Greg to spill his guts.

"Don't you think Glenn is scared now with this lightening and thunder?" she asked. Greg nodded his head quickly.

"Please tell me why he is not coming down out of the tree when I call him. Could he be stuck, or hurt?" Cathy questioned. "Have you ever been up in his hiding tree?"

"No," Greg said with the look on his face to infer that a hiding tree is so sacred that even your own brother is not allowed to visit.

"I don't think he is stuck," he said, "maybe he is hiding from Mike."

"I know Glenn doesn't like Mike, but why would he hide from him?"

Greg tried to break the eye-to-eye contact his grandmother was demanding. She firmly took his chin and turned his face so he would have to look her in the eye while maintaining the gentle squeeze on his arm. Cathy could tell by his expression that he was trying to make a big decision. She was growing more frantic with each howl of the wind and clap of thunder. She was fighting the urge to shake it out of him. She knew she had to give him the time it would take to tell her what she prayed was the answer to where Glenny was.

"One time Glenn saw Mike behind the old outhouse. Mike said that if he told anyone he was there that he would hurt his little sister. And he told Glenn that if he ever saw him again that he would steal him and then go hurt Kimmie."

"Sweet Jesus," Cathy murmured. "Is that why Glenny didn't want to come and stay at Grandma and Papa Tim's house anymore?"

Greg only nodded his head.

This new knowledge jerked Cathy into action. She stood up and went to the counter. She opened her purse and rummaged for her keys. She walked to the broom closet, grabbed a flashlight, and stashed it under her arm. With a key, she opened the guest closet and motioned Greg to come to her side.

"Look, Honey," she said. "I have to go and look for Glenn. Grandma has to know in her heart that you are safe or she can't leave you. I want you to stay in the closet with the door locked. Here, take this flashlight so you won't be in the dark. I would give you the phone but it's not working with the electricity out, and we don't want a cord going under the door to warn anyone that someone might be in the closet."

"Sweetie, you must stay inside with the door locked and not make any noise. You can open the door from the inside so you can get out, but you must NOT open the door to anyone! It is only safe to open it for Grandma, Tim, or your mother. Don't even open the door if a man says he is the sheriff. Do you understand Grandma?" Greg nodded his head and his eyes were moist. The poor child was holding back the tears.

"Now give Grandma a hug. Grandma is promising you that she will be back soon with Glenn. I won't forget you are here.. Please do exactly as Grandma says. Go ahead into the closet."

Greg gave her the hug and stepped reluctantly into the closet. She could hear him suck in a breath and fight back a sob. Cathy grabbed a children's book that had been left on the floor, and handed it to Greg before she locked him in.

"Can you hear Grandma?" she asked through the locked door.

"Yes." said a small-frightened voice.

"Remember, Sweetheart, only answer to Grandma, Papa Tim, or your mother. No one is to know you are in the closet. Do you understand?" she asked.

"Yes, Grandma, I promise."

"I'm proud of you. I promise to be back soon."

Cathy felt like a child abuser locking this sweet child in the closet. The thought crossed her mind that if Mike hadn't stolen all their coins and guns from that very same closet there wouldn't have been room for Greg to hide in there.

She went into the back bathroom, opened the closet door and pulled out the drawer that held all the seldom used and expired medications, finger nail polish, band-aids, and miscellaneous crap that she had been too lazy to chuck-out. In the very back of the drawer, Cathy pulled out the loaded gun that was hiding there. Tim had told her it was a thirty-eight. She would take his word for it. The only thing she feared more than the gun was the fear of what might have happened to Glenn. She grabbed a rain jacket and her cell phone as she left the house.

She started calling Glenn's name again as she punched the auto dial on the cell phone and tried to reach Tim at the baseball game. She wondered what the weather was like in San Diego because it certainly was black here, and the lightning and thunder just kept exploding in the sky.

She got Tim's voice mail. She looked at her watch and realized the game was about to end if it had not been called because of rain. Was he out of service or didn't he hear it? She left a message and told him that Greg was in the locked closet and she was out looking for Glenny. She also said that she had seen Mike's van going up the Miller's driveway. She told him that Greg had said that Mike had threatened to steal Glenny and hurt Kimmie. She hated leaving all this on his voice mail but at this point, he needed to know how serious Glenny's disappearance was, and he needed this information in case something happened to her. As a last tidbit of information she told him she had the gun. That should push him over the edge, she thought. She knew that he knew how dangerous she was with a gun! She might just shoot her foot off, or worse!

As Cathy continued to call Glenn's name the dogs appeared and ran barking up the driveway. Thank God, she thought, Tim is home. She stood there watching for his green truck when a white van started down the driveway with the dogs following and now barking wildly. Just what I need, she thought. That SOB has to be insane to come here now!

Mike stepped out of his van with his phony look of concern on his face and started walking towards Cathy. The dogs were growling and barking. The hair on their backs was standing up in a ridge. Those dogs are smarter than most humans are, she thought, they know evil when they smell it. I wish my own husband had that the same instinct.

He stopped, and with a look of hurt on his face had the audacity to ask Cathy to tell the dogs to shut-up. She called them off, fantasizing the boys lunging for his balls. Having that wish become a reality unfortunately wouldn't give her the information she needed. Where was Glenn, did he take him? she kept asking herself.

"What are you doing here?" she demanded.

"I heard you calling for Glenn. Is he lost?"

That was obviously not the answer to her question but Cathy decided that any answer from this thief was not worth the effort. She only wanted to know what had happened to her precious grandson.

"No," she lied. "The boys were playing hide and seek with me, and he still thinks the game is going on. I want him to come in out of the storm before the rain begins."

Mike continued walking towards her with that mock look of concern on his face. She wanted to slap it off. Her fear of him getting closer to the house and Greg locked in the closet stopped her breath.

"Stop!" she yelled. The noise of the storm, and her fear, made her demand seem impotent. He kept walking. She drew an invisible line with the toe of her shoe on the driveway. "Don't cross this line! You have reached the end of the road, no closer!" He looked at where she had scraped her foot and defiantly took a mother-may-I giant step. He looked her in the eye and smiled.

Cathy knew she was beginning to drown in her own fear and he was inching towards the house. Somewhere in the back of her mind, she was able to pull out something she had learned years ago in a psychology class. She remembered humans were only capable of one emotion at a time. She was feeling fear, and it was her fear that Mike was feeding on. She needed to be angry, and he needed to know she was one angry pissed off bitch! She remembered the gun in her pocket. She put her hand inside her rain jacket and slowly raised the gun and pointed it at Mike. His smile widened across his face.

"Oh, you're so funny pointing that finger at me," he mocked. "Pretending you have a gun. Some bluff, but it won't work with me. You and I both know I took all your guns," he chided, taunting her with each statement. The smirk on his face infuriated her.

There was his confession! Just standing there confessing that he had indeed stolen the coins and guns from them. Just because they couldn't prove it, or convince the deputy they owned guns and had a coin collection, didn't make it any less true. That son of a bitch, she kept repeating to herself, each time building up more anger. Now you are here taunting me while I look for my grandson. You SON OF A BITCH, she screamed silently. Now she was not afraid! She was angry, and she had become one wild lioness protecting her cubs. He was going to be sorry!

Cathy slowly removed the gun from its hiding place and showed Mike that she was indeed pointing the real thing at him. Very controlled and very quietly she started to speak. She prayed that the noise of the storm, and her air control would not fail her.

"Look you son of a bitch, you have been told never to darken this place with your presence! Now you show up and confess to your crime! I want you to leave! I said LEAVE!" she demanded.

"What's your problem? You sure aren't being neighborly," he cajoled. "Both you and I know you would never use that thing. The way I heard it, the last time you played with a gun you shot the legs off Tim's grandmother's antique nesting tables." His voice was smooth, syrupy, and taunting. "Where did you get that thing? I stole all your guns. How do I know that one is real?"

Cathy was enraged! This thief knowing her ignorance of guns and taunting her with the information brought her to the boiling point, and she felt betrayed by her own husband. Had he told this creep about the time she had indeed shot the legs off the tables while he was out of state and she was feeling very vulnerable and isolated? Was Tim's need for a friend greater than their safety? Had he bugged their house and been listening to everything?

Cathy looked Mike in the eye and smiled. She thought she would give him back some of his own sugar and phoniness. She was feeling the power she had now that she had the gun out of its hiding place. She slowly moved her arm slightly to the left and pulled the trigger. The gun went off and the noise startled Mike into jumping behind her invisible line. Luckily the recoil brought the barrel pointing directly back on him. She continued to smile and look him directly in the eye.

"Yup," she said, "the gun is real, and this is one gun you didn't steal. It wasn't in the closet. And, since you crawled in through the doggie door I have been target practicing when I am in San Diego, taking lessons so I can pick off intruding vermin. This here baby and I have become dear friends. If you want to see what a good shot I have become I will show you by target practicing with the big toe of your left foot. I bet I can hit it dead-on, even with your shoe on." This of course was not the truth, but she felt empowered giving him this tale of crap in a snotty voice that reminded her of some seven year old fighting with her classmate. In fact, she still didn't know diddlysquat about guns, she only knew her fear of them. Mike didn't need to know this or her bluff wouldn't work. He looked from his feet to her eyes and said nothing. The smile was finally gone from his face.

"Now, if you are a smart thieving son of a bitch," she continued in that taunting snotty tone, "I would suggest you climb into your van and get your ass far away from here!" Mike didn't move so Cathy started walking toward him. The distance between the gun and Mike was closing. He started to back up the driveway watching Cathy and the gun, the dogs following him happily as if begging for food. Cathy stepped forward to keep the distance between Mike and the gun close enough so she wouldn't miss if she had to use it, and remain far enough away so he couldn't jump at her and knock the gun from her hand.

"Hey," she shouted as the thunder continued to explode the sky, "I want to look inside your little crime-mobile before you leave my life for the last time."

Mike's face showed fear for the first time. Was it fear or controlled rage? He was a hard man to read. Was Glenn inside? She needed to know before he drove away. Now fear was beginning to control her again. Cathy mentally slapped her face to get back in control. I have to keep this bluff going! I have to see if he has Glenn. Glenny would be gone forever if he was allowed to drive away with him! Now her fear of what poor little Glenn might be experiencing was making her hand shake. She couldn't let Mike see her fear. The gun felt so heavy to hold and her deepening fear was making this bluff almost impossible to pull off! She was determined that nothing was going to harm that sweet child while it was her watch! Just push one more of my buttons, you son of a bitch, and see what I will do!

"I said open the door!" Mike slowly started to open the driver's door never taking his eyes off the gun.

"No, not that door, open the back doors." Mike stood frozen with his hand on the handle.

"I am going to look inside, with or with out your help." she stated mater of factly. "Show me the inside, and then you can back up the driveway and leave forever. Don't show me, and the sheriff can hose your blood off the driveway tomorrow. At this point it makes no difference to me." Cathy could tell that Mike was weighing his options, and her ability and determination to use the gun.

He walked to the back of the van and opened the doors. She was surprised that they weren't locked. She motioned him to step aside so she had an unobstructed view of the interior. She made him stand in front of one of the open doors, within easy range so she couldn't miss. She knew at that moment that she would and could kill him if she found Glenny inside. The new knowledge she just learned about Catherine Louise Spalding, and what was worth killing for was just a plain and simple fact. This new knowledge cleared her mind. Knowing this about herself calmed her. There were no decisions; she knew that squeezing the trigger would be a reflex. In that same instant she knew she would let him go if Glenn was not in the van. God, help me if I truly overreacted!

She was raging mad that this SOB had turned their lives upside down by continually showing up, stealing from them, and threatening Glenn. For Gods sake, he was just an innocent five-year old! Yet part of her anger was that law enforcement treated them as if they were the local crazies. Treated them like they had just made up the theft, for either the insurance money or the attention. Cathy believed that at some level of her internal psyche that a power far greater than herself would take care of this Bastard. She hoped she could be patient enough to wait it out while fearing she would always wonder if she would ever know. Yes, she said to herself, God will get you!

As she looked inside the van, she noted the cupboards and drawers lining the walls. Near the front, there was a built in bench and table, and there was some kind of a folding door so she could not see out through to the windshield. The aisle was clear and unobstructed. It was unsettling not seeing Glenn. Where was he if not in here? Cathy calculated the thickness of the cupboards to estimate if they were deep enough to hide a child. The thought of that precious child in one of those cupboards made her eyes water. Mike shifted his weight to the other foot and this movement caught Cathy with her guard down, caught her peering into the van engulfed with fear.

They had never spoken that the search inside the van was for her to look for Glenn. Quickly their eyes met and parted. She knew that Mike knew what she was looking for. She was looking for her missing grandchild. Was that why he had allowed her to look? To prove to her that even he was not evil enough to harm a child! On the other hand, was it the fear that she might just shoot him if he hadn't allowed her to search? Screw it, she thought; I don't care what his reasons are. I am wasting valuable time with this bastard!

"Climb into the driver's seat and drive away, and I mean FOREVER!" she yelled. She watched him slide the accordion door open, climb into the seat, and reach for the keys that were hanging in the ignition. He turned around and looked at Cathy through the open back doors. Cathy descended the few feet to the van, closed the doors, and knocked on them, still pointing the gun at the back window. She backed off the pavement and kept the gun pointed at the van. He backed up the driveway, turned the van around at the top, and continued up the hill. The dogs resumed their barking and chasing the van. Cathy stood there at attention with the gun pointed until he was no longer in sight.

"GOD WILL GET YOU FOR THIS!" She screamed as loud as she could. He didn't hear her, she had screamed into the wind and he was gone. The screaming clearing her head and she needed to believe it.

Cathy's mind was racing and she was torn apart with both fear and rage. She felt like she was trying to keep her balance on a tight wire while she was fighting to keep the gun from blowing a large hole in the SOB's chest, or at least the side of the van. She still wanted to pull the trigger and she knew that she would have if she knew Glenn was safe. She was enraged this creep kept coming into their lives and undermining everything she and Tim held dear. He had turned their lives upside down in their special place in the forest, stolen their possessions, and threatened an innocent five-year-old. And, with Glenny missing she was terrified for his safety, and seething that he may have some knowledge of where he was. Had he done something with her precious Glenn?

Oh God, she thought, I am so tired and I need to go find Glenn. I'm just one person in this huge forest, all alone in the rain, so cold and afraid. A voice inside herself told her to stop feeling sorry for herself and go find the kid! She knew that she was all Glenny had at this moment and he needed her to find him, and pronto! She let the gun fall to her side and shook out her arms to get the blood flowing again. Her shoulders slumped and she dropped her head to her chest and started to cry. She stood there with her chest rising and falling, the rain soaking her hair, the back of her neck, running off her raincoat and sliding down her arms and onto the gun. She raised the gun and looked at it as though seeing it for the first time. She noticed how slick it had become with the sweat from her nervous hand and the rain. She tried wiping it dry with her other hand before she placed it back into her pocket. The phone started to ring. It was Tim.

"Jesus Christ, Cathy, what are you trying to do to me, leaving me a voice mail like that?" Tim snapped. Cathy couldn't speak, the sobs still stealing her breath. "Hey Baby, are you crying?" his voice instantly becoming sweet and supportive. "Take a deep breath and tell me what's going on. Did you find Glenny?"

"No, I can't find him. Shit, I can't even look for him. I have been holding Mike at gun point."

"What did you just say?" Tim screamed into the cell phone. "You've got the gun? Did you call the sheriff?"

"I haven't had a chance, and besides you know how much they helped us last time we called! I got Mike to leave without killing him. By God, I would have killed him if Glenny had been in his van. Can you believe he actually admitted to taking your coins and guns? He thought your thirty-eight was a toy. Boy did I show him it was real when I pulled the trigger! The sound of it about scared us both to death." She chuckled at the memory of the loud blast and started to unwind with Tim on the other end of the line.

"Calm down, calm down Baby, you are not making any sense." Tim's voice was now full of concern and support again. "There is a tree down blocking the road and all traffic is stopped. I will probably see Mike stopped on the other side. I will watch for him. How long ago did he leave?

"Mike? Ah... he left just left a couple of minutes ago."

"The phone is back in service now and we can talk again. I am going to hang up so you can call the sheriff. Call the sheriff now, then go and look for Glenny!"

"OK, OK, I am better now, just talking to you made me better." Cathy murmured as she kept gulping small breaths of air. She was beginning to feel weak with the loss of adrenalin pumping through her veins. "I have to look for Glenn. You know how I hate to call the sheriff. They treat us like we keep calling them because we want attention. I haven't even called Elaine and told her I can't find Glenn. I wasn't afraid for Glenn until I ran into Mike and I looked and he didn't have him in his van. Oh Tim, where could he be? Did Mike hurt him and leave him somewhere? Oh God, how can I ever tell Elaine? I need you here now!"

"Cathy, go look for Glenn, the phone call to Elaine can wait until you have some kind of answer. I am stuck on the other side of this huge tree with a bunch of stranded commuters; the road is completely blocked. I wish I had my fucking chain saw with me. I would cut the damn tree into pieces myself!"

"Does anyone know how long it will take the road crew to clear away the tree?"

"First, they have to get here! Right now, we are backed up against the downed tree, just stopped and blocking traffic worse. Come on Cathy, you have to get hold of yourself. I know I can count on you, Glenn definitely is. Hang in there, and I will be there as soon as I can." Tim hung up and Cathy had never felt so alone in her whole life.

Cathy yelled Glenn's name a couple of times and stopped to listen and see if she could hear him answer her. She dialed 911 on her cell phone and waited for a connection. She hurried back into the house and up to the closet where she had locked Greg.

"Honey, it's Grandma, you OK?" she asked in her sweetest grandma voice as she held the phone to her ear.

"I'm OK, can I come out now?"

"Not right yet, I'm still looking for Glenny and it has started to rain really hard. Grandma still needs to know you are safe. Please stay quiet and in the closet. I will be back again soon. OK, sweetheart?"

"Grandma," a frightened little voice pleaded, "is it really important for me to stay here? I could help you look."

"Oh God, yes Greg, it's really important," she said with a pain in her heart.

"OK, just find Glenny soon. I hate it in here."

"Soon sweetheart, soon," she promised. "I am going to look again now." Cathy still held the cell phone to her ear and she quickly moved away from the closet door. She didn't want Greg to hear her plead with the sheriff when she was lucky enough to reach him. The TV was black so the electricity was still off. It was beginning to get dark. What time was it? Was it dark from the storm or had that much time elapsed?

She was back outside again calling Glenn's name. She decided to walk along the creek since Greg had said his hiding tree was there. It was hard walking in the rain, the steep terrain, the new mud, let alone looking for a missing child with a wet cell phone to her ear. She prayed the battery would last. She had the gun in her pocket and the dogs were running innocently at her feet. They thought the rain great fun.

"Hello, this is the California Highway Patrol. You dialed 911?" a perturbed voice said.

"Well yes, but I wanted the sheriff here in Julian." Cathy lamented.

"The Highway Patrol handles all 911 cell phone calls. We are swamped with calls so please explain your problem quickly," the voice on the other end snapped.

"My grandson is missing and a man whom we have reported previously to have stolen our coins and guns was here on the property. My other grandson said this man threatened my missing grandson if he ever saw him again. I am afraid something horrible has happened to him, he is only five. I held a gun to the man, and then I made him leave. His name is Mike Jenkins. I looked in his van and I didn't see Glenny."

"Lady, Lady, calm down. You are not making any sense," the voice said. "We are really busy so please don't ramble. What's your name and address, and the name of the missing child?"

"I am sick and tired of people telling me to calm down when I have a missing kid, his brother locked in the closet for his safety, my husband gone and this thief on our property again. It is raining like a cow pissing on a flat rock and if I am not hit by lightning before I find this kid, God will get me for the evil hate I have for having to talk to an arrogant son of a bitch like you! My name is Cathy Spalding and I live at the bottom of North Peak on the north side, south of Julian. I am standing by the creek where they found the skeleton of that unlucky lumberman that was murdered on this very spot about a hundred years ago. Get hold of the sheriff in Julian and he will know where I live and tell him I said to get out here NOW." Cathy very clearly screamed her cell phone number into the phone. With that, she hung up and put the cell phone back into her pocket. Boy, she thought, that conversation sure unwound the knot in the back of my neck! I'd better get busy because it looks like I won't be getting any help anytime soon!

"Where could he be? Glenn please answer Grandma and tell me where you are hiding." She wasn't calling him any more, just talking out loud.

"Hey, boys," she said to the dogs, "where is Glenny?" They both looked up at her excitedly wagging their tails. "Where is Glenn?" Andy cocked his drenched head keeping his eyes half closed to keep the rain out of them. "Come on boys, earn your feed. Give me a sign." With that command, Andy walked over to a tree, sniffed, and lifted his leg.

Some help, she thought but she moved to stand under the huge tree next to Andy and looked up, half looking for Glenn and half looking for a miracle. Just then, lightning struck simultaneously with a crash of thunder making the ground shake. She instinctively covered her head with her arms believing the tree above her would begin to fall. Then it was so dark and quiet and she realized the scorching white light had momentarily blinded her. "Dear God," she pleaded, "don't make this the hiding tree."

When Cathy started to unfold and get her senses back, lightening struck again and set her dancing in place, the ground alive with electricity.

She felt it enter through her shoes and leave through her fingertips. She heard Andy yelp and saw him speed away from the tree. She blinked and flexed her fingers, feeling strangely invigorated and free from her fears for the first time in months. She knew she would find Glenn and this horrible day would turn out OK. Did she loose all common sense with the jolt of lightening? Maybe, her doom and gloom mood had only been hormonal, a chemical imbalance in the first place. Did she only need a jump-start to get back to her old relaxed self, or was she floating out there somewhere in the aftermath of Mother Nature's shock therapy?

A tree crashed nearby sounding like it was destroying the forest. She could hear a limb break and as it fell, she heard another limb break. The sound was so near, the ripping of timber so thunderous. She could imagine trees falling like dominos in the forest, falling on each other knocking the next tree over, each creating a new path of destruction. Cathy slumped against the trunk with her arms still covering her head. She knew that Glenny must be scared to death too.

It became obvious to her that being out in the forest, standing under a tree in a lightening storm, was more than dangerous, it was life threatening! So much for her recent mood alteration, a little fear of Mother Nature might keep them both alive! With all that noise, electricity, and destruction she wondered why she was still standing when it sounded like the rest of the forest was crashing around her feet. Was there some force greater than Mother Nature keeping her from being zapped? "Thank you, God," she said as she looked up through the limbs.

A shoe hit her on her head and bounced near her feet. It was muddy but she recognized it. It was Glenny's shoe. Cathy called Glenn's name again. Then she yelled, "Answer your Grandma and come down out of that tree before the next bolt of lightning fries your little butt." There was only silence. She reconsidered her tactics and began again with a different tone.

"Glenn, Grandma is right here. Please come down out of the tree. It is safe, and Grandma will not let that Bad Man Mike hurt you or Kimmie," she was pleading now. "I have a gun and I will shoot him if he tries to hurt you!"

A little voice from overhead said, "Grandma, where's Greg, did Mike take Greg?"

"Oh, Honey, he's safe in the house. He's waiting for you."

With that answer, Cathy saw first a sock, than a shoe from the other foot, then a pant leg as he began the descent from the tree. Very slowly, Glenn slid down the rain slick tree into his grandmother's arms. She grabbed him and hugged him tight against her ample breast, hugged him with her whole heart. He was safe! Their whole world was safe again. She would free his older brother from the closet, build a fire in the fireplace and dry this cold wet child. Perhaps they would pop popcorn over the fire or roast marshmallows. She wondered how long it would take the sheriff to come, or Tim to get home. She would call the sheriff back when Glenn was safe in the house and Greg was out of the closet.

Glenny could have walked back to the house but Cathy didn't want to let him go. He held on tight to her with his wet head nestled into her neck. God, he had gotten heavy, she thought. Cathy was trudging up the hill and was finally beginning to unwind. They had weathered the storm. They had all survived. In her mind, she was already pulling the video out of her memory box, and editing it for when she replayed it for Elaine. She knew she would have to be very careful about how she told Elaine what had happened here today. Now that they were safe, that old fear flared again. Elaine would never again trust her to watch her children. She saw herself in her mind's video, the part about Mike and her with the gun. She felt pleased that she had pulled the bluff. He was gone, and they were safe. Elaine hated guns even more than her mother did, she would not like the bluff at all!

Chapter Twenty-One
Safe and Snug

Cathy knocked loudly on the door to the closet and told Greg to come out. The door popped open and Cathy could see a scared little boy emerge and run to hug his brother. "Yuck," Greg groaned, "you made me all wet."

"Grandma is going to get some towels and dry off Glenn. Greg you can stack the wood on the grate and build a fire all by yourself. Do you boys want popcorn or marshmallows once the fire is going?" A dumb question, she thought, because she knew the answer was going to be marshmallows. They loved the drama of the flame and they already had the straightened coat hangers out for torching the marshmallows. She knew dinner was out of the question when Elaine got here late to pick up the boys. She hoped Tim would arrive soon. She needed to call the sheriff back.

So many thoughts raced through Cathy's mind as she went for the towels. It felt good to be able to think again, even if there were too many thoughts running rampant through her brain. She accepted this as better than the alternative when she seemed paralyzed with fear. As she grabbed the towels from the bathroom, she started to put the gun back into the drawer. She hated the feel of it with its weight hanging in her pocket and she hated what it represented. She looked at it, and pulled the hand towel off the bar and wiped the gun clean. She knew this gesture was more symbolic than sanitary, sort of like erasing all the prints of this afternoon from her memory. She closed the drawer and put it back in the pocket of her pants. I'll keep it until Tim or the sheriff arrive, she said to herself.

The dogs were back and standing on the hearth waiting for the warmth the fire would give them. They often stood there to melt the snow off their legs after they had been playing in the forest in winter.

"How am I going to build a fire and make you guys warm if you are in my way?" Greg explained to two very soaked schnauzers. The dogs had a great time today and they were happy that Greg was talking to them. The more he tried to move them from the hearth the closer they leaned into his face, and the faster their cropped tails wagged.

Cathy let Greg light the candles with the barbeque lighter after he had the fire going. She wanted to show him how grown up he had been this afternoon by staying in the closet. She knew how frightened he had been. They had been through so much today that she couldn't say he was not old enough to light the candles when she was right there to supervise.

Cathy towel dried Glenny after she had pulled his wet and muddy clothes off his little body. His skin looked almost transparent and blue. He seemed more than just cold to her, she thought he looked a little shell-shocked.

"Grandma, can I have a warm bubble bath?" Glenn asked.

"Oh, Sweetie, I wish you could but we don't have any water without electricity, only what Grandma collected in the plastic bottles. Soon the fire will help you to get warm. You OK, big guy?" she asked. He just shrugged with his arms hanging loose and his palms pointing forward. She tried to dress him quickly and pulled his sweatshirt on over his shirt. She hoped this would help until the heat of the fire took hold.

"You sure gave me a scare when I couldn't find you with the storm coming and all. You're safe now. I made Mike go away and never come back!" He stood there looking up at her but the expression on his sweet little face changed from fatigue and cold, to one of fear.

"Greg told me about your hiding tree." She continued talking, trying to calm him as she rubbed his head with the towel. "He also told me that Mike said he would take you and hurt Kimmie if you said anything. Is that true?" Glenny just nodded his head and began to cry quietly. If his lower lip had not been sticking out it would be hard for Cathy to know he was holding back the tears.

Cathy knew her Glenn; they had developed a bond. It had not been easy to get this child to trust her and at one time she was a stranger. She was just the name Grandma. It had taken most of his young years for him to know the meaning of her name. Hours spent, stories shared, games played, but still he just tolerated her when his mother was away. It was after watching Grandma care for baby Kimmie, changing her pants, feeding her, washing her face and talking baby talk to her, he knew that they would be safe while Mom was away. He knew she would never leave them alone, or lie to him. He had learned, especially today, that he must always tell her the truth too.

That was why he was crying. He was crying because he had kept such a secret, a secret out of fear, fear of Kimmie being hurt. He kept his secret because he knew if Kimmie were hurt, his Mom would be crushed. He knew his Mom loved him, but he knew that Mom loved Kimmie so, so much. He had to believe that she loved him just as much. He didn't have to be loved more, just loved as much. If Kimmie was hurt and Mom was crushed, she wouldn't love him anymore because Mom's heart would be broken. He didn't think he could bear not being loved by Mom anymore.

Grandma held him tight. He loved her holding him even though Greg said that hugging grown-ups was for babies. He wanted to be baby enough to hug Grandma when Mom was gone. She stroked his head and spoke softly to him.

"You're safe sweetheart, Kimmie is with Mom and she is OK too. Mom will be here in a couple of hours and you boys can go home just as soon as the road is open again. That horrible old Mike is gone and he will never be coming back. Grandma promises you that!"

Glenn pulled out of Cathy's arms and looked her in the eye. He had a terrified look on his face and he took a deep breath and weighed the truth he was about to speak. "Grandma, he is not gone, he went to his camping."

Cathy sat up straight, her heart skipped a beat, and a knot began to form in her gut. What information did this child have that she did not? "What are you telling me?" Cathy demanded of her five-year old grandson. This child she had searched for in the storm. This child that was hardly dry and warm.

Glenn straightened his little back, held his head straight, and knew that he had to tell Grandma the truth. "Mike is at his camp. He left your house and drove to his camp."

"What camp, what are you talking about?" she asked. "How do you know this?"

"I could see him from my hiding tree."

"Did you see me with him in the driveway?" she asked, feeling like her safe little world was blown apart again.

"I didn't see him but I heard a loud shot." He said, his eyes growing large as he answered her. "It was louder than the thunder."

"Did you see him drive away, out of the driveway?"

"Yeah." he said, nodding his head.

"Then where did you see him go?" she pleaded

"He drove into the trees. I know, Grandma, he didn't really drive into the trees it just looks like that," he said. "Then I saw him coming down the other road, you know, the road where we go for walks."

"Just where is this camp of his?" she pleaded further.

"Across the creek, it's across from my hiding tree. It's really neat, and he has a telescope on legs and I looked through it. I could see your house through the trees but everything was green."

"How do you know all this?" Cathy prodded Glenn, and the tale began to fall from him in jumbles with excitement, and now uninhibited.

"I went to see it. I never told you 'cause you said to stay on this side of the creek but it was so close, only eight giant steps across the creek. One time I saw him by the outhouse. He had a big metal circle with a stick on it and it made fast beep, beep sounds. He got really mad when he saw me. He said to stay way, far away from him, and if he ever saw me again he would steal me and then hurt my little sister." The words just continued to fall from the frightened child with the large eyes and the stiff back.

Sweet Jesus, Cathy thought. He had a metal detector and a night vision scope. No wonder we can't even fart without this sicko watching us. This knowledge gave her pure nausea. Here she thought they were safe, and now she learns she could just about throw a rock from the deck into his camp across the creek.

She jumped up and started locking the doors to the house. Cathy started making a mental list of all she must do to keep them safe until help arrived. They would stay inside the living room with the blinds down and she would shut the doors from the bedrooms into the hall. He couldn't see in with the doors shut. She knew the dogs would let her know if anyone came onto the deck. Either Tim or the sheriff would be here soon, and she prayed that Elaine would arrive after them. She had better try calling her. She put her hand on her hip and felt the gun in her pocket. She was glad that it was still there. At this moment, they were safe.

She pulled out the cell phone and dialed 911 again. Maybe I should have been a little nicer the last time I called, she said to herself. She cancelled the call and decided to call Tim first and tell him she had found Glenny. I think he needs to call the sheriff this time, she thought, I am still recovering from that bad case of *foot in mouth disease*.

She looked down at the dial and the low battery icon was illuminated and pulsing on the face. "Oh, shit" she said softly. "Now we are truly isolated!" She could recharge her battery in the car but she was not going to leave the house, with or without the kids. She thought of driving away with the kids, but she was afraid Mike might be waiting for her now that it was dark on the long drive to the road. Dear God, she prayed, please let Elaine not be the first one here and run into Mike.

The kids were having a great time with the dogs while they sat in front of the fire. Cathy marveled at their quick recovery. Such innocence, she thought, why not let them bask in it.

"How about some dinner?" she asked. "I could make some Kraft Macaroni and Cheese. The stove works but the oven doesn't." She was always amazed at how they could eat macaroni and cheese three times a day. She wondered how many of those blue boxes she had opened and prepared over the years, and how many gallons of water she had used to boil the macaroni. She remembered how her children had loved it too, and how she had only paid twenty-five cents a box for it then. That memory made her feel really old!

"Grandma, will the ice cream in the freezer go mushy when your electricity goes out?" Greg had his little engineer's look on his face when he asked her this question. Cathy always delighted in all the questions he would ask her about how something worked. Her answers usually sounded rather dumb, and she soon realized that he had pretty much known the ins' and outs' of an object before he had asked the question.

"If it is out long enough, Sweetie," she said. Cathy was now pouring water from the plastic gallon jug into a pan and turning on the burner. The activity of cooking, something she knew so well seemed to calm her.

"How about we have an ice cream party after you eat your macaroni and cheese? Grandma has vanilla ice cream, chocolate and butterscotch syrup, some bananas, and a can of whipping cream. I think I even have a jar of those red cherries to put on top. We can even use those special ice cream dishes, just like in the restaurant." The boys began the discussion on what kind of syrup they were going to have on their ice cream.

Cathy was pouring water she had heated into the dishpan when the lights came back on. In the light, she began to think that maybe the situation didn't look so bleak. She turned on the faucet and the water pumped freely into the sink. She squirted a little detergent into the water and watched it begin to foam. She marveled at the simplicity of the task that she did several times a day. It seemed so easy when all the pieces of technology worked, something as simple as running water. Since they had moved to the mountains, she had learned the value of electricity. When they had first moved to their place they had a generator and when it wasn't running they were without water, and lights. Being a city girl, she had never considered such problems.

The phone now worked and she vowed that they were going to get a good old-fashioned phone, the kind that didn't need electricity. This cordless stuff was great but when the electricity went out, they were useless. She plugged her cell phone into the battery charger and her voice mail beeper began to signal her she had messages. She called her voice mail and learned she had three messages from Tim, one from Elaine, but none from the sheriff.

Tim's last message said he was checking to see if Glenny was found and safe. He was so worried when he couldn't reach her that he decided to turn around and go back to the city and would take the road north through Ramona. He had not seen any sign of Mike waiting on the other side. Cathy punched the time log to see when he had made the last call. She calculated that he would be home in about 45 minutes if the road were clear through Ramona.

Elaine's message said she had been on her way when the storm hit and the lightning and thunder was scaring Kimberly. She heard on the car radio the road was closed so she turned around and went back home. She would be back in the morning when the sun was out. She said she hoped keeping the boys one more night was not too much of a problem.

Cathy called Tim, and he answered the phone on the first ring. "What's happened?" He pleaded. She could hear the fear in his voice.

"I honestly was too busy to call, and then my battery went dead. Glenn is safe; he was up hiding in a tree."

"Thank God, he is safe!" Tim sighed with relief.

"Honey, Glenn said that Mike drove to the other side of the property and he has a camp there with a night vision telescope. I am scared to death he might come back. I don't trust that creep. He has been watching us. Why would he be doing that?"

"Jesus," Tim said, and she could hear the air escaped from his lips. "Has the sheriff been there yet? I'm about 10 minutes until I turn off for the house. I will honk three short times to let you know it's me when I start down the driveway. I hope you still have the gun close by. Please hang tough, Baby. Are the boys doing OK?"

"Yeah, once Glenny got warm and told me everything he seemed to settle down. Greg is in charge of the fire and roasting the marshmallows. He was more worried about the ice cream melting when the electricity was out. I have been so scared for so long I am wiped-out. I am dying to see you!"

"Have you heard from the sheriff?"

"No, but I wasn't too nice to the man who took my message, I was sort of hoping you would call them back when you got home."

"Oh Cathy, this was definitely not a good time for you to blow up at the Sheriff's Department." He hung up and kept his eyes searching for any movement in the forest, and looking for a white van as he turned down the driveway. He was almost home. He thought it was one of the longest days of his life, and his damn Padres had lost, too.

Chapter Twenty-Two
The Hiding Tree

Cathy sat up with a jolt, sweating with fear. Had she screamed out loud or screamed in a dream? She looked over at Tim and saw that he was sleeping peacefully. She looked around the bedroom, at the kids on the floor, and then out the windows into the forest. The sun had risen in a clear sky, making the trees sparkle as it dried the moisture from yesterday's storm. How much better her world looked this morning with the clear sky and the golden trees.

The fear was still pounding in her veins, her pulse still rapid as she swung her feet off the bed in dreaded pursuit of taking on one more day with a frightened heart. This premonition was more than real to her; it had been a loud voice. Yet she had it when she was sleeping, did that make it technically a dream? It was more like insight, one of those videos in her mind. It was a rerun of yesterday, but with new knowledge of what was going to happen.

Tim rose up on one elbow and gave her a sleepy smile. She loved the way he smiled; it softened his features and lit up his face. She had fallen in love with that smile. This morning he drove a little of the fear from her veins with that smile. She felt safe when she was with him.

"You hitting the floor so early, Babe?" He questioned as he reached for her arm to pull her back for a good morning kiss.

"I had a long night. I was afraid to sleep soundly, always listening to any sound in the forest because Mike might come back. Then I guess I fell into a deep sleep because I had this horrible dream. It was about Mike when he was here yesterday. It frightened me so much that I awoke because I couldn't handle what he was thinking. I actually could hear what he was thinking yesterday in my dream."

"Really, what was he thinking?" Tim was rubbing her arm trying to coax her back into bed so they could curl up together and wait for the sun to clear the pump house. It was a time of sharing they both loved. He often seemed receptive to listen to her plans for the day, the details of a dream, or just to lie quietly together as he drifted back to sleep and her brain kicked into high gear.

"It was so real to me that I am not sure you want to hear it, or I want to hear you try to talk me out of what I now believe to be true." Her words had come out with more of a sting than she had intended. She was trying to fight her fears as she listened to her friends' advice about giving Tim a little slack about believing her premonitions. She sat while he continued to stroke her arm. Was he going back to sleep, or ask her to explain herself?

"Why don't you let me decide if I have married a witch or not? Do you spell it with a W or a B?" He pinched her elbow and gave her a little boy lazy grin. His grin was almost his *wanna*? grin. She doubted he was being amorous with the kids asleep on the floor beside the bed. They had insisted they sleep in the same room with them last night in case Mike returned. The gun was under Tim's pillow. She hoped he hadn't forgotten the kids were there.

"When I had the gun pointed at Mike and asked him to open his van so I could look inside, he had the strangest look come over his face.

At first, I thought I finally had him scared. I had been working so hard on pulling off this bluff with the gun, and hiding my fear. Then he gives me this award winning hurt look on his face. For a second it caught me off guard, but I could see through it. His look was so phony to me. For a split second, I wondered if he was scared or enraged, but I was too busy to waste any more time on him. I only wanted him gone so I could look for Glenn. Then in my dream, yesterday was a rerun. However, in my dream I could hear everything he was thinking, as if he was talking out loud. It scared me so much I woke up. We have to plan for his return." Cathy spoke quietly and wondered if he would release her arm if she gently pulled away and got up. His eyes were closed, and she was not sure if he had even registered what she had said in his half-asleep state.

"What do you mean his return? Why would he be coming back after he told you he had stolen all our stuff?" Tim's eyes were now wide open and looking directly at her.

"He is coming back because he came here yesterday to kill me. When he found out Glenny was here too he was going to add him to his list." Hearing her voice out loud in the bedroom sounded so frightening and bizarre. How was Tim going to take what she had said? Please God, don't let the kids hear what I have just said.

"List, what is this shit about a list?" Tim was now standing beside the bed, his back to the window and he appeared to Cathy as a looming silhouette. She was thankful he was talking or he would have taken on an evil form to her.

"Shush," she whispered and gestured for them to leave the kids asleep and have this conversation out of their earshot. He followed her to the kitchen and stood silently watching her fill the coffeemaker and slide the switch to on. When she had completed the task, they sat in their favorite chairs in the living room waiting to speak after they had consumed their first swallow.

"List?" he asked again unable to wait for the coffee.

"I just know I heard him and he said I was on his 'Things To Do Today' list. And since the little brat was there today he wouldn't mind adding one more item to the list." Cathy was always amazed how Tim always only remembered the last thing she said, hardly ever the important contents of her conversation. Had he truly missed what she had said about his coming to kill her? It was hard to believe he had missed that! Missed the part about when she told him about the threat on her life, but since they had many such fragmented discussions; she could believe it.

"Did you hear me tell you that he had come to our house to kill me?" She repeated what she believed to be the punch line. She sat quietly waiting for his reaction.

"Let me get this straight. From your dream, you could read his mind, or hear him talking? He was standing outside his van and you heard his mind saying that he drove all the way from San Diego to kill you. Did his mind, or your dream, say how he was going to do it?" Tim's voice had slipped into his best "I have definitely married either a witch or an idiot" voice.

"Yeah, well sort of. When I sent him away, his thoughts said it was OK, just a change of plans. He was going to drive away, go to the west side of the property where he always hides his van and walk back across the creek. After I find the little *brat,* that is what he kept calling Glenn, he was going to wait until we were all *snuggy,* also his word, in the house and then sneak in and use his belt to strangle me and then kill Glenn!" The pitch of her voice now rose. She had begun to speak fast, telling him everything before he could scoff at her. She no longer cared if he believed her or not because she had been on her own yesterday, and if it was necessary to protect the kids again today she would do it!

"Mike also said, or thought out loud, he actually liked me, but I had stepped over the line when I demanded you not let him into the house.

He said a whole lot of other stuff I couldn't understand. I could hear his mind talking to me clearly, but I didn't know what he was going on about. He did say he had as much right to be here as we did!" Cathy sat back in her chair and watched Tim to see what his reaction was going to be after this diatribe.

"Hum," he muttered as he was thinking. He sat quietly in his chair appearing to be listening to the sound of the coffeemaker. "Let's not tell the deputy when he arrives here this morning, not tell him the part about reading a mind in a dream. Please, don't get angry with me because I tell you this; but this definitely is the most off the wall thriller I have ever heard you recite!" He jumped up immediately after this plea and went into the kitchen to pour them both a cup of coffee. He didn't want to see her jaw tighten as she processed what he had just said.

She was so frustrated and hurt that she could not get him to see the evil of this Mike. She knew her dream was way off base, but it was so clear and it made so much sense to her. She could still hear his voice in her head; hear all that he had said. Not what he actually said to her yesterday, but what he was thinking yesterday.

"Oh yeah," she said with her voice loud enough for Tim to hear in the kitchen. "He also said that yesterday was his last day in the good ole USA. He was starting a new life in Mexico. He just had to complete one more thing on his list before he left. He had to kill me." The thoughts from Mike just kept filling her head. She knew that this was new information; she hadn't heard this in her dream. This new voice running through her head she would keep to herself.

"Please Cathy; promise me you won't tell this tale to the deputy." Tim poked his head around the corner of the kitchen and looked at her sitting quietly in her chair, waiting for her morning coffee. "If I can promise you that I won't let Mike in our house why can't you promise me you won't sound like a crazy woman to the deputy? We already have lost all credibility with the Sheriff's Station. Obviously there is a leak in security there because the whole town, all one thousand five hundred of them already thinks we are crazy!"

"OK, I will promise you that I will not mention my dream. I will tell him about what he said in the driveway, and I will tell him what Glenny said when he threatened him. Is that OK with you?" She loved him, and more than anything, she needed his trust. She was tired of this fear, and this aversion with this evil Mike and the hassle of Tim not seeing him as a threat. She knew she would never sleep peacefully until he was arrested. She feared she would grow to hate her forest because he could always be lurking behind some tree, listening to them from across the creek.

"Can I be sure you can tell the difference between your dream and what actually took place yesterday?" Tim was pleading with her. He wanted all this to stop as bad as she did. To her it seemed as simple as what he perceived stop to mean, and how she perceived stop to happen.

"I have always known the difference. In addition, if I might be so bold to say…it is one thing not to have your trust and support when I feel someone to be evil, warn you away from him. But, what really hurts is when you start to belittle me for my beliefs, perceptions, even scoffing my premonitions. I will take your advice about what I say to the deputy, it is valid. I will continue to listen to how you perceive my observations, take your opinions under advisement, as they say. But, get one thing straight Timothy Spalding! Don't, for one minute begin to think that I have accepted your opinions to be true, accurate, or gospel! If you want me to just stop telling you what I think, or feel, just say the word and mum is my new MO." She had now begun to finish her pronouncement through clenched teeth. How dare he, she fumed!

"Shit, Cathy, let's not get in an argument before we have our first sip of coffee, right before the deputy arrives. We have to be a team on this. I believe you when you say that Mike confessed to the theft, and I believe you when you say he threatened Glenn. I always want you to say any and everything to me. I love to listen to how your mind works, it's one reason I fell in love with you. I knew my life would never be dull!" He couldn't understand why she was so mad at him; he didn't understand where he had stepped over the line.

"OK, truce. We have a far bigger problem lurking in the forest. Whether you believe my dream to be accurate or not it is not worth the argument. I am going to take what Mike told me in my dream as true. Mostly because I believe it, and it is in my best interest to believe that he intends to kill me. He even said that if he couldn't pull it off in the two hours he still had left he would decide then what he was going to do." That was new information that just flew into her head and off her tongue. All these thoughts flying around were scaring her.

The mood of the conversation changed and they discussed how they would handle the day. The deputy was coming and Elaine would be here to pick up the kids. She was dreading telling her about losing Glen in the storm yesterday and locking Greg in the closet. She hoped that when Elaine saw her children safe and happy she wouldn't become unglued.

They were watching the local news and learning about the destruction the storm had caused when Glenn and Greg woke up all excited and wanted to go outside and play in the creek before breakfast. A knot of terror gripped Cathy in her gut. She had not been outside since she locked them all in after Glenn was found. She was not about to let the boys outside when she had no clue where Mike was hiding. She looked at Tim to see his reaction. She half believed he would think wading in the creek was just what the boys needed to wash away yesterday's traumas. She eyed him, waiting for a response. If he said they could go, she would go against him in front of the kids, and tell them a big NO!

"Not this morning guys, we are waiting for your Mom to come and I am sure she won't want to wait while we wash all the mud off."

Cathy put in this opinion quickly before Tim could give them permission, and she had to go against him in front of the grandkids.

"Gee, this is the first time this summer there has been any water in the creek. We thought the pond would be finished and you said we could play there every time we came to visit you." Greg was using his most convincing guilt tactic on his grandparents.

"Yup, I agree. First time we have had water this summer. I know I did make you the promise but the pond is not finished and if you play there you will make a bigger mess the men will have to undue when they come back to work." Oh, he is good Cathy thought. She hoped her reason would hold the kids off.

"How about we sit in the sled and slide down the hill in the wet leaves and pine needles?" Greg was now giving her his plan B.

"Your Mom will be here soon, and she will have wanted you to eat breakfast before the long drive home. Do you know how late you two slept?" Cathy would try any ploy to keep from telling the boys that she would not let them out until Mike had been found and put away. It made her heart ache to think they may never be able to come stay with Grandma and Papa Tim again if they didn't know where Mike was.

What if Mike had left, made it into Mexico, given up on killing her, and she was still waiting in fear for him to return? How were they going to live their lives in the future? Were they going to have to pack up and move, hope he could never find them? She took a deep breath and let it escape through her mouth and puff out her lips as she exhaled. She hoped it would release some tension. Tim and the boys must have taken the giant sigh as a sign not to push her, leave her alone.

"Can I have macaroni and cheese for breakfast?" pleaded Greg, changing the subject.

"Sure Honey, do you want it cold or heated in the microwave? What do you want Glenn, Honey Nut Cheerios?" He nodded yes to the bowl of cold cereal and Greg wanted his macaroni cold.

The boys were eating second helpings of their breakfast when the deputy arrived. Tim met him at the door and unlocked it, and held it wide for him to enter. It was Deputy Johnston. Right now Cathy wished they lived in a big city and got someone different each time they had a call. She was still roaring mad at Deputy Johnston since he had come about the theft of the food, coins, and guns.

"Morning, Mrs. Spalding." He nodded to Cathy as he entered into the family room. "Quite a storm we had yesterday, that creek of yours running today?"

"We had more than the storm here yesterday." Cathy was in no mood for his small talk. She wanted to cut to the chase and have him take their information and check it out. She knew she would have to watch him unbutton the flap of his lapel pocket and take out the little notebook. She remembered how this automatic gesture intrigued her the first time she had seen him do it. Today she wanted to rip the damn button off the flap and throw it across the room! He always seemed to be stuck, lost in time as he unbuttoned the flap. She was trying desperately to fight her impatience. She vowed she would not mention all she had learned from her dream, and she vowed, to herself, she would not sit back quietly, act the little lady, and let the men run with the questions and answers. She was here with the kids alone yesterday, alone to have to deal with Glenn lost, Greg locked in the empty closet and Mike threatening them. By God, the deputy would have to deal with her!

"I want you to hear it first from the Grandkids, hear what Mike said to little Glenn and what he has seen across the creek. I want you to talk to them first so I won't be blamed for putting words into their mouth. Then I will tell you what I experienced, learned and did yesterday."

Cathy had jumped right in before the deputy had a chance to direct the investigation into his vague question and answer session. His question and answer session deficient with enough information to solve one single simple question.

She felt she was walking on a tightrope. Trying to keep her balance between impatience with the deputy's laid back, don't rush a trained professional style, and the rage she felt because she knew from her last experience with him that he ever so sweetly dug his heels into the investigation and came to a complete stop when she had taken control. She was weighing her options about whom she would contact if he played his little passive aggressive game on her today.

"Sure, Mrs. Spalding, but what do you want me to ask?" He looked at her as if she was trying to control him, tie his hands behind his back.

"That's my point. Just talk to the kid, ask him questions; get to know what level of observation he is functioning on. He is five, but damn smart! If I gave you the questions to ask it would look like I had prepared him for your visit." Cathy was trying to get this jackass to move in one direction or the other before Mike had made it to South America on his hands and knees.

"Start by asking his name, that is always a good beginning. Ask him if I told him you were coming today." Cathy walked away from the dining room table where the kids were finishing their breakfast and where they had watched the sparring between their Grandmother and the Deputy. Their eyes shot between the two grownups as if they were watching a tennis match. Tim now had a clear shot at Cathy and he gave her a look that told her she had better behave if they expected any cooperation from this guy. She shot him back a glance that said, *dare me to sit back and let this idiot run my show when I have been threatened and robbed.* Tim decided it best to sit back and sip his coffee. He knew that look.

"My name is Deputy Johnston," he said as he looked to Greg. "What is your name?" the deputy asked Glenn.

"My name is Glenn."

"How old are you?" the deputy asked.

"I'm five, and I will be in Kindergarten when school starts." Glenn proudly answered the deputy's question as if he was giving his first speech on his first day of school. He was melting Cathy's heart, and she was pleased he had decided to talk.

"My name is Greg. My birthday is on Thanksgiving and I am going to be eight." Greg jumped in not wanting to be left out of the morning discussion.

"I want to ask you boys some questions, OK?" The kids nodded and Glenn picked up the bowl that had held his cereal and drank the remaining milk.

"You said your birthday was on Thanksgiving. Is it always on Thanksgiving?"

"No, not every year. This year it will be." Greg looked at the deputy like even an almost eight-year-old kid knew that birthday's fell on different days of the week each year.

"Do you come and visit your Grandparents often?" The deputy asked, changing his direction.

"We come lots, but I didn't want to come after that Mike told me he was going to steal me and hurt my little sister. My Mom made us come this time." Glenn looked at his Grandmother as if he hoped it was OK to tell the Deputy. They had told him in Pre-School that kids were to trust the police. He had promised himself to always tell the whole truth to his Grandmother yesterday too. She nodded with her eyes to encourage him to continue.

"Who is this Mike you are talking about?"

"We met him one day in front of the market. He stopped us to talk to us. We were staying with Grandma because my Mom was walking for breast cancer. Grandma had bought us candy apples, the big red ones." Greg was giving the deputy a run down on their introduction to Mike.

"I told Grandma he was bad, I didn't like him." Glenn said rather emphatically to the officer.

"Bad you say, why did you think that?"

"Just the way he looked at me, my little sister, and he kept looking at Grandma's ring." Glenn was now opening up, remembering how he had come to make his judgment.

"He had a big smile and I liked him. I saw him when we were leaving town. He had a cool van. It was white with trick wheels." Greg was already into the lingo of boys and cars. It was obvious to Cathy that he had been listening to the older neighborhood boys.

"Any other reason why you liked him?"

"Well…he was super friendly and bowed down and took Grandma's hand like he was a real gentleman, just like in the cartoons. He even asked her how big her ring was."

"What did he say then?" The deputy plowed deeper.

"Oh nothing, he just disappeared. Presto…gone. Well, until we saw him driving away." Gregg continued to inform him.

"Did you ever see or talk to him at your Grandma's place?" He continued to question Greg and turn his attention away from Glenn. Cathy wanted to tell him he had the wrong kid.

"No, but Glenny did. You tell him, Glenny." Glenn began to squirm on his chair and look to his Grandmother for support. She wanted to run to him and whisper it was OK to tell him everything he knew about Mike.

"What do you have to say young man?" Glenn looked at his empty bowl and started pushing his toast crumbs around into little piles on the wooden table as he talked towards the saltshaker, not giving the deputy eye contact.

"One time I was playing with the dogs when I saw that man walking behind the outhouse with a big stick with a circle on the bottom. He had on headphones so he didn't hear us running and playing."

"What do you think he was doing with the headphones on?" The deputy was evaluating how astute a five-year-old kid could be.

"He was scanning for treasure." Glenn said without a blink, as he now looked directly at the deputy.

"Did your Grandma tell you that was what he was doing?"

"No! I saw a commercial on TV and they showed all the neat things you would find when you swing the circle back and forth. You wear the headphones so you can hear when you pass over the treasure. I bet Captain Hook wished he had a treasure finder." Glenny's observation about the pirate brought a smile to the deputy's lips.

"Last year I was Captain Hook for Halloween and Glenn was Peter Pan. I got to wear my costume to school and the Carnival. We didn't get to go to very many houses Trick or Treating. It was a school night, my Dad said. We still dress up and play pirates in the back yard. We turn over the patio table and pretend it's the pirate ship, and the grass is the water. The hook that came with my costume is real cool." Greg was now on a roll telling all the family secrets to this Deputy.

"OK, boys, that sounds like fun but I want to talk about Julian where your Grandma and Grandpa live, and talk about that man you saw. What did the man do when he saw you playing with the dogs?"

"First, I saw he got mad in the face. Then he said if he ever saw me again he would steal me and hurt my little sister!" Glenn told the deputy what he was told as if he believed Mike would do just that if he had ever been seen again.

"Did he ever see you again and try to hurt you?"

"I never let him see me! I didn't want him to hurt my little sister." Glenn answered.

"Did you see him when he didn't see you?"

"Just this time because I stayed away from Grandma and Papa Tim's house. I played like I had a bad stomach ache and we all stayed home." He told his story with guilt written all over his face. He looked to Grandma and looked so sad that he had lied to stay away.

"Where were you when you saw him and he didn't see you?" The deputy was getting tired of talking to a couple of kids. He had almost completely stopped writing in his notebook. Cathy could tell he was wondering why he had been conned into pumping little kids for information. So far, he only had some guy with a metal detector on the Spalding's property. He knew he was trespassing and threatened the kid to keep his mouth shut. It was common knowledge the place once had the old mill, especially since the whole county saw that dumb feature on Channel 8 when the skeleton was found.

"I was in my hiding tree. Greg was hogging the train so I just climbed up in my tree and watched the wind and the clouds. I can see everything from up there."

"And young man, just where is this tree of yours?"

"It's by the creek. It has a huge branch and when I climb way up Greg can't even see me. I kept it a secret until yesterday when Grandma couldn't find me. I heard her calling and calling me. I answered her but she didn't hear me. Then I saw Mike drive out from across the creek and come down Grandma's driveway and stop next door. He left but he came back again. I was afraid to come down 'cause I was afraid Mike had taken Greg and was looking for me." Glenn continued talking to the deputy as the deputy wrote again in his notebook.

"I just held on tight to my tree and closed my eyes. The thunder got louder and louder and the lightning was so white. I waited until Grandma came to get me." Glenn seemed to deflate now that he had finished his tale about yesterday. Cathy wanted to hold him and let him know that yesterday was in the past and tell him how sorry she was that he was so frightened.

"And you young man, what were you doing while your brother was in a tree and your Grandma was looking for him?" The deputy had slipped back into that same sarcastic tone he had used when they had told him about the guns and the coins that were stolen. She wanted him to leave that tone out of his voice, out of any conversation he had with her grandchildren. She could handle that tone, but a couple of young boys would not understand the subtle disbelief he was insinuating. He had worked on getting their trust, and getting them to open up and talk to him, and now he was acting as if they were not believable. Cathy was ready to jump in, and call a halt to this line of questioning. He had just about run out of time with them.

"I was locked in the closet." Greg answered before she could respond and stop that insulting tone in his voice.

"What closet?" The deputy looked up from his notebook and directly at Greg. The sudden attention made Greg more guarded when he began again.

"That closet right there." Greg pointed to the infamous closet. The deputy had definitely been acquainted with the very same closet on a previous visit. He swallowed hard.

"May I ask why your Grandmother would lock you in a closet?" He looked at Cathy for the answer to this incredulous statement, not believing any answer that had rolled cheerfully from a small child.

"She wanted me safe from Mike when she went to look for Glenn." He said it as a matter of fact. The deputy still looked at Cathy and she took that as her lead to tell her rendition of yesterday's events.

"Are you finished speaking with the children?" She wanted to ask if he was finished with his interrogation but she was trying to choose her words wisely. She wanted his full attention and anticipated that he would fill many pages in that little book of his with her information.

"Is there anything else they can tell me?" He was showing her he was heavily into CYA, and he did not want them to think he had left a stone unturned. This whole interview with the kids had taken longer than he had anticipated and didn't amount to much. He looked directly at the two boys and waited. He was thinking about how he could slide out of the house and back into his patrol car.

"Mike has a cool camp with a telescope that makes everything turn green. He has a big dish with headphones. It looks like Papa's Tim's satellite dish 'cept it has legs and sits on the ground. Oh yeah, he has a folding camping chair too." Glenn chirped this information as he was climbing down from the chair and took his cereal bowl into the kitchen. Cathy smiled at his mannerly gesture because he certainly never returned a bowl to the kitchen at his house. Then she caught on. Going into the kitchen was Glenn's way to end the interview, maybe even a five year old caught on that it had turned into an interrogation.

"Where is this camp of his?" The deputy was waiting to write the answer in his notebook, trying to show his interest.

"Across the creek, it is real close and almost under my tree. I can see him and his camp from my tree." Glenn had no trouble telling all his secrets from the kitchen as he stood next to the sink. "He parks his van real close but I can't see it from my tree. I can hear it really loud when he drives in or goes out."

"Before I talk to you Mrs. Spalding, do you mind if we check out this tree and the camp?" He could feel the tension in the house and was tired of filling his notebook. It felt like he had been there for hours and needed some air.

Cathy was elated that finally someone was going to search for evidence that Mike really existed. The way her luck had been running, she was afraid Mike had packed up his camp before the storm had hit, and driven away with all the evidence. She knew the rain would have washed away all traces of footprints or tire tracks.

"Sure, proving Mike is real has been my goal for months. I just hope we can find something today. I am afraid he has driven off only to return when I am alone."

"I won't get into that fear of yours now," he said, with an Oh God, here we go again tone in his voice. "Can the kids show me where the camp is?" He put the notebook back into his pocket and stood waiting for an answer, and an indication from the Spaldings on how flexible they were. He hoped the answer led them outside, outside in the fresh air.

Cathy looked to Tim to see if he believed it was safe to go to the creek. He only lifted one eyebrow. Then Tim put a hand on his pocket to signal he had the gun hidden there. The boys jumped up ready to show the Deputy where the camp was, glad to be free of the constraints of the house. When is Elaine coming and free these children from this mess? Cathy was still terrified to go outside and have the children accompany them.

"Give us all a few minutes to put on some hiking shoes." Tim announced. He had taken charge and informed the deputy they would all remain together. Cathy began to relax, just a little. The mad scramble was on to find socks and shoes.

Tim was the last to leave by the back door and Cathy stepped back to ask if he had his key. He looked at her, not understanding her question.

"I am not going to leave this house unlocked for one second!" She informed him emphatically. Tim reached inside, took the keys off the hook, slid them into his pocket, and flipped the button on the door into the locked position as he stepped out. Tim shrugged his shoulders and refused to give her eye contact.

Cathy realized she was walking in fear on her own deck. She was trying to keep up with the kids who were merrily skipping and running toward the creek. It was still her watch and she was having a hard time letting go and trusting Tim and the deputy to help protect them. She knew she would only feel the children were safe when Elaine called her from their house and told her they had all arrived safely. She caught Tim's eye and motioned with her eyes for him to help with the kids. He nodded and patted his hip, reminding her he had the gun. She gave him a half smile in return as thanks for his protection. Oh how she loved that man at that moment knowing he took his job as family protector very seriously. He wanted her to know he was on watch now. She was now able to look past the backs of the kids and into their forest, relaxing just a little.

The sun was out and warming up the day. Every tree, rock and leaf was washed from yesterday's rain. The ground shimmered gold where the sun shone directly on the fallen leaves, the shadows making dappled shade upon the damp earth. Cathy felt so alive to be able to see the beauty of the forest again, to breathe the clean air. As she walked near the creek, she could see that the water would soon disappear again as quickly as it had appeared with the rain. There was a small pool where the men had dug. The kids stomped through the water with the dogs following, turning the cool pond into a brown mess. The deputy, Cathy and Tim crossed the creek, walking on top of the old dam. As they climbed the hill, they used trees as a help to pull themselves up, and give support against the incline and the wet mulch. The children and dogs ran merrily ahead unaided and energetic with Cathy and Tim forging frantically, beyond their endurance, to keep the grandkids within sight.

"Boys don't run too far ahead. Stay with us to show us where the camp is." Cathy tried to sound cheerful, trying to keep her fear from creeping into her voice as they neared the area where Mike had been stalking them.

Once on level ground and across the creek, Glenn stopped abruptly, held his arms out, and slowly turned around with his head looking towards the sky. They stopped short of the small clearing, watching, and waiting for Glenn to announce to them where the camp was. The dogs sat by Glenn's feet looking up in the same direction as the twirling child. He began to twirl faster and faster. Cathy, Tim, and the deputy began to look at each other. Was this a game and they had been taken for a ride? That was the look Cathy detected written all over the deputy's face. She couldn't understand what Glenny was doing but she knew he had told the deputy the truth.

"That's my hiding tree." Glenn stopped abruptly and pointed up and across the creek towards a huge tree that grew at an angle and hung over the creek. The group turned and looked to where he was pointing, including the dogs. Cathy let out a deep breath, feeling relieved.

"That's Mike's camp, right here." Glenn marched in place squishing the leaves as he stepped up and down. The clearing was empty, no sign of man or beast having ever left a mark. They all now stepped into the small area and they slowly turned and twirled around, the same as Glenn had. From the clearing, Cathy could see the hiding tree but more importantly, she could see their house and deck. It was easy to see the house when she angled herself and looked between the trees.

"Look here, Deputy Johnston, you can see our house from here," Cathy was pointing in the direction of the house as she called the deputy to her side.

"I see it. What is the significance of that?" The deputy questioned.

"This is his camp so he can sit and watch and listen to us." Cathy tried desperately to convince the deputy of their danger.

"Why would anyone want to do that?" The deputy questioned. The tone of his voice implied that two middle-aged people would not be worth eavesdropping on. He implied that this Mike must have had better things to do than that. Cathy took the implied tone to mean that he had better things to do than listen to more stories from this couple. Now they even involved a couple of little boys.

"Grandma, can we look for Mike's van?" Greg asked.

"Sure, Sweetie, just as long as you stay close to us." Cathy was so proud of Greg, keeping on track, keeping the issue of a thief and potential kidnapper in the forefront of the outing. She knew the deputy would have to go along with the search. It had come down to CYA. Cathy knew that he knew she would not go away.

The boys ran into the trees and the adults lost sight of them. Cathy gasped, the fear once again controlling her. She was about to yell for them to come back when she heard Glenn.

"No, it's this way." As Glenn spoke, she could see the boys clearly, this time skirting along the creek.

"I see it. Right over there." Greg was instructing Glenn where he had found the van.

She looked towards the voices of the kids and waved the two men in their direction. My God, Mike may be hiding in his van. What if he was waiting for them, waiting to kill Cathy and snatch the kids and escape. Her heart was pounding, her breath gone. She had to grab a tree to remain standing. At that moment, she realized all the months she had been fearful of Mike, were just mere anxiety. She now was seized with mortal fear! As she clung to the tree, she tried to fill her lungs with air. Breathe, breathe, she kept telling herself. Get back in control and listen for any voices from behind the trees. She only heard a rook of crows noisily squawking from across the creek. "Shut up, you damn birds," she yelled across the creek; "can't you understand I have to listen."

As quickly as the men and boys had disappeared into the trees, they returned to the clearing. Oh, God, they are all safe, she said to herself. The deputy even looked good to her.

"The van is parked there, unlocked and empty. Fits the description the kids gave, right down to the *cool* wheels. Not a sign of the owner, I doubt he could be too far." The deputy informed Cathy of his find in the forest, with the same detached coolness of an abandoned snow sled in August.

"He's had about sixteen hour's head start. He could be a long way off." Cathy cried this because she wanted it to be true. True that Mike had walked out, hitchhiked or crawled. She didn't care she just wanted him gone!

"I think he would have taken his vehicle, no reason not to. It still runs, we started it right up. The key is in the ignition," informed the deputy.

"Yesterday when I told him to leave I noticed he kept the keys in the ignition too." Cathy said.

"You talked to this Mike yesterday?" The deputy asked Cathy as he reached for his button on his lapel pocket.

"Please, Deputy Johnston, we are all in danger standing in the middle of the forest while you ask questions and make notes in that notebook of yours. That thief is stalking us! You told us yourself that he couldn't be far. Can't you at least run the license plates, dust for prints, call for backup, and make a search of the forest? Talk to the neighbors; ask if they have seen him hanging around. How could he just sneak into here when he has to drive by the nosiest neighbors in all of Julian? Talk to them!" Cathy was pleading, demanding the deputy to do something, anything but write again in that damn little notebook of his.

She had done it again! Told him to get moving and do his job. Would she ever learn? Now what kind of a passive aggressive game was the deputy going to play while they all remained in danger?

"I think Cathy has come up with a lot of good suggestions to start the investigation. I particularly like the one about talking to the neighbors. We could go back to the house and call them ourselves. If we get any information, we will inform you and you can take over. That will free you to work with your fellow deputies. The boys' mother is due here to take them home any minute. Do you need to talk to them further?" Tim had taken the lead and defused the tension in the air from Cathy's pleas.

"No, I think everything they told me checks out." The deputy stood with his hand still on his buttoned pocket, called back from the depth of his anger. He couldn't disagree with Mrs. Spalding and what needed to be done. It was just that he wasn't going to take any orders from some hysterical woman. Why did they keep calling the Department? They had been nothing but trouble since that damn lumberman was unburied on their property. He couldn't believe it was just a few months ago. Seemed like an eternity ago to him. "Do you feel able to get back to your house on your own? I will put a call in to the Department from here and hang around the van."

"Come on boys, let's all go back to the house and wait for your mother." Tim had taken charge again and the dogs followed behind obediently.

Once across the creek and on the final climb to the house they could see Elaine leaning against the Sheriff's car with her arms folded across her chest. She watched Kim run up and down the driveway. The kids yelled for her as they ran the last yards uphill and into her arms. Her body language did not look good to Cathy. The sheriff's car was a dead give away about the trouble. Tim and Cathy looked at each other and simultaneously took a deep breath to fortify themselves against the recent events they were going to have to explain.

The boys excitedly told her about the loud lightning and thunder, the hiding tree, the locked closet and finding the van. They explained their recent experiences with the same happiness and enthusiasm they generally saved for a description of Disneyland. The whole time they explained about yesterday they kept interrupting each other or adding their version of the events.

Elaine stood listening to her children without interruption but watching her mother for any confirmation that the events were factual and not the fantasy of two young boys who had been playing make-believe. She absently took her purse off her shoulder and set it on the hood of the sheriff's car. When she placed her purse on the black hood, she instantly was back to the present and realized there had to be truth to their story or the patrol car would not be here now.

"Why is the sheriff here?" When Elaine spoke, that was all she asked. Cathy scratched her nose where her glasses rested trying to choose her answer carefully.

"He is looking for Mike across the creek. We found his van." It was the answer coming from Greg. Cathy was momentarily off the hook.

"Who is Mike?" Elaine asked, still looking to her mother for an answer, any answer. Kimmie was more interested in running up and down the driveway than greeting her brothers who had been away from her the last few days. Cathy was watching her and the surrounding perimeter in fear that Mike might make good on his threat and hurt her.

Cathy finally assumed responsibility for an explanation to her daughter. She had been in charge, and the children were in danger. All of them had been threatened in one way or another. She hoped the way she explained the events, the details she curiously choose to omit at this time, and the bright and beautiful day would make it easy for Elaine to swallow.

She definitely decided to omit her premonition, or dream, and the gun. Cathy was sure the boys would somehow someday mention it, but today she was sure it was TMI. Too Much Information.

"Let's all go inside and I will explain it all to you." Cathy began.

"Since when did you start locking your house in the middle of the day?" Elaine questioned with an edge to her voice.

"Since yesterday, when Mike threatened your mother." Tim answered, warning Elaine not to push her mother or she would also have to deal with him. Oh, I love this man, Cathy thought.

Tim unlocked the door and Elaine and Cathy herded the kids and the dogs into the house. Kim wanted to continue running her marathon up and down the driveway. Cathy bribed the kids into the house with Popsicles and she hoped they were refrozen in the correct shape after the power had been out so long yesterday.

Once the Popsicles were extracted from the freezer and the paper removed, the kids started dragging out the toys. Cathy was about to tell them to stop, but thought their play might distract them from hearing the explanation to their Mother. She realized there were so many details about which the kids were clueless.

Elaine sat patiently on the couch sucking on her own Popsicle while she let her mother talk. A couple of times she interrupted and asked a question, trying to get the facts in order. When Cathy had finished she sat back and waited for the assault her daughter would most likely unleash. She would take it because she knew what she had explained to Elaine had almost taken her children from her. Cathy's heart was breaking. Having to tell her daughter what a dangerous line they had walked while the storm raged yesterday was the most difficult thing she ever remembered doing. She could hear her own Mother in her head criticizing her. She had grown up being told that everything bad that happened to someone was brought on by their own behavior. Cathy had lived her whole life trying to shake that criticism from her brain. Never once did she try to pass that belief on to her own children. Elaine had always reminded her so much of her own mother that she was ready for the same wrath she feared had been genetically released, skipping a generation.

Cathy didn't believe that God punished people that way. If her mother's theory was right, wouldn't innocent people live and bad people die. So often in her life she had witnessed horrible things happening to good and wonderful people, and good things happening to bad people. Was this all her fault because she didn't like Mike, and made Tim promise not to let him into their house? Even though this was true, she wouldn't accept the responsibility for Mike being evil. She accepted the responsibility for her wrongs when she had done them, but not this time. Mike had tried to squeeze into their lives; she had refused him, and that was as far as she would go in the responsibility department for the recent events. She tempered herself for Elaine's reaction.

Elaine was now chewing on the stick. She took it from her mouth and looked at it as if the flavored ice had fallen from the stick, not quickly eaten. She got up, and on the way to the trash, she stopped off at her Mother's chair, bent down, and gave her a big hug.

"Jesus, Mom, yesterday must have been pure hell for you. You must have been scared to death and felt so alone. I thank you, and God; it all worked out fine. The kids seemed to have survived it well." Elaine proceeded to the kitchen and popped the stick into the trash. Cathy sat with big tears running down her cheeks, her nose now running.

"Ah, come on Mom; don't get all mushy on me now. I have to get the kids together and on our way home. They start back with swimming lessons today." Elaine started picking up the kids clothes and stuffing them into the duffle bag. "OK boys, pick up the toys, we have to go."

"Honey, if we have to stay in town tonight could the dogs stay at your house?" Cathy had dried her face and regained her voice.

"Can we take them now?" It was Greg, all excited because he was always trying to talk his Grandma into bringing the dogs to his house.

"Only if we have to come to town tonight. We need the dogs with us today to tell us when we get company." Cathy hoped this was enough of an explanation to quiet Greg.

Within twenty minutes, Tim and Cathy locked the dogs into the house and followed Elaine and the kids up the driveway in their truck. They followed them all the way to the main road. Tim still had the gun in his pocket and they were not going to take any chances that Mike might be hiding on the way to the road. Elaine promised to call them the minute they were home and safe. Cathy slid next to Tim in the truck and he put his arm around her and squeezed her shoulder. As they drove home, she felt like they were teenage sweethearts. She prayed they would have many years ahead, years without fear.

Chapter Twenty-Three
The Mighty Oak

As the truck rolled down the driveway to a stop, Cathy looked over and saw the sheriff's car still parked in the same position. She knew the empty car would still be there, they had only been gone a short time, but somewhere internally she had pushed the fear of Mike lurking somewhere deep inside. Then when she had hugged and kissed the kids, and watched them drive away with their mother to safety, she had felt freed of her fear. Now it was back, the fear had returned quickly, and the patrol car was the symbol of the danger. Reminding her Mike was probably still close, probably hiding behind some tree, right under their noses. Why had Mike left his car yesterday in the storm, where had he gone?

It was hard to believe all that had transpired the last eighteen hours. Losing Glenn, locking Greg in the closet, the storm, Mike's visit, his confession, Cathy's bluff and the knowledge of how Mike had threatened them. Then there was the matter of the dream and Cathy's ability to hear what he had been thinking. As all these thoughts roared through her mind she closed her eyes and slowly shook her head. It was all too much to comprehend, all too bizarre.

"Honey, you OK?" Tim sweetly asked as he gently put his hand on her arm.

"Yes," she quietly said as she opened her eyes and looked beyond the windshield and into the forest. "I was just reliving the last eighteen hours and even I can't believe all that happened. Only by the grace of God are we all OK. Are we OK?" Cathy turned to look at Tim with pleading in her voice, hoping for confirmation of their safety. His face looked blank so she looked back into the forest.

She loved the color of the freshly washed trees and earth. The woods were still wet and the trees shimmered in the morning sun. The storm had come and left quickly and the ground had been too hard to absorb the assault of the instant downpour. The rain had quickly run off and scurried into the dry creek. Only the dried leaves covering the earth were still filled with yesterday's moisture. Cathy marveled at the resilience of the forest, the trees that were over a hundred years old and had survived all of nature's perils. How many fires, droughts and snows had they witnessed as they continued to give beauty, shade, and sanctuary to the abundant wildlife? She could feel their strength, their permanence. Could people survive that many assaults and still look unchanged: continue to thrive? With the doors to the truck locked, she felt impervious to Mike, isolated and safe with Tim and his gun.

"Tim, when I was crushed against a tree yesterday looking for Glenny, a large jolt of lightning struck and I felt it through my feet. I know we had a tree struck and it knocked down some others. Do you think it is safe for us to go see what was damaged?"

Tim scrunched up his mouth and rotated his chin. He was trying to choose his words carefully before he answered Cathy's question. Truth was, he didn't really know how to answer her. He was a jumble of contradictions. When he made mental lists of what he had seen and heard he thought this whole ugly set of events were just a bunch of unrelated incidents. He tried hard to see Cathy's fear, hear her pleas for trust and support, believe her premonitions. God knew how hard he tried, but he couldn't see what she had seen. He had to see something concrete before he could believe it. Why couldn't he just accept it as a matter of faith? He loved her dearly, but this *Mike Thing* was more than he could grab his brain around. Then, there was Glenny telling the sheriff how Mike had threatened him, he had heard that himself. He saw the abandoned car, the empty closet with his guns and coins missing. He knew that Cathy had told the truth about the confession from Mike on the driveway at gunpoint. All of those events he believed. Then she had told him of her dream and he was back to unbelieving again. Why would Mike want to kill her? The pieces just didn't fit for him. Was there a whole bunch of puzzle pieces he didn't have?

He could feel her stir under his hand and he knew she was patiently waiting for his answer. God, how he loved her but he wanted his old life back, a life with a sane woman, a quiet retreat in the forest, a baseball game where the Padres won. Was that too much to ask?

"I wish I could promise you safety. I could say the words but I know you would just think I was giving you lip service. I was going to, but I knew that would be an insult to your intelligence. I will give my life for you, but I can't promise you much right now, just my best. OK Sweetheart?" Tim said this to Cathy with the kindest tone in his voice as he softly stroked her arm.

"I know you always give your best. I just wish I could share my fear with you. I know that sounds stupid, but if I felt you were scared too, I would know we were definitely on the same team." Cathy spoke quietly trying to get him to believe how scared she was.

"Oh God, Cathy, we are definitely on the same team! I understand what you and the kids went through yesterday. Do not for one minute think I am not scared too! I am still trying to figure out why Mike would want to kill you, and how you learned about that from one of your dreams. Can you cut me a little slack on this Babe?" Tim had a pleading tone in his voice and was looking deep into Cathy's greenish eyes, waiting for her answer. He loved her eyes because they were so expressive to him. He could always sense her moods and feelings through her eyes. Sometimes she scared the shit out of him with the daggers she could throw at him with those eyes. Today he could see she was genuinely scared, and yet they took on the color of the forest, green with flecks of gold. He looked out through the windshield to verify the colors were the same.

Cathy flashed back to the night at the restaurant with her friends and their advice about just that, cutting Tim a little slack because he couldn't understand her premonitions.

"I can cut you all the slack you need. Can I bargain, plead, or whatever term I need use to get you to *act* as if Mike wants to kill me? If I felt like you had my fear about his intent to kill me we would base our behavior on our safety first."

"Well put. Don't ever think I would not protect you! How about we stick together, let the boys out of the house, and do some checking ourselves. I want to check out any storm damage too." Tim was touching Cathy's arm while he spoke. He wanted her to understand how he would do anything to protect her and their life here in the forest. He turned and looked back into the forest silently planning his next move.

"Shouldn't we be able to see the outhouse from here?" Tim said as he was furrowing his brow to see deeper into the forest. Cathy leaned a little forward and tried to see what Tim was, or was not seeing.

"Isn't that our Mighty Oak blocking our view of the outhouse?" Cathy said as a pang of fear shot through her heart. She was in fear of her favorite tree. "Please God, not my favorite tree."

The oak was so huge and sturdy they had actually begun calling it *Mighty* the first time they walked the property prior to their purchase. Instantly they loved its size, shape, and the scars it bore. The trunk was almost split in two because of the charring from a long ago fire, and one large branch grew almost horizontal to the ground. Suspended on the horizontal branch was a large dead pine that had fallen and had been held aloft by the branch of the oak all these years. There were indistinguishable carved initials in the trunk, perhaps from lovers over a hundred years ago. Through all the insults the tree has thrived and grown, never giving up, always growing a canopy of leaves in the summer to shade her roots, loosing her leaves in winter as she goes dormant. Not to mention the splendor of autumn and the show of colors, or spring with the new leaves that sprout coral before they unfold and become green? This tree inspires men to write poetry while they sit in her shade. The kind of tree where promises are whispered, couples become lovers, and children are conceived. Were Tim and Cathy looking at their *Mighty Oak* or one of her many cousins? It was hard to tell at this distance through the windshield.

They looked away from the forest and at each other with awareness that yesterday's storm might have destroyed something very precious to them. Just when you thought one danger had passed there seemed always to be some new threat lurking, another shoe to drop and remind you how life appeared to be spinning out of control in the forest. Her thoughts about the shoe dropping reminded her of yesterday when Glenn's shoe hit her on the head. That had turned out all right. The tree is probably OK too, she thought, becoming more relaxed. Then she felt a little guilty worrying about a tree when their lives may still be in danger, maybe the life of the deputy too. Cathy knew her life was getting closer to normal if she could worry about a tree. It was their favorite tree, but they had a least a hundred other oak trees, and she could name any or all of them when this *Mike Thing* was over. At least she finally had the deputy believing that there was a Mike, and he drove a white van.

"Should we contact the neighbors first? We promised the deputy we would make a few calls." Cathy asked Tim. She wanted him to call the shots.

"The calls can wait. Let's yell across the creek and tell the deputy we are back and going to check around the house." Tim informed. When he took control, Cathy felt like the most protected and cherished woman in the world.

After they climbed from the truck, Tim went and released the dogs from the house and relocked it. The boys ran around in search of the kids. They followed their scent half way up the driveway and returned slowly. Cory had his head down as if he was sad they were gone. Cathy watched him as he processed the absence of the kids. She could see the sorrow in his body language, and understood his feelings because she always felt the same when Elaine drove up the driveway and the sweet faces blew her kisses through the closed windows.

Today was different; today she feared for their safety, she felt only relief when they left. She also understood why God gives the children to the young. She felt too old and too tired for all the responsibility right now.

Cathy was lost in her thoughts as she watched Cory. His little head jerked up and looked into the forest. Within an instant, he was running and barking profusely, his buddy joining him in song as they ran towards the Mighty Oak. Her eyes followed the path of the two Schnauzers in hot pursuit of prey.

"What do you think they found this time?" Tim asked the question but spoke towards the tree.

When the dogs neared the giant oak, they came to an abrupt stop as a rook of crows took flight and began their noisy screeching. The birds flitted and darted from limb, to branch, to flight again as they continued to warn the dogs with their noise. Slowly, ever so cautiously they crept closer to the dogs, listening for any unfamiliar sound.

Upon closer examination, it appeared a large part of the Mighty Oak was struck by lightning. A large hunk of the trunk had split off and had taken several large branches with it. The large trunk of the dead pine was now visible and lying on the ground tangled within the broken branches of the old oak. It seemed as though the lightning had frightened the Mighty Oak into releasing the heavy burden after all these years. Cathy was awed at the contradiction of nature here on the mountain.

"Did the tree squash the outhouse?" Tim asked the forest as he crept closer. Cathy watched him as he skirted the perimeter of the downed tree branches, still giving a wide berth to the limbs. He was touching the gun in his pocket unconsciously. He looked up at the Mighty Oak, surveyed the lightning damage, slowly turned three hundred sixty degrees, and stopped, facing Cathy. "I think she will continue to thrive, maybe relax with the release of the pine, just one more scar to her history. The outhouse is history, flatter than a pancake! I don't think I will be able to use any of the wood for more than firewood; kindling would be about all, perhaps toothpicks. The force of nature sure makes a believer out of me. Thank God, Glenny wasn't hiding in the outhouse!"

"We will rebuild it though, won't we?" Cathy wanted everything in her forest to remain the same. They had never used it but she still wanted an outhouse. She had plans to have a campground near, with a picnic table under the mighty oak. She wanted the boys to pitch a tent and camp here when they were a little older. They would need that outhouse and now it was squashed, ruined, flatter than a pancake!

"Sure Babe, any kind you want, bigger, better, and more beautiful". Tim was now teasing her. "How about a brick shit house?"

She knew he would build her one if that was what she wanted. She loved him for his generosity, and knew that by spoiling her with material things was one way he could show her his love.

"How about I make a stained glass moon window for the door?" Cathy was continuing the fantasy because it was familiar and a way they communicated their love to one another. "We could make it a pay toilet, and within fifty years or so we could recoup our money for the construction."

"Who is going to drop the coin into the slot? I sure would hate to be dancing in front of the door with no money in my pocket!"

"We could potty train the animals in the forest, or maybe market it to the hikers by putting up large neon signs directing them to our brick shit house. There must be a number of creative ways to finance the building. We could show nature videos to the hikers while they used the facility, which would cost extra of course." So they continued with their silly fantasy as they watched and listened in the forest, always keeping track of the dogs for any early warning. Tim continued to skirt the damage while Cathy stood planted, just watching him. The boys were running merrily with Tim and had circled the perimeter three times to Tim's once.

The crows had perched in the upper branches of the forest canopy and kept a continual nagging at their intrusion. Occasionally one would dive and dart between Tim and the downed branches warning him to stay back, out of his territory. A crow had floated to the ground and stood sassing Andy. Andy took a flying leap, pushing off with his back legs, almost catching the crow within his mouth. The crow was quick too, and jerked his head quickly to the side to miss the assault from the dog. Andy looked both startled and pleased he had missed the bird. What would he have done with the bird if he had caught it? He knew this was no little bird. These large crows were not anything like the birds that flitted from bird feeder to birdbath on the edge of the deck. He was a purebred Schnauzer and he knew that only ground prey was instinctual to him. The cat had trained him to hunt birds but she had never trained him to catch a bird as tall as he. Better stick to the lessons learned.

The bird pranced and danced on the ground refusing to take flight and did a little dance of intimidation. Andy was now curious and tried his style of intimidation; sniffing, lunging, ducking while he whined with excitement. Tim was standing near the dog and the bird, watching and smiling. Cathy came to his side to see why each creature was claiming some territory. Then they saw it; saw the shoes. Two muddy tennis shoes were sticking out from beneath the downed limbs.

Cathy's hand flew to her mouth as she stifled a scream. She knew who lie trapped beneath the limb; she recognized the shoes. She would know those shoes anywhere! Tim jerked his head to catch the motion of her hand and pleaded with her with his eyes.

"Is it Mike?" He asked in a whisper, afraid to wake up the man covered with the damage from the storm. He poked the sole of one shoe with the tip of his boot to see if he was sleeping or dead. He knew the answer before he had stepped forward. Cathy nodded as she bit on her index finger, trying to control the sounds and emotions that were welling up from deep within. Tim touched her arm but she stepped back, recoiling from his touch. She took several more steps back fearing that Mike was playing possum and would jump up and grab her ankle, a ploy to get the opportunity to get close enough to kill her. Her face was white and her eyes now shone dark and luminous. Tim decided he liked it better when her eyes were the color of the forest. Oh, how he wanted to hold her and tell her it was over, tell her they were safe, but he knew she had to process Mike's death before she could understand.

Tim walked twenty paces to the west and bellowed for the deputy to come. He listened for a few seconds, waiting for an answer and yelled again. Cathy had only heard him use that volume when he yelled angrily at an umpire at a game. He was so loud he sent the crows flying from the trees and they responded to his calls with those of their own. When they listened for the response from the deputy, it was now impossible to hear. Tim's bellowing set off the raucous screeching from the rook. Cathy now held her ears, she wanted peace, she wanted quiet. The video that was about to begin she understood, it would be a rerun of the time the skeleton was found. She pressed her hands tight against her ears as if they were the pause buttons and she could control the machine from going from still into play.

She knew she was about to lose it. Was she scared at the sight of a dead man in their yard again? Was she relieved Mike was dead? Did she want anyone to die? She remembered how she could have killed him yesterday when Glenn was missing, and she knew they would have no peace until she had proof that he was unable to return. No, she was not sad he was dead, but not glad either. What a conflict of emotions! She had carried the fear of his evil since she had first met him on Opening Day, and now that he was dead, literally at her feet, it was too soon to digest it all. Too soon, to release her anxiety that she had held and nurtured for months. Would she ever be able to relax again? She would try to relax, she would try right now before the deputy arrived and started asking a million questions. She took a huge deep breath, shook her hands limp at the end of her dangling arms, marched in place, and jiggled her whole body to loosen up. She did this little dance while she fixed her eyes on the shoes that protruded from the dark green foliage. Tim watched her from his twenty paces as he continued his bellowing for the deputy. He knew her dance; he had seen her do it before, especially when she felt she had a headache coming. He knew she would be OK. That's my Cathy, he thought. He could always count on her to keep it together.

Then it started, quiet at first and then with a roar, she was laughing, laughing with her whole heart and soul. He rushed to her side and tried to quiet the guffaws and her dance. Had she lost it? Would he have to deal with the deputy alone? He put his arms around her shoulder and pulled her to his chest. She came out of her hysteria and looked directly at him as if he was a stranger.

"You OK? Tell me what's so damn funny?" He was really afraid of what her answer might be, but it was better than her crazy behavior.

"Don't you see it?" She asked. "It is so similar it made me crack up. I just love God's sense of humor." She now was calm and continued to smile, as if she had control of a private joke and he was not allowed to know the punch line.

"A N D?" he asked, waiting for her reply to give him some insight, any damn sign to know what was going on in that brain of hers.

"Come on now, you have truly got to see the similarity! Just look at the big scene and tell me where you have seen it before."

He could tell she was getting impatient with his inability to grasp the punch line. He was walking carefully around her now, afraid to set her off and wanting desperately to move onto the next step of getting their life back to normal. Crazy scenes and punch lines was not where he wanted to go. He looked at her, saw the smile on her face and decided it was better to play along.

"God, Cathy, you have got to give me a clue! You know how I can't even find the Cheerios on the counter, and you want me to figure out some scene in a movie?" How bizarre, he thought, for two middle-aged people to be playing a game at the feet of a dead man who had literally torn their life upside down the last few months. Was she off the deep end, or was he for humoring her?

"Somewhere over the rainbow, blue birds fly. Birds fly over the rainbow, why then, oh why, can't I?" Cathy sang in her best Judy Garland voice as she smiled at him drawing him deeper into the game. It was a clue.

"You give me some stupid line from a song? I was looking for a clue from a movie." Tim complained in his best pouting voice as she continued to sing and started the chorus. "What does a rainbow have to do with this? Do you see a rainbow, a pot of gold? Give me a break, stop this silly game before the deputy shows up and sees us acting like runaways from the loony bin!"

"OK, OK, I'm sorry you can't see the humor in this bizarre little scene. I should have caught on that you couldn't, long before now. Thanks for humoring me anyway." Cathy informed him in the sanest voice he had heard in weeks.

"Now you are just being mean! I still don't get your joke. Give me the answer!"

"*The Wizard of Oz*. Don't you remember the scene where the tornado blows the house on the Wicked Witch and all you can see are her feet sticking out?" Her voice sounded disappointed, disappointed that he couldn't figure out her clue.

"I know this is no house...but the lightning did break the branches that smashed the outhouse that came down and squashed the Wicked Mike. That was similar enough for me to bust up laughing. Besides, I screamed at him yesterday as he drove away. 'God will get you!' Don't you see? God did just that!"

Chapter Twenty-Four
The Buried Treasure

It had been the longest summer of Cathy's life. Had it really been the longest summer or had it been the heat, the drought, and the forest fires? Maybe, it seemed like the longest summer because of the found skeleton, the theft, the afternoon with Glenny missing, and finally ending with the death of Mike Jenkins. She tried not to dwell on it; she tried to not get caught in the trap of reliving it each day, each incident replaying in her mind. When she did start to remember and lapsed into a daydream, her stomach would knot and her anxiety would return. Oh, how hard she had fought to release her constant anxiety. She had been fighting to release her anxiety since she had watched the coroner's assistants use a chain saw to pull Mike's body from under the limbs of the lightning-struck tree.

She and Tim had been there to identify the body, answer the million questions, and tell their story again, and again. Fortunately, the body under the tree had only become a quick blurb in the media. His death had left them with so many unanswered questions, and their emotions so frazzled they didn't pursue the authorities for answers. They had accepted his death and worked hard to restore peace on their little plot of land at the end of the road.

The whole spring and summer had become a video in Cathy's mind. Each time it replayed, the lines etched deeper in her brain, the scenes tweaked tighter into focus, the colors becoming more vivid. Oh, how she longed to bury the video deep in the bottom of that box in the back of her mind. About the time she thought she had mastered control of her subconscious it would float to the surface and begin to play in garish Technicolor with a close-up of Mike's face grinning at her. Her spine would stiffen, her stomach would twirl, and she could hear his sinister voice. She would snap herself from her daydreams and rely on her surroundings, and thank God for his quick and simple justice. God always made her smile with his sense of humor, his gifts, and the beauty that surrounded her in her life.

The season would evolve into autumn soon and she was anticipating the many visible changes and relying on the invisible ones, the continuation of life. Cathy was particularly looking forward to the changing of the leaves, the cooler days, and the chilly nights. She had been able to feel the chill of the evening air the last few nights, a subtle hint of what was to come.

Isn't that just the way life works, she thought! When the days turn cool, the pond will be finished. The men had finally started working again and although progress was slow, it would be finished soon. She longed to see the grandkids splash in the cool water before they had to wear parkas, galoshes and mittens.

Today a crew had shown up to help Tim cut the downed limbs into fireplace size logs and clean up the rubble of the smashed outhouse. She could watch the men work through the trees and hear their voices through the open windows. She liked the sounds they added to the forest, the voices in both English and Spanish. She wondered if similar sounds had come from the lumber mill long ago. She guessed the second language would have been Russian. Then she lapsed into the memory of the day the lumberman was found murdered. So many unanswered questions had come with the discovery of his remains. She quickly pulled herself from her daydream and walked back into the present when she stepped out on the deck to watch the men work. She listened to the chainsaw slice easily through the thick branches. The sounds of the men silenced while the sound of the saw drowned out all sounds of men, birds, and wildlife.

Cathy leaned against the house and planted her feet wide as she watched the men work. She could smell the heat of the saw as it strained against a limb and smell the hot new sawdust as it flew free on a breeze before it fell to earth. The scent of the hot wood was so fresh, so full of promise that Cathy knew the removal of the limbs that had killed Mike would free them of the whole ordeal; acknowledge they were indeed now safe.

She knew her feelings about the clean up were only symbolic, but she had been after Tim for weeks to get rid of the downed limbs. Each time she saw them they reminded her of what had happened there, and with each day the bright green leaves turned a little darker as they dried and shriveled, reminding her of death. Each time they drove down the driveway, they could see the pile of desiccating leaves held prisoner beneath the rotting pine trunk. She couldn't avoid the scene to be replayed each time they returned home, and eventually Tim had seen the necessity to hire a crew to help him rid the area of all scars of the storm.

Cathy stood in the shade the eaves provided, only her extended feet in direct sun, her sandals leaving crisscross patterns of un-tanned marks on her feet. She felt the warmth of the sun and looked down to see her feet browning. She smiled at the warmth and relaxed a little more as she slid a couple of inches down the side of the house, wedging herself in absence of a chair. She loved how she felt at this moment, not a care in the world, feeling truly safe while she watched the men work. She felt sort of like a voyeur and then curdled at the thought of how Mike had been watching and listening to them for God only knows how long. She took a deep breath and relaxed again knowing that watching someone in plain view was not the same.

The men worked diligently without speaking, the sound of the chain saw consuming the forest. Each man with a task; one cut, one moved, one stacked the branches, carrying the leaves and twigs too small for firewood to a nearby clearing. The piles burned when the weather conditions were right; the fire hazard too great this time of the year. Perhaps they would burn the leaves when there was snow on the ground. She could visualize the bonfire this winter, enjoying its warmth. She liked her idea, and continued to plan the event. Perhaps they would invite the kids and grandkids and make an official ceremony of the clean up, eat a big bowl of chili after the fire, and the kids could roast marshmallows. That would be the last remains of their ordeal. "I think I will pray for an early snow this year," she said to the forest, "have it all over in this calendar year."

Now she had planned the final ritual of their anguish and she felt free of anxiety, totally free. She loved this feeling within, it gave her a spurt of energy and she began to plan lunch for the men. She would surprise them, her secret reward to them for ridding her of the reminder of the storm, Evil Mike's death, and the severe injury to the Mighty Oak. She liked the symbolism of the stack of firewood close to the tree from which it had fallen.

She would not deliver the lunch to the men, they would come to the deck to eat, she was not about to squash the calm feeling she had recently acquired by walking to the place they were working.

Cathy had to work hard to push her body away from the house and into the standing position. Her knees had become locked and it was hard to get leverage against the wall with her hands. She was glad the men didn't notice her struggle. She added one more item to her list of things not to try again now that she was in her fifty's. This getting old is a bunch of shit, she thought to herself. Who was the idiot who called these years golden? The only gold we ever had was Tim's coin collection and it was stolen from us! She felt so good today she secretly smiled at how ridiculous her thoughts ran, but more ridiculous was how she must have looked fighting with herself to stand upright. She quietly went inside.

She set the food on the deck, yelled to the men the first chance the saw was silent. They climbed the hill, washed and ate, gregariously sharing stories and teaching Tim to understand their humor and a few words in Spanish. Cathy remained in the house while they ate, checking periodically to see if the food or drinks need to be replenished. She loved the relaxed voices and knew it was good for Tim to be working with the men, removing the debris.

"*Por nada.*" she answered when the men thanked her for the lunch and went about cleaning off the table.

Tim was pleased with her gesture of the unexpected meal and the fat Ziploc bag filled with her fresh homemade cookies to eat on their *descanso* later. Tim opened the refrigerator, filled a small picnic cooler with ice, and then filled a quart mayonnaise jar with milk and half buried the jar in the ice.

"The men will want to drink this when they eat your cookies." He leaned toward Cathy, who was putting the remains of the meal in Ziploc bags, and whispered ever so sweetly, "I love you, and the mess will be cleaned up within the next hour or so. I hope before my back or my knees give out."

"I have been watching you, and you have been trying to keep up with men half your age. Let them do the bending and stacking. It's OK for you to be *El Patron.* Throw one of the folding chairs in the green garden cart and take it with you down the hill. That way you can throw the broken siding from the outhouse into it and save all of you a thousand steps." Cathy was trying to give her suggestion on using the cart casually. She didn't want Tim to bristle because she could see an easier way to do the job. He nodded as he stepped out the door and she watched in the shadows to see if he took her suggestion or not.

Cathy had figured out when she was a young woman that it was a woman who had invented the wheel. Men were so busy being macho and marking their territory that they never got the rock moved from point A to point B. Then one day, when they were so distracted with showing each other their biceps and boasting about who could lift the biggest rock: a woman set a rock on edge and it rolled into position without the rock ever leaving the ground. Since that day men have been threatened with the superiority of women's ability to seize upon a problem and just go for it! Therefore, to keep peace women have been pampering the man's hurt ego and pretending that the discovery of the wheel was his.

This video Cathy played in her mind over the years. It would often float to the surface of her conscious. The more Chauvinistic a man became, the more she liked to visualize his rock rolling over him and flattening him like a scene in a *Roadrunner* cartoon. This internal belief about the discovery of the wheel she obviously kept to herself as her own private joke. It often helped her deal with bosses, little bureaucrats and insecure men in general, sometimes even her dear husband.

It was not long after lunch that the chain saw was still. The tree limbs sliced into manageable size logs for next year's fire. She could see the men begin work on the remains of the outhouse while Tim sat in the lawn chair with his bad leg propped up on a log, the men loading and dumping the lumber into two neat piles. Occasionally she could hear a hammer breaking apart the framing from the siding, and then she could hear the wood landing in the cart. The steady drone of work drifted through the forest, interrupted occasionally by Tim's voice giving the men directions. Occasionally she heard the men laugh, it was a good sound, men working and laughing, being productive, turning a pile of branches into something useful. Men making firewood for next winter's fire, the downed trees becoming fuel to warm them from their fireplace. She wanted to stop the video playing in her head of the storm exploding the tree, and the limb crushing a man with its force.

Therein lies my dilemma, Cathy thought. She thanked God daily for his punishment and justice for what Mike had done to them, and yet she had a hard time accepting God striking him dead. Had what he had done to them been worth a death sentence? Or, was his death as simple as being in the wrong place at the wrong time? Was this paradox a test from God about her faith? On the other hand, was the whole incident a random force of nature that proves a theory? A theory that a mass of unstable rising warm air hitting a loft of cooler air sets up electrical charges, which build up causing lightning? Was it a sign from God to be careful about what you wish for, you might just get it? She had asked and He had answered!

Does God strike others when someone demands? She truly doubted it. Her self-contradiction going back to good things happening to bad people and bad things happening to good people; did God pull those strings? She just stood staring out into the forest and not seeing beyond the inside of her eyelids, nothing registering visually as her mind kept ruminating on life and all her experiences. So many questions kept rising to the surface and remained unanswered. Sort of like the unstable air, she thought.

Tim was excitedly calling Cathy from the demolished outhouse. The men were making a loud ruckus and jumping up and down as they joined Tim. She stuck her head out the sliding glass door to see about the excitement. She thought they had probably uncovered a nest of snakes. They certainly would not be making that kind of noise if they were watching deer and wanted her to come see them. They would have scared off a pack of aggressive wolves with all their movements and noise! When they saw her, they signaled for her to come to where they were, and by their exaggerated gestures, they wanted her to come quickly.

"It had better be good," she said to the forest, knowing they could not hear her over their shouts, "or I'm going to be pissed! The last thing I want to do is walk down there, down to that place. I am not yet ready to visit that place. I don't know when I will be ready, but I am sure it is not today!" She said this in the men's direction as both a complaint and a ruse to keep up her courage as she continued walking towards them. "Just give the forest a little more time to heal." Then she knew she was the one who wanted time to heal. When she neared the men, they stopped their movements and silence controlled the forest. The silence was unnerving because the men had silenced every bird and breeze with their shouts and gestures. They stood frozen, looking at her with broad smiles on their faces.

"Y E S," she said as she raised her eyebrows with a warning to inform the men that fat old ladies do not hike here on some whim. The men stood frozen as if they were playing some child's game. She scanned the earth with her eyes looking for a clue to their excited behavior but only seeing the neat piles the men had stacked; the ground they had raked. They had obliterated the scars from the storm. The only thing remaining was the cement block foundation of the outhouse. It apparently had survived the tree smashing, and the rectangular walls were the only mark left by man in the forest. The sun was shining on the blocks and the walls reflected the afternoon sun in defiant silver.

"It looks great! Thanks for giving me back my forest. Are you finished?" Cathy asked. Her eyes scanned the area again and realized she was pleased she had hiked to the site. There was no anxiety radiating up through her shoes, no whisper of evil from the trees. She finally knew the ordeal was over. Her subconscious had grasped the finality of it all. She was sure she would still have the bonfire ceremony in the winter and she would make it a festival filled with love, family, and external rituals. Just for fun, it would be an occasion to get together, and eat lots of good food.

The men looked to Tim for instruction and Tim looked to Cathy like she had to be blind. Tim took her gently by the elbow, led her to the edge of the foundation, and pointed. There it was! The guns and the coins were all lying in a scrambled heap within the foundation of the smashed outhouse, and rising above the top layer of coin folders lay the ring of the metal detector reflecting the sunlight.

Chapter Twenty-Five
The Mystery Solved

Tim was unloading the contents of the green garden cart into the closet. The cart filled with the stolen and now found coin collection. He carefully catalogued each coin folder he pulled free from the loose coins and cans dumped into the cart, and compared the coin against the mark that had been made in *The Official Red Book*. It was time consuming but he loved every second of it, like the prodigal collection that has come home. He vowed he would never take the years and money invested for granted again. Carefully he wiped each folder free of any signs of the storm before he placed it upright in chronological order on the shelf. The gold coins placed on one shelf, the silver on another shelf; the proofs separated from the uncirculated, and the commemorative sets filling another shelf. Cathy enjoyed watching Tim unload and catalogue the collection, because she knew he was truly happy again and she loved hearing him hum as he worked. Soon everything would be placed in the exact location.

They were amazed how it all turned out, leaving them unscathed, physically and financially at least. The psychological scars were healing rather quickly now that the threat was gone and the stolen items found.

"Honey, do you think you should call the sheriff and tell him of our find under the outhouse?" Cathy asked Tim as she watched him unload the cart of another coin folder.

"Mmmm, probably." Tim was busy looking up a coin in the *Red Book* and could only give his concentration to one task at a time.

"When do you think you will be finished so you can call the sheriff?" Cathy said sweetly, knowing he did not want anything to interrupt his inventory. Cathy did not want to call the sheriff because she feared her anger would flare and she would catch that same virus she was so susceptible to, that dreaded old *foot in mouth disease*.

She was sure they even recognized her voice when she called. She was positive she could hear the deputy suck in his breath in fear that he might have to come to their place again. She could visualize him scrunching up his shoulders and holding his eyes shut tight with his jaw locked while he waited for her to tell another wild story. Maybe, she was reading too much into all the experiences she had with the local substation, but she had never forgiven Deputy Johnston for what he said when they had him out about the theft of the coins and the guns. In addition, she was still extremely angry from when she discovered he had not called for backup when the van was found. He had only hung around acting as if he was searching the forest.

She went back to slicing the mushrooms and olives for pasta salad. She was putting them into her egg slicer and loved the way the pieces of vegetables extruded through the fine wires in exact sizes. It was the mind numbing kind of busy work she loved. She experimented with the olives and discovered she could cut four olives at one time; it actually worked better than one or two. She admitted to herself she loved gadgets, and scanned her kitchen and saw that it was full of items purchased from infomercials and gourmet shops. Tim loved to tease her when she brought home a new gadget. Every drawer and cupboard was full. She had reminded him how full the coin closet was, and they both agreed they had better not point a finger when they each were just as guilty. Tim's closet had been empty far too long, and she was thrilled he could fill it again.

She continued to weigh all the reasons in her mind why Tim should call the deputy, and all the reasons she hated to call. She was relieved to know that the call wasn't going to be an emergency call this time, just an informational call. She would finish making her pasta salad first. By then, Tim might have finished sorting his coins or be ready to take a break. Dreaming, she acknowledged, she knew in her heart she would have to make the call.

"Honey, are you going to take a break soon?" She still had hope that he might make the call if she set up the opportunity, and hoped he would take her suggestion. Fat chance, she thought again to herself.

"Mmmm," Tim hummed as a response to let her know he had heard her.

"Are you getting hungry?" She knew she could always get his attention when she offered him food.

"Sure," he said into the closet barely audible to Cathy.

"How about grilled cheese and the pasta salad I just made. We can eat some with lunch but it will be better tomorrow after the pasta sucks up all the flavor of the dressing." Cathy was talking more to herself than to Tim as she opened the refrigerator and started looking for the sliced cheese and butter.

"Mmmm," Tim mumbled again.

"Do you think the deputy will come to the house to take a report on the found items?" Cathy was asking questions about the phone call to keep the call to the station in Tim's conscious.

"Don't knoooow," he hummed in response as his mind concentrated on finding the listing of the coin in the book.

Tim sat at the dining room table while he ate his lunch and continued thumbing through the *Red Book.* He was very careful not to leave any greasy smudges from the grilled cheese on the pages with his fingers. He continually wiped his hands on his napkin before he touched the book again. Tim treated books with great respect and this, *The Official Red Book, A guide Book of United States Coins* he placed in his highest esteem. It was his bible to his coin collection. Damn, Cathy thought, not even my pasta salad has pulled him from his coins. She sat next to him at the table knowing she could be eating anywhere and he would not have noticed she was not sitting down to a meal beside him. He was truly mesmerized with his beloved coins.

"Are you going to call the sheriff when you finish your sandwich?" She was very careful about the tone of her voice because she wanted Tim to believe it was his duty, as the man of the house, to make the call. Fat chance, she thought again.

"Mmmm," he said with pasta salad in his mouth.

"Do you want me to make the call?" She hoped he would feel guilty making her cross into his territory if she made the call.

"Sure, go ahead." This he said clearly with pasta salad still in his mouth. It was obvious he had been stalling and ignoring her the whole time she pelted him with the question about the phone call. "I think it is important that we place the call today to look like we are not hiding anything. You know, just in case the workers tell someone about their find. In this small town the gossip blows faster than the wind through the trees".

"OK, I'll call as soon as I clean up the lunch mess." Cathy sat there taking little bites of melted cheese off the edge of her sandwich while she silently grew angry because he had dumped the call back in her lap. OK, she said to herself, just get it done and don't catch that old virus.

Cathy cleared the table, stashed the pasta salad in the refrigerator, and washed the few dishes, table, and counters. She knew it was a stall tactic to keep from making the call. As if the sheriff would care if her kitchen was clean or not while she called the station on the phone. She dried her hands, filled a glass with ice before filling it with water, and sat down with a pen and paper. She had been a secretary for years and never picked up the receiver on the phone without being prepared. She had memorized the telephone number to the station these last few months as she circled the number, again and again, in the Orange Phone Book, with her ever-ready pen as she waited on hold. The circles were sort of a doodle she created as she waited. Something visual to look at while she tried to hear the words she would use when she had to speak. She was starting to feel like the teenager who was afraid to ask the most handsome boy in school to accompany her to a dance. Why did she feel this way about calling the sheriff? They had done nothing wrong! It was just a courtesy call to inform them to tear up the report of the theft, or at least amend the report, and CLOSE THE CASE!

"Julian Sheriff's Department, may I help you?" It was a man, a real live person and not some electronic voice message system. Something to be said for a small community, she thought.

"Hello, this is Mrs. Spalding. We live beyond Cedar Grove, where the old lumber mill once stood."

"Oh yes, I know the place, and who you are." The deep voice interrupted. Cathy didn't know if knowing who she was, was a good thing or not. She started to lose her courage. She fought the urge to just hang up and slink away. She knew they had been the *joke* of Julian for some time now.

"W e l l," she sort of exhaled the word before she began to speak again, "when we were clearing up the mess of the tree that was hit by lightning, the very tree that killed that man that had threatened us, we found all of my husband's coins and guns in the rubble of the old outhouse." The longer her explanation, the faster she spoke, hoping to keep him interested until she had finished.

"Mrs. Spalding, I am so glad you called today. I was just talking to Deputy Johnston about you and your husband, and not just five minutes ago. It must be some kind of telepathy. Deputy Johnston said he believed you had some kind of strange ability, yes I believe that was the way he put it, to know that man you found under the tree was evil. We have been putting the puzzle together and have come up with some pretty astonishing pieces." The deputy was so cheerful on the phone, treating Cathy as if she was some long lost friend.

"Just what kind of pieces do you mean?" Cathy was starting to unwind because his manner was so friendly. She was still leery because of her history with the Department. Maybe, it was her history with Deputy Johnston that kept her wound up.

"Let's see here, wait while I grab Deputy Johnston's little notebook and see what I can pass on. He just stepped out for a cup of coffee, ran to the Donut Chalet." He paused while he was obviously trying to make out the notes in the little book.

Cathy could see Deputy Johnston unbuttoning his lapel pocket, removing the notebook and writing. She could also imagine him looking into the display case at the Donut Chalet and choosing what kind of donut he wanted. Maybe he was a man of habit, and when the clerk saw him coming, she had his donut on top of the counter, sitting on one of those wax papers with his coffee poured. How many times had she been down this road in her mind remembering each of his gestures? Too many times, answering her own question and now she was hoping they had come to the end of the road, their strange relationship terminating. Then her mind floated into the image of her selling a lot to every visitor who came to Julian for the weekend. When all the properties were occupied, the town would have grown enough to increase the men who protected and served the residents of the backcountry. Then, if she ever had to call the Sheriff's Department again, another man would come out to their house for the report!

"I haven't left you," he started to speak again and brought her mind back to the telephone call. "I am having a hell of a time trying to figure out his notes. Oh, I see him coming now. Did you know he took two weeks of vacation so he could do research on that man that was killed on your property? Worked all through his vacation, that man had become some kind of obsession with him. Here he is now. Hey Bob, Mrs. Spalding is on the phone for you."

Cathy's stomach took a quick spasm in dread of a conversation with Deputy Johnston, but her curiosity definitely had shifted into high gear. She was trying to overcome her hesitation because of this new information she had just learned about his vacation and research. She promised herself to be sweet while she listened to him. No easy task, she admitted to herself.

"Hello, Deputy Johnston here," he said in a familiar tone that sent a jolt of stomach acid directly to her throat.

"This is Mrs. Spalding. I called to inform your department that we found the coins and guns buried under the rubble of the outhouse yesterday." She had a hard time speaking in a natural tone because she was fighting the effects of the acid, her eyes beginning to water. She had originally wanted to inform him of their find so they could close the case about the theft. However, this newly acquired information changed everything. She prayed he would share it with her. Instantly she made the decision that she would get the information from him one way or the other. Didn't they have a right to know? It had happened to them, and the grandkids, right here on their property! She could now visualize trying to pry Tim away from his coins to drive into the substation while they did a sit-in until they got the story. She would take a bowl of her pasta salad as a gift to wear the deputies down.

"Oh yes, Mrs. Spalding. I was planning to call you but this is just my second day back from vacation. I was trying to catch up with some unfinished business before I called. I almost had to throw a fit to get time off in the summer when it's tourist season up here. We usually take vacations in the winter when the town is quiet and the fire hazard is low." He was chatting with her as if she was his next-door neighbor. Something had really changed! Was it good news for them? Was he ever going to get to the point and tell her what he had discovered?

"Yes, the deputy who answered the phone, I didn't catch his name, said you had been investigating the man that was killed on our property." She hoped this introduction would get him back on track.

"Yes I was. I spent most of the last two weeks in San Diego going through the county records, working with the FBI, San Diego Police, and the archives at the Historical Society. I had the grandest of times doing all this research and learning from the men who helped me. My wife took the kids to the Zoo, Sea World, the beach, and all the museums while I was busy doing research. I believe it was our best family vacation ever." He spoke with such energy that he sounded like a little boy who had his first pony ride.

"A N D," she said trying not to show her impatience, and wondering what kind of a family vacation has the father off doing something else while the mother schleps the kids to all the standard tourist attractions. Family vacation my ass, she thought, just a change in scenery!

"Let me look in my little notebook here. I have pages and pages of information. I haven't had time to write any official report yet; well actually, I don't even have to write one since I did all this on my own. I will though, only when I have extra time of course, because I strongly believe this new information is pertinent to all that happened on your property. I was hoping to write it up real soon and then call you when I had put it all together in some sort of logical order. But since I have you on the phone I will fill you in if you don't mind it being out of order?" He was excited and in his glory as he flipped the pages in his little notebook. He was actually happy she had called and he could inform them of his research and findings.

"I don't mind at all. That was really nice of you to do all that for us." Cathy was pleased he had taken on an investigation but also angry that no one had spent any time earlier. Maybe the whole *Mike Thing* would not have escalated if he were stopped sooner. What was it going to take to get him to start telling her what he had discovered? "What did you learn?"

"Well, first thing I learned was that Mike Jenkins is really Yuri Miller. We got his real identity from his fingerprints. His van was stolen in Texas almost two years ago and the plates he had on it were also stolen. We talked to your neighbor to the southwest and found that he had tried to run him off the property once because someone had been stealing his eggs. At first, he thought it was a landscaper on the wrong road. He knew you were doing all that work on your pond." The deputy continued to give information and Cathy quickly wrote in her hybrid shorthand. She didn't want to miss one tiny piece to this puzzle!

"Really?" Cathy murmured hoping to oil his memory and keep him talking.

"Then we found the sliding glass door unlocked and the alarm disabled at your next door neighbor's. Mike, err…Yuri; lets call him Mike because that is how you knew him, had been using the cabin next door. The refrigerator had fresh food in it so we talked to the Castle's, and they said they haven't been to their cabin in over a year. He had night vision binoculars and a listening device just like your grandson said. We also found some binoculars he used for the daytime. That grandson of yours is one smart little kid, got everything exactly right."

"Uh huh," Cathy replied. The smart kid part was one thing she agreed with him on. Staying at the Castle's and stealing eggs made her skin crawl. He had been right under their nose all along.

"Then, here's the real kicker, Mrs. Spalding. Hold on to your seat! The coroner found two very important things on his body. One was a wadded piece of paper he still held in his hand, it was wet and muddy but the writing was still visible. It was from one of those preprinted tablets that said *Things to do Today*. He had written on it and the #1 line had 'kill Cathy' and the #2 line had 'kill the brat,' and the #3 line said 'leave the USA for Mexico.' I would not have believed it if I had not seen it for myself! It appears you were really in danger. It looks like he was going to leave the country after he had killed you and your grandson. I hope this new information doesn't scare the…ah, hair right off your head?" He paused as if he almost said, "Scared the shit right out of you," but caught himself in time. He was quiet and waiting for a response from the other end of the phone.

"I knew that, I am glad someone finally believes me," Cathy answered with total relief in her voice. Finally, she thought, I had prayed I would live to see the day that someone, somewhere didn't think she was some crazy woman. She didn't say how she knew it from a dream. Don't go too far and blow your credibility now. "That was actually three pieces of information you said there were two?"

"Oh yes, excuse me, I often get off track. Thanks for redirecting me." He said apologetically.

Was he sorry for getting off track, or sorry for believing he had scared the…hair right off her head, as he put it? Was this the same Deputy Johnston? He sounded the same but he was certainly a changed man!

"I was counting the list as one item. Number 2 is really astonishing! Mike was wearing, around his neck, a heavy gold chain and through the chain was a ring exactly like the one that was found on the finger of the skeleton. Can you believe that in a hundred years?" He told her this as if he had just guessed the numbers and won the lottery. "That ring was what got me truly interested and demanding a vacation. I had agencies all over the country digging up leads for me."

"Wow, that is astonishing," She wanted to fuel his enthusiasm and keep on giving her more information. She was writing like crazy, trying to keep up.

"Once I found out his true identity, I learned that he had been born in Norfolk, Virginia. His father was in the Navy, never married the girl. Can you believe we found him and he is still alive! He was rather upset when we called! He said the mother was a one-night stand, a paid prostitute, doubted he was even the father but she had kept dogging him for support. She even went to his C.O. and he did time in the brig for not supporting the kid. Forty some years later and he is still mad as hell! Pointed out that today's DNA would have gotten him off the hook."

"We got the mother's name from his birth certificate, and found she had quite a record of petty crimes, shoplifting, writing bad checks, prostitution, and similar stuff. It looks like she hung out with the worst of men. Her boyfriend actually killed her in a fight and Yuri, sorry Mike, then killed the boyfriend when he was only twelve. The official report said it was probably self-defense. The kid went to a foster home and ran away from there. He resurfaced when caught on a burglary charge and did fifteen months in a juvenile facility. He was sixteen at the time. He is wanted today for the murder of an old man in Jacksonville, Florida. The police in Jacksonville believe he broke in and found the old man and thought he had to kill him so not to leave a witness. Years ago, they found Yuri's DNA on some skin under the old man's fingernails and a couple of hairs on the old man's robe. The lab has been keeping it all these years. They cross-matched it with the DNA from the body, it all matched and it was the same! They put it all together with CODUS, the national DNA databank. They have been watching him and his girlfriend for years. Just couldn't prove anything. He steals the jewelry and she redesigns it and sells it as an artist. They have actually become rich from their crimes. They invested in Real Estate with the cash from the sale of the jewelry."

"My God," Cathy said quietly as she continued to write. She thought of stopping and only listening but she wanted to get each word written down to tell Tim.

"Come to find out, his mother was born in San Diego and was the up and coming hooker when the boyfriend killed the Grandmother. They could never prove if he actually hit her or she had fallen. They couldn't pin her death on him and they left town in a hurry, and didn't surface until the mother was beaten to death." He was on a roll now and speaking quickly. She could hear the pages flip back and forth in his little notebook. He was trying to give her all his information in chronological order.

"Mary, Mother of God," escaped from her lips as she continued to listen and write. Tim stood transfixed with a coin folder in one hand and the *Red Book* under his arm listening to her responses and watching her write.

"Then I worked on finding out about the grandmother. I got her name from the police report when she died and off the mother's birth certificate. She was born in Russia and emigrated to the U.S. as a young girl. She actually ended up in Julian and was the housekeeper for a Harvey Luce. He was the manager of the Stonewall mine at one time and listed as the father of Yuri's mother. I found no records of them ever marrying. He was registered as married to one Olivia Mitchell in Maine before Mr. Luce ever worked in Julian. They had three children, all born in San Diego, and ended up in La Mesa. I did find that his grandmother came from the same small village as the lumbermen who worked the mill in the early nineteen hundreds. God, isn't it amazing what you can uncover with some help and the computer!"

"Whew," is all Cathy could let blow through her lips. She felt like she had been kicked in the gut. Harvey Luce was her grandfather too, her mother's father. She could still see him in her memories, his weathered face, and kind deep voice. That made Yuri her cousin; half cousin would be more accurate. Dear God, that evil man had been a relative!

"I am taking a giant leap here, but what the hell. I think that Yuri was the Great-Grandson of the skeleton we found on your property last spring!"

"How?" she quickly gasped. She was trying to put all the pieces together, weighing the significance of this new information along with a family tie. She had a hard time breathing and was sure she had misunderstood what he was saying.

"Well, there's this whole line of people, records, and of course the matching rings. Am I totally crazy on this one?" Deputy Johnston asked. Was he actually asking Cathy if she thought he was crazy? She wanted to reach through the phone and hit him for every time he acted as if she was!

"Well, no." She was trying to grasp it all and write simultaneously. When she took dictation as a secretary, she didn't have to think. Just listen and write, then of course, there was no emotion involved.

"I'm glad you could follow the line of people. I gave this explanation to the deputies here at the station and everyone laughed. I thought it was pretty obvious, but maybe I didn't explain it too good." He was now trying to get credibility with her and it was obvious her approval was very important to him. Cathy realized she was still holding some anger towards him, let alone him informing her of a family link. This whole turn around of Deputy Johnston had left her almost speechless. Had he really had a turn around with them, or was he just pleased with himself about his research and his vacation? Should she continue to be wary?

"Yes," she said realizing that any short reply was enough to jump-start his conversation with her again.

"I went back over all the notes I had written each time I came to your place. I just kept staring at them; they weren't making any sense to me. I knew there had to be some connection, some reason why this man was threatening you. So, I started tearing out the pages in my notebooks and moving them around on the table like each page was a piece to a puzzle. I believe he came to your place when he saw the ring on the news and knew that it belong to his Great-Grandfather. Why he stayed and stalked you people I can't quite figure. Maybe he overheard Tim talk about his coin collection and guns. You understand he was a pickpocket and burglar?"

"I know, I saw him on that video from the stadium. Remember, I told you about that segment on Channel 8?" Cathy replied.

"I did remember. I checked out that lead you gave me about the feature on pickpockets. I ran the footage a hundred times trying to see if it was Mike. I had never seen him when he was alive so I couldn't really identify him from the tape. I had the tech enlarge areas of the video and then I scanned those with my magnifying glass. I could pick out a heavy gold chain around his neck. It was rather expensive looking and unique. Sure enough, the gold chain was the same as the one found on his body, and that proved to me that he was the pickpocket. I wonder how many people would have kept their money if I had checked him out sooner. I apologize, Mrs. Spalding, for not checking out your report. There is no excuse for my attitude and I am taking all this as a learning experience. I guess I have been working in a small community too long, where nothing happens much but a traffic accident or a fire. Will you at least think about accepting my long overdue apology?" He was now pleading with Cathy to accept his half-ass investigational skills. Now she felt guilty; she was not ready to let go of her anger towards him. Why was it so hard to let go of her anger? Was it anger towards the deputy she was feeling or fear of an evil gene lying dormant in her family? There had never been any deviant behavior in *her* family. The evil must have come from Yuri's mother side. Cathy relaxed after scanning her memory of her extended family.

"I'm working on it, which is all I can promise now." She tried to soften her voice so as not to sound bitter. She wanted to scream at him for all that he had neglected to believe and do. Scream at him for informing her that the evil man who had turned their life upside down was related to her. Would informing him of his insults, Chauvinistic attitude, and general stubborn slow down, going to change this man? He was what he was! She knew if she told him why she was hurt and angry, and pointed out all he could have done he would become defensive. The whole cycle would begin again. Better to let go, and pray they would never have to deal with him again. After all, they were building a new Sheriff's Station next to the Veterinarian. The Sheriff's Department must be planning to expand the employees there, maybe they would draw another deputy next time they had trouble. Let me pray we never have trouble again!

She was now embarrassed with herself for her mean thoughts. He was trying to change and he didn't have a clue about the family connection. That bit of information she would definitely keep to herself! She should be thankful for his efforts; and knew she had no right to set the bar on what changes in his behavior were enough to accept his apology.

"Thank you," he quietly said. "You called to say you found the gun and coin collection? I'm sorry I was so excited to give you my news that I ran away and wasn't listening."

"Yes we did, it was buried under the rubble of the outhouse which was under the limbs that had flown off the tree in the storm. It appears everything is there. Tim is taking an inventory as we speak, checking it off against the marks in the margins of *The Red Book.* Do you need to come out and see it now that we can actually show you we had a collection?" Cathy was hoping he would say no.

"I will amend the report about the man found penned under the tree on your property, identified as Yuri Miller, and that the stolen goods were hidden in the outhouse. We know what happened to the thief, a report would do quite nicely. Did you know the lightning didn't kill him?"

"No, if it wasn't lightning, what did, a branch hitting him on the head?" Cathy kept seeing the shoes protruding from under the fallen limbs. She had been trying to erase the image in her mind, and now the deputy was reminding her again.

"The ME's Report said he died of hypothermia, he wasn't really hurt at all from the branches falling on him. It looked like he was imprisoned under all the debris, laid there all-night and died sometime in the morning, probably around the time I arrived at your place. I hope that murdering SOB had lots of time to ponder his life and have a good talk with his maker!" The deputy kept talking with wild abandonment and quickly changed directions. "Did you ever see the metal detector that your grandson was talking about?"

"Oh yes, it was half buried with the coins and guns in the foundation of the outhouse. Do you need it for evidence?" Cathy answered quickly as her mind tried to answer his question and take in the details about Mike's death and the link to her family. Dear God, she shuddered, he lie outside all night held down by the fallen limbs, and we were all locked in the house in fear of him returning. She remembered how much the wind blew and the temperature dropped that night, dropped enough to have a fire in the fireplace in the middle of summer. She got a chill up her spine, and tried to shake the image from her mind. The new image of Mike and her sharing a grandfather was still too new to put in perspective.

"Naawh, keep it for at least ninety days and then do what you want with it. I would like to see that antique gun of Tim's sometime. The one his relative used in the Revolutionary War. The gun was with the others, wasn't it?"

"Yes, it appears everything is here, he didn't take anything off the property." Cathy answered.

"If it would be all right with you folks, sometime when I was in the area, I could stop by and Tim could show it to me. I just want to touch a piece of American History. I think I am becoming an old softy, especially after 9-11."

"Sure, anytime," she said. She knew she was letting go of some of that anger when the thought of him dropping by didn't set her stomach into a knot. "Thanks for the information. Call us anytime." Cathy hung up and stacked her notes into a neat little pile.

"Well, what did he say? You were on the phone and writing forever. Come clean and fill me in!" The sound of the receiver setting back into the cradle had pulled him next to her waiting for a reply. She handed him the stack of papers as if he could read her pidginized shorthand. He looked at her notes and then directly at her, shoving the stack back into her hands. She smiled at him and began to read the conversation back to him in its entirety, word for word, minus her replies of course, and all the thoughts that had run through her mind as she listened to Deputy Johnston. Cathy didn't tell Tim that her Grandfather was also Mike's Grandfather. She would tell him, but she needed time to process all the information from the deputy. What would it all mean to her?

Chapter Twenty-Six
Split Commission

As Cathy sat in her lawn chair watching the grandkids splash in the pond she smiled. Replaying the video of last spring and summer in her mind had taken on a surreal glow. Hey, it all worked out fine, and she had accomplished her dream. The kids were having a grand time!

The pond was finally finished, and right now, she felt more relief than joy. She had removed the cross with the vine and berries painted on it before the kids came that morning. She was not about to sit and watch the kids play with that shrine casting a shadow over the new pond. He had been dead for almost a hundred years, and if Deputy Johnston was right about who the skeleton had been, nothing but bad people were spawned from that man who had been dug up. She would bet the murdered man had done something illegal and was murdered because of it. That was just a feeling, or perhaps a rationalization; she had no premonition this time.

Elaine and Carmen had run into town to buy a couple of apple pies. Carmen was having her new love over for dinner tonight and wanted to serve a piece of that famous pie from Julian. Elaine would take home the leftovers for Brian. Tim was playing with the metal detector while the kids squealed, splashed water on each other, and occasionally splashed their grandmother as she hid from the heat under a giant oak. Each time they caught Cathy off guard she responded with a loud squeal of her own, and acted as if she was wounded. The cold-water torture brought her out of her daydreams and into the present.

Cathy kept rolling over in her mind her affection for Carmen. Each time she went into the office she looked for her, and hoped she would stop in while Cathy was there. Lately they had been making lunch appointments, and sharing news and updates on their Real Estate transactions. Cathy had secretly adopted Carmen because she truly liked her, let alone all the crazy times she made Cathy laugh. She knew she could only invite Carmen into their family and hope she would begin to consider them special too. Cathy felt pleased that Carmen was making more and more time to include them in her life.

Today Carmen had confided that she had new love in her life and that the relationship was progressing nicely. A little step closer into their lives, Cathy thought. They all had agreed that a slice of Julian Apple Pie would certainly win over any reticent love. The young women went to town to purchase the pie, while Cathy remained at home watching the children splash.

It was obvious the kids were cold, their lips were blue, and their teeth were chattering. Glenny was jumping up and down with his arms crossed to stay warm. Cathy insisted they take a break for lunch. The moans and groans were as loud as the squawking of the crows sitting in the oak that had become known as the Hiding Tree. Once pried from the new pool, each child waited in line while she dried their arms and bodies, blotted their hair and gave them a big hug. Then she whispered something in their ear about hot cocoa topped with whipped cream. She loved to hold each child close, smell their hair, and have their undivided attention as she promised a treat she knew they would love.

She had completely forgotten to whisper in the children's ears when she was so worried about Mike and what he might be scheming against them. They never asked for her whispers, they accepted the change when she seemed stressed. They had become sensitive to her fears and anxieties, and Cathy's heart ached to know how her tension had become theirs'. They were all back to their old selves again. Cathy knew that life was good, and had finally returned to normal.

As Cathy was scooping out powdered cocoa mix into the cups, Tim came back into the house carrying a rusty can partially crusted with dirt. He excitedly showed it to Cathy.

"Look! I found this with the metal detector while I was looking for loose coins the men may have missed in the clean up. The can was completely buried in the foundation of the old outhouse; the metal detector showed me where it was. God, Cathy it looks like it has been buried for years." His voice quivered with excitement and he walked away from Cathy towards his desk. She squirted whipped cream on top of the hot chocolate. It was fun for her to see Tim so excited about a find with the metal detector, but she couldn't fathom what was so special about a rusty old can.

Elaine and Carmen returned from town with their pies and some vanilla ice cream. The activity of slicing the pie and scooping out the hard ice cream, with three active children, filled the house with laughter and noise. Carmen was being a clown. She had put on hats and boots from the laundry room and paraded in front of the kids. She was acting silly and juggling baseballs from Tim's mini baseball shrine he had displayed in the family room. The boys looked at her with wide eyes because they knew that Papa Tim's baseballs were sacred. They knew those balls had been signed by very famous baseball players and no one could play with them. The boys looked to Papa Tim and back to Carmen before they had the courage to laugh freely. It was safe to laugh because Papa Tim was busy at his desk with his back turned. Carmen deliberately dropped a ball as part of her routine and when she picked it up she read the signature. She knew immediately what she had done when she recognized the name. Carmen loved baseball as much as Tim, and often accompanied him to a game.

Being the eternal entertainer, she made a big act about putting round balls back on a flat shelf. She did all this with the children laughing at the falling balls while she ended her skit quickly, Tim never realizing she had entertained the children with his baseball memorabilia. He was removing coins from the can and had entered another world.

The kids took their pie and ice cream outside on paper plates, and the grownups ate theirs in the living room. Cathy brought Tim's pie to his desk. When she placed his plate on the desk, she slid several stacks of coins to the center. He reached out and grabbed her hand. When she tried to pull it free from his grasp, she noted the strangest look on his face.

"You OK?" She quietly asked so as not to draw any attention to their little exchange in the corner of the living room.

"I'm just great! Isn't this the best day ever?" He replied, and looked into her eyes. Cathy tried to understand Tim's expression but he only grinned at her. He looked like the cat that had swallowed the canary.

Cathy sat in her chair, picked up her plate, began to pull an apple slice from the crust, and sucked the sweet sauce from the apple before she chewed the wedge and swallowed it. One by one, she ate the apple pieces then spooned the ice cream over the crust until it was soggy. When the crust was soggy, she cut it into small pieces with the edge of her spoon and placed them into her mouth. She did her eating automatically while she listened to the young women talk about the high cost of living in San Diego.

Elaine's complaint always centered on the fact that it took two salaries to own a house in San Diego, and a mother with young children should not warehouse her kids in daycare so she can put a roof over their heads.

Carmen's lament was that she worked hard; often six days a week, selling houses for other people, and she could barely pay her bills because her rent kept increasing every six months. She had been placed right out of the housing market, the market where she sold the dream to other people. She needed her own place where she could lock in her payments. All she needed was to come up with enough money for a down payment. Fat chance, the two women agreed!

"It's so embarrassing, selling houses when I don't even have one. It is like being a Veterinarian and not owning a dog, a Marriage Counselor without being married, an Obstetrician without having a child." Carmen was off on a roll with her voice changing with each example. "A Dentist with no..." Elaine's hands flew up to her chest in a gesture to stop! That was all the notice Carmen needed to quit her routine, and sit back and take another bite of her pie.

Cathy grinned to herself, wondering how many examples Carmen could have come up with if Elaine hadn't called her off. She didn't want to throw her frustrations into the pot. Her complaint would be what it was like, being at the other end of your earning power, Tim retired and all. Any increase in income would have to come from her, and she wanted to mostly stay home with her new husband and enjoy her grandchildren when she could. She sat there silent and gave both women sympathy. Once, she added how easy it had been to buy a house when she was a young married woman because the prices were so low and the interest rate a little over four percent. She didn't point out how small her first house was, with only one bathroom, and a single car garage. What was really scary, is that people are now buying that same house for over two hundred fifty thousand and they had paid fifteen. The housing prices in San Diego were outrageous and still climbing through their mortgaged roofs!

Many years had passed and that reminded Cathy how old she had become, too many years of experiences, too much personal history, too many old friends gone. She wasn't sad the years had slipped by so quickly; she was content to roll with each day and thank God for it. She still remembered the energy and ambition she had when she was the age of the two young women sitting in her living room. She was glad she was now in a different place in her life.

"Brian and I would take a big family vacation if we had the extra money. We all need a get-away with a change of scenery, a fun place for the kids. We dream of a family cruise but it is *way* out of the question. We will probably be able to afford it when the kids graduate from college. I guess then we will be paying for Kim's wedding." She said all this with longing in her voice but Cathy knew her daughter was happy with her husband and family.

"I would have you help me find the perfect condo. I get my place and we split the commission." Carmen lapsed into her Old Russian Lady accent. "Two birds, one stone." She deliberately pronounced her words to make it hard to understand. "I have been paying horrible rent for that stupid little apartment. Think what I could buy if I had the down payment." Carmen spoke sadly that her housing dilemma was just out of her reach; she said her last statement in pure and unaccented English.

"I want lots of stuff, but most of it can wait now that I can listen to my waterfall. I still want one hundred red tulips to bloom next spring outside the dining room window. New carpet, of course, central air, and one more kitchen gadget, that has yet to be invented." Cathy was sort of dreaming out loud. She believed every wish had to be said *out loud*, in the light of day before it became an official wish. She believed that when one hears their wish *out loud*, something inside your soul marks the wish and your subconscious starts working to make the dream take shape. "But if I had a hunk of found money I would invite a whole lot of family and friends on a cruise and I would treat everyone. That way everyone could have their own room, do what they wanted, and I could still see everyone at mealtime. And, I wouldn't even have to cook!" Cathy told this wish to Tim, who still had his back to them as he worked on his coins.

"That sounds like winning the Lottery." Elaine said.

"Nah, no more than Carmen's down payment for a condo. If I had the money, I would give it to Carmen. That's way more important than the Grand Vacation. I could just invite everyone here for a big party and have it catered." Cathy explained.

"Geez, Cathy, that is about the sweetest thing I have ever had offered to me, even if it was just pure fantasy. Of course we still split the commission." Carmen said with genuine gratitude in her voice.

"Of course, that's how I am going to pay the caterer." Cathy quipped.

"Hey Tim, what would you do if you won the Lottery? Elaine asked, trying to draw Tim into their fantasy conversation.

"I hate to tell you girls how many hours I have spent in this old lifetime of mine fantasizing, spending my winnings. I even have percentages of my winnings all delegated to family and friends. I did have to do a revision when I married your mother, she deserves fifty percent, it is California you know." Tim was twisting his body around in his chair as he delivered his answer from the corner of the room.

"Him fantasizing about winning the lottery is second only to counting his coins." Cathy said affectionately.

"Ah, but a coin is something real, something you can put in your hand, something to look at. Then you can look it up in the *Red Book* and chart its value." Tim said all this with great affection in his voice. His voice sounded as if he was selling his love of coins to the masses from the pulpit.

"Can you spend them?" Carmen asked.

"Ah, but will he spend them?" Cathy replied.

"Don't make fun of my hobby, albeit an expensive one. I promise it will bring pleasure to all my special people." Tim solemnly responded.

"How do we get on his special people list?" Elaine jested.

"Forget it; he will have changed his list a hundred times by the time he dies." Cathy informed the two women. Tim looked to Cathy with an exaggerated hurt look on his face, as if she was making fun of him about his collection possibly being his *first* love.

"Here, apply this towards your condo." He said, and pelted Carmen with a coin. Carmen jerked into action and caught the coin on the fly. She slowly rolled it over in her hand and held it to the light for a closer look.

"Thanks Tim, but a twenty-dollar coin won't even fill my gas tank these days." Carmen whined, acting hurt by his generous gesture.

"Don't pooh-pooh my gift too quickly." Tim started throwing coins in Carmen's direction as Elaine and Cathy laughed at the awkward movements of her trying to catch them. "These are old gold coins and not one of them is worth any less than four hundred and fifty dollars. One of them is worth almost three thousand. I bet I can get you interested in collecting coins now, Ms. Smarty Pants."

"Hey, I already have a coin collection. Papa gave the boys his old collection a couple of weeks ago. I am always open to learning about a new hobby." Elaine was teasing her mother's new husband.

"Want to learn more now girls?" Tim teased as he started throwing coins toward Elaine and now occasionally towards Carmen. When they thought he was finished he started pelting them again. The laughter rocked the room and the two women had a hard time catching the coins while laughing so hard. Carmen and Elaine now had several stacks piled next to their chairs. It looked like winnings from a poker game.

"That was fun, much more fun than spending time dreaming about winning the Lottery. Playing catch got my heart pumping. You were right, you can get your hand around a coin real easy, look it over up close too." Carmen picked up her stacks with both hands and gently sat them back on

Tim's desk. "Thanks for your understanding, I feel so lucky to be able to be part of your family. You treat me like I am one of yours. With all my brothers and sisters living so far away, it is nice to be part of your wild bunch on holidays. You all mean a lot to me!" Carmen returned to her chair and looked at Elaine's stack with longing. Touching all that money was fun but it still didn't solve her condo dream.

"I gave you those for your down payment. Cathy would love to help you find the perfect place, and help you get the loan you need. Not that you really need any help, you being a trained professional and all, but Cathy just loves being in the middle of the action." Tim returned the stacks of coins to Carmen, this time dropping them into her lap. "Don't forget to split the commission!"

"What will I do with them? Just put them in escrow when I find a place?" Carmen was beginning to understand the power the coins would have in her life.

"You will have to sell them first. Scout out a buyer, either private or a coin shop. If you want my help, I can instruct you. I know you are too smart to let some shyster buy them at below market value. By the time you are moving into your new place you will certainly know way more than you ever dreamed possible about old coins."

"How will I explain how I got them? I will have to do some explaining won't I? Are they hot?" She was beginning to see all the ramifications of these little piles now stacked again on the end table.

"If they are hot, it was about a hundred years ago. I think the lumberman buried the coins where the outhouse is now. Maybe someone knew he had the gold and wanted it. Maybe that's why he was murdered. I bet that is why Mike, or Yuri, had the metal detector up here. He was looking for his Great-Grandfather's buried gold. Imagine that!" Tim shook his head and let out a snort. "Yuri was looking everywhere for the buried treasure and when he hid my coins and guns in the old outhouse he must have been standing right over what he had been searching for. What a great little irony!"

"Do you think that's really what happened?" Elaine asked.

"That is just my humble opinion. It's probably best to keep all this speculation to ourselves, and just enjoy my find." Tim was thinking more out loud than speaking to Elaine. He had the look on his face that finally said he had put the pieces together and understood the events they had endured.

"If anyone asks you where you got your coins, just tell them your father gave them to you so you could buy your own place. Tell them they have been in the family for years, saved for just such an occasion." Tim looked at Cathy for reassurance. It was just impossible for him to lie or twist the facts. Wasn't it technically true that Cathy shared the same family as Yuri? He knew Cathy was the rightful heir, even though he had been the person who unearthed the coins in the rusty can. He felt confident she would agree to how he began to disburse the treasure. Carmen and Elaine didn't have a clue how his mind had taken such a giant leap, never learning that Yuri was Cathy's cousin. They believed this was the story they were to tell if ever asked.

Cathy had followed Tim's giant leap. She could read his mind as he thought through the events that formed the story he told the young women. She gave him a reassuring grin.

Carmen jumped up, went to Tim, and gave him a big hug. Tears were trickling down her cheeks. She didn't say a word, hung from his neck, and hugged him a little tighter.

Tim enjoyed being squeezed by Carmen in the throws of appreciation. He was beginning to choke-up; especially when he saw tears begin to roll down Cathy's cheeks. Elaine was watching this emotional scene with an expectant look on her face.

As Carmen hung from Tim's neck, he looked directly at Elaine and said, "Don't you dare say anything to me young lady, just decide how to enjoy your stack of coins with your husband and kids. Don't let Brian go all-conservative on you and try to pay off some bill, or he will have to answer to me. This money is for one hundred percent fun!"

Cathy was watching her husband as she absently stuck her tongue out of the corner of her mouth to catch a tear. The tears, of course, made her nose run. She hated it when she cried happy tears, because it always wiped her out as if she had taken some kind of tranquilizer. She became all flat and placid, wanting to curl up and take a nap. Happy tears were for celebrating, not for napping. She had married a good man, kind and generous. She was beginning to wonder what he had really found in that can.

"Anything left for me in that rusty old can of yours?" Cathy asked more as a question than a request. She wiped away her tears with the back of her hands, and then the bottom of her T-shirt. She still snuffed her nose.

"Oh, Babe, when these young ones here leave I will show you everything I have in my old rusty can." Tim spoke with an exaggerated lecherous tone in his voice.

The two young women looked at each other as if it was time to take their coins, pie, and run.

"Hey, Mom, please wait for us to leave. This is definitely TMI!" chided Elaine. She called to the kids, picked up the beach bag, and started stuffing the kids' wet clothes inside.

Cathy smiled at her husband, and thought, with those rosy cheeks and the white beard he looked a lot like Santa today. She knew he was making her a promise, and she had never been disappointed when his eyes twinkled and he flirted with her.

THE END

Printed in the United States
40001LVS00004BC/22